SOME OTHER AMAZONIANS:

PERSPECTIVES ON MODERN AMAZONIA

Some Other Amazonians:

Perspectives on Modern Amazonia

Edited by
Stephen Nugent and Mark Harris

Institute for the Study of the Americas
Senate House, Malet Street, London WC1E 7HU
Web: www.sas.ac.uk/americas

British Library Cataloguing-in-Publication Data
A catalogue record for this book is available
from the British Library

ISBN   1 900039 55 9

INSTITUTE FOR THE STUDY OF THE
A M E R I C A S

Institute for the Study of the Americas
Senate House
Malet Street
London WC1E 7HU

Telephone: 020 7862 8870
Fax: 020 7862 8886

Email: americas@sas.ac.uk
Web: www.sas.ac.uk/americas

TABLE OF CONTENTS

LIST OF CONTRIBUTORS

Scott Douglas Anderson first came to the Amazon as a Peace Corps Volunteer working in rural development. He was then employed as a computer systems analyst at the Amazon Regional Development Bank and a state planning agency. He left to carry out graduate study in Geography at the University of Chicago and returned to work as a research fellow at the Goeldi Museum, Belém. He has published on the themes of social change, rural development, natural resources, traditional technology and industrial archaeology in the context of Amazonia. Currently he is Coordinator of the Tide-Energy Project near the Mouth of the Amazon.

Edna Maria Ramos de Castro received her doctorate in the sociology of development from the Ecole des Hautes Etudes en Sciences Sociales, Paris, France. She teaches at the Núcleo de Altos Estudos Amazônicos at the Federal University of Pará, Belém. Her publications include *Faces do tropico umido e estado* (Editora CEJUP, 1998) and *Saúde, trabalho e meio ambiente políticas públicas na Amazônia* (NAEA, Pará, 1999, edited with Rosa Carmina Couto and Rosa Acevedo Marin). She is the joint co-ordinator of the project to map the rural black communities in the state of Pará.

Neide Esterci is a Professor of Anthropology at the Federal University of Rio de Janeiro. Her publications include *Conflito no Araguaia: peões e posseiros contra a grande empresa* (Vozes, 1987) and *Escravos da desigualdade: um estudo sobre o uso repressivo da força de trabalho no Brasil* (Cedi, 1994). Currently she is coordinating Rede Amazônia and researching and writing on the social implications of new environmental projects in the Brazilian Amazonia.

Mark Harris teaches at the University of St Andrews; he has also held posts at the Federal University of Pará in Belém, the London School of Economics and the University of Manchester. His publications include *Life on the Amazon* (Oxford University Press, 2000) and *The Child in the City* (Prickly Pear Pamphlets, 2000, edited with Anna Grimshaw). Currently he is researching colonial and imperial Amazonia.

Deborah de Magalhães Lima received her PhD in anthropology from the University of Cambridge in 1992. She currently teaches anthropology at the Fluminense Federal University and has been attached to the Federal University of Pará since 1987. She has written articles on the social category *caboclo* and on environmental issues related to peasant and Indian populations in the Amazon. She has worked extensively on the social component of environmental projects and was responsible for the design and implementation of the social part of the Mamirauá Reserve, one of the first to integrate human populations in the Amazon.

David McGrath teaches political ecology at the Núcleo de Altos Estudos Amazônicos of the Federal University of Pará in Belém, Pará, Brazil and is an Associate Scientist at the Woods Hole Research Center, Woods Hole, MA. He also coordinates projects in the community management of forest and floodplain resources through the Instituto de Pesquisa Ambiental da Amazônia. His scientific work has focused on community-based management of floodplain fisheries and of community forests in the Santarém region of Pará, Brazil.

Rosa Elizabeth Acevedo Marin received her doctorate in history and civilisation from the Ecole des Hautes Etudes en Sciences Sociales, Paris. She teaches at the Núcleo de Altos Estudos Amazônicos at the Federal University of Pará, Belém, and is the coordinator of the Association of Universities in Amazonia (UNAMAZ). Her books include *Escrita da história paraense* (editor) (NAEA–UFPA, 1998), *Negros do Trombetas: guardiaes de matas e rios* (edited with Edna Maria Ramos de Castro, UFPA/NAEA, 1993) and *Saúde, trabalho e meio ambiente políticas públicas na Amazônia* (NAEA, Pará, 1999, edited with Rosa Carmina Couto and Edna Maria Ramos de Castro). She is the joint coordinator of the project to map the rural black communities in the state of Pará.

Raymundo Heraldo Maués has taught anthropology at Federal University of Pará in Belém, Pará, since 1972. His publications include *Padres, pajés, santos e festas: Catolicismo popular e controle eclesiástico* (CEJUP, 1995) and *'Uma outra invenção' da Amazônia: religiões, histórias, identidades* (CEJUP, 1999). At the moment he is researching the Renovação Carismática Católica (Catholic charismatic) movement in Belém, Pará.

Stephen Nugent teaches at Goldsmiths College, University of London, and the Institute of Latin American Studies, University of London. He has written on the Amazon, peasants and anthropological theory, including *Big Mouth: the Amazon Speaks* (Fourth Estate, 1989); *Amazonian Caboclo Society: An Essay on Invisibility and Peasant Economy* (Berg, 1993); *Anthropology and Cultural Studies* (edited with Cris Shore, Pluto, 1997); and *Elite Cultures: Anthropological Perspectives* (edited with Cris Shore, Routledge, 2002).

Gregory Prang is a Lecturer at Wayne State University. Between 1994 and 1999, he was Visiting Professor at the Universidade Federal do Amazonas where he also served as coordinator of a multi-disciplinary research and extension project 'Piaba' (ornamental fish). He has published several articles on the ornamental trade and is the co-editor of Conservation and Management of Ornamental Fish Resources of the Rio Negro Basin, Amazonia, Brazil: Project Piaba. Although he continues his research in the Brazilian Amazon, he is currently expanding his research into consumer aspects of the aquarium hobby and the international aquarium fish supply chain.

List of Figures

LIST OF TABLES

Introduction: Some Other Amazonians

Stephen Nugent

There is a tendency in much writing about Amazonia — and the current offering is no exception — to succumb to generalisations that upon brief reflection must be highly qualified. The 'forest' itself, for instance, because it is the largest extant tropical example, is not an inaccurate gloss, yet it embraces *cerrado*, flood plains, wetlands, river systems and numerous examples of anthropogenic modification, all of which challenge the unifying notion of 'the Amazon forest'. And yet the macro-structures of the region — both natural and social — encourage monumentalist starting points.

One consequence of this compulsive 'big picture' approach is that it is easy to lose sight of the relationship between the micro and the macro. The surge of ecologically-informed research in recent decades has gone some way to revealing the complexity of such relations within the biome, but that is much less the case in terms of the field — anthropology — that has borne most of the responsibility for documentation and analysis of Amazonian social landscapes. Anthropological studies have traditionally been ethnographic, often indicative (as in the case of studies of peasant Amazonia) and more often implicitly representative (as in the case of studies of Amerindian societies).

This collection represents the former: case study examples of societies and peoples that fall outside the traditional Amazonian anthropological remit (Amerindians), Amazonian, yet bearing the inscriptions of a history often different from that of the original Amazonians. These are peoples whose Amazonianness is shaped by more than the primordialism of the Amazonian 'big picture': recent and long-standing immigrants from Brazil and abroad; Afro-Brazilian refugees from slave plantations; petty producers of tropical preciosities; river merchants; labourers who are their own bosses.

Attempts to incorporate the study of ersatz Amazonian societies into the canon of Amazonian anthropology have not been completely neglected, and since the inception of the Transamazon Highway and related development schemes the plausibility of the denial of the relevance of such studies has been manifestly untenable, but the 'big picture' take on the region is only gradually being deconstructed. Following Wagley's path-breaking monograph (*Amazon Town,* 1953) it was 30 years until a new neo-

Amazonian literature began to appear, one that systematically addressed this forgotten aspect of Amazonia, an Amazonia that first emerged before European eyes as the New World; then became the (Victorian) Lost World; transformed after the collapse of the rubber industry into the abandoned world; and re-emerged in the late twentieth century as, again, the New World: a planetary resource, replete this time less with gold (although that element has hardly been inconsequential) than 'systems resources' (biodiversity), cheap commodities (iron ore) and esoterica (cancer cures).

Behind the filters of the New World, Lost World, Abandoned World, New World MkII there is a quotidian Amazonia revealed in the contributions to this volume. This is an Amazonia without hubris, indeed, an Amazonia that is hardly recognised as a consequential aspect of the 'big picture'.

Some Background

Since 1970, with the onset of an aggressive programme of modernisation in the region, Amazonia has been the subject of a novel phase of intense research by social and natural scientists. In some cases this research has pursued long-established lines of inquiry, following up the pioneering inventories of the Victorian naturalists Bates, Spruce and Wallace, for example, or continuing the search for tropical preciosities of commercial and pharmaceutical value. In other cases, this research has reflected less the specifically Amazonian than it has reflected global scarcity of mundane — yet strategic — primary products.

In the case of the human and social sciences as well as the natural, research trajectories have been strongly informed by the emergence of an ecological discourse which offers both a common reference point as well as — at times—a specious unity. One of the benefits of this eco-discourse has been the emergence of a cross-disciplinarity within which previously segmented research (that of botanists and that of anthropologists, for example) finds a focus. One of the shortcomings has been that the many different Amazonias have become an imagined whole, one whose coherence, articulated by licensed, respectable and perceptive experts, often renders a dynamic, contradictory Amazonia mute.

The coherent — imagined — Amazonia portrayed in the research literature of the past three decades contains within it a special sub-clause: a cardinal quality of Amazonia's distinctiveness is its toleration of anomaly. Hence we have a variety of synecdoches which allow us to leap from the particular to the general without much processing intervention: piranha, noble savage, lungs of the earth, green hell, opera house in Manaus, biodiversity, *tanga*, Col. Fawcett.

One thing that this assemblage of key images attests to is ignorance (and its spurring corollary: more research required), but it might also suggest something else: is it possible that a region integrated into the world system for 500 years is still such an inchoate, marginal part of that world system?

Social Science

In narrowly anthropological terms, Amazonia is hardly inchoate or marginal. From the pioneering studies of Nimuendajú to the encyclopaedic efforts of Steward, to the work of Ricardo Cardoso de Oliveira, to Lévi-Strauss, to the post-WWII cohorts of US, UK, French and Brazilian indigenists, the ethnographic record is fulsome, and no less impressive is the degree to which anthropological activity has contributed directly to indigenous rights campaigns which forestalled the complete eradication of indigenous Brazilian societies.

The extension of the anthropological remit to include non-indigenous Amazonian societies has a chequered career. From the perspective of many indigenists, non-indigenous Amazonians are less the tolerable co-residents than they are advance parties of a national society which has little desire to acknowledge the rights of indigenous peoples. *Caboclos* may not be the enemy per se, but they are widely identified and portrayed as the agents of pathological change within Amazonia.

Anthropological portrayals of non-indigenous Amazonian societies are few. There is only a handful of monographs — a testament to the focal notion: Amazonian society=indigenous society — and the passing references to *caboclos* (and ersatz others) in the standard anthropological literature clearly position such Amazonians as awkward co-residents, and ones hardly worthy of attention. Three examples:

1. The rubber industry drew into Amazonia a large number of labourers from the north-east. This was not a passing phenomenon; it was not (only) a boom. It was an extractive industry which for almost a century made available to industrial manufacturers a unique product key to the development of the electrical and automative industries. There are two major monographs in English (Dean, Weinstein), one in Portuguese (Santos). And that's it.[1]

2. Japanese colonists in Amazonia are closely associated with the town of Tomé-Açu in the state of Para. One of the few development suc-

---

1   Dean (1987); Weinstein (1983a); Santos (1980).

cess stories of Amazonian colonisation (introduction of black pepper), Tomé-Açu has been the subject of one monograph (Staniford).[2]

3. Although the Jewish community in Amazonia dates from the early nineteenth century, it was immigration in the early twentieth century — mainly from Morocco — that formed the base of a contemporary community poorly accommodated by stereotypical portrayals of Amazonian society.

These three examples make the point that the social landscape of the region is not accurately filled by available stereotypes (Indians, predatory colonists), but these few new examples are hardly representative or exhaustive. The diversity of Amazonians/Amazonian societies simply has not been on the agenda.

This volume is preliminary. It is meant to indicate in a broad way the diversity of what has to date been a social landscape reduced to stereotype, but it seeks to do so not in the name of restoring balance, but in terms of recalibrating conceits about 'Amazonian society'. That there are concurrent non-indigenous Amazonias is hardly an issue, and all who work in Amazonia recognise the limitations of the crude nature versus culture framework which has prevailed, but there exist few attempts to address directly the greyscales of the Amazonian social landscape, and that fact is not surprising: the material is too voluminous, the conceits are too well-entrenched, the basic research has not been done. Instead, one finds — understandably — a retreat to manageable ground or recourse to programmatic if provisional synthesis. Wilson (1999), for example, in *Indigenous South Americans of the Past and Present* presents a cohesive post-Stewardian account in which the subject is not so much the societies of Amazonia, but the character of natural constraints which sharply direct social possibility. Roosevelt's (1994) *Amazonian Indians: from Prehistory to the Present* proposes an ambitious synthesis of archaeology, history and ethnography with the aim of establishing the empirical accuracy of modern views about the relationship between pre- and post-conquest Amazonia. Balée's (1999) *Advances in Historical Ecology* (although not wholly devoted to Amazonia) argues for a new kind of collaboration between history and the social and natural sciences.

This volume aims to fulfil quite a different task: to present some Amazonian societies which fall outside the standard terms of reference — classic or revisionist, societies which evade easy inclusion in the debates currently dominating Amazonian studies.

2. Staniford (1973).

Evading Inclusion

The chapters in this volume represent Amazonians who are peripheral in several senses. First of all, they are peripheral to the major idioms of contemporary Amazonian research as defined by the academy and the development institutions which shape the contemporary agenda. They include, for example, runaway slave communities, syndicalists, long-distance river traders, *caboclo* fishermen, rum distillers exploiting tidal power, *varzea* eco-managers, none of whom is a privileged player in the new Amazonian research environment.

Second, they are peripheral to Brazilian national society: they live in Amazonia, a region whose proximity to Brazil is highly negotiable. Amazonia is as close to Brazil from the standpoint of Europe, but from the standpoint of, say, Rio, it is hardly close at all.

Third, they are peripheral in terms of the 'officially' marginal Brazilian citizenry: they are neither closely affiliated with Brazilian indigenes nor with Brazilian New Social Movements (e.g. MST).

They are, for better or worse, neither one thing nor another in national terms — neither indigenous (true Amazonians) nor allocthanous (neo-Amazonias), but actual, existing Amazonian societies which repudiate many of the levelling orthodoxies of the official literature, and what links them thematically is modernity.

Modernity in Amazonia is typically represented in incomplete and narrow form through only one aspect: modernisation. While modernisation is certainly a compelling feature of the region — especially since 1970, and the extension of Kubitschek's developmentalist programme into the interior of Brazil — it is not exhaustive of Amazonian modernity. First of all, the colonial occupation of the region, commencing in the sixteenth century, effectively expunged native American social formations. Although some survived and even, by some measures, thrive today, for the past several hundred years the Amazonian landscape has been dominated not by promordialism or traditionalism, but by experiments in modernity, from new labour regimes to policies of racial miscegenation to republican movements to a pan-Amazonian mercantile network to urbanisation to the brutalities of rapid developmentalism. These amplified aspects of modernity have largely been overshadowed by the techno-economic modernisation.

Second, modernity in Amazonia has not been well represented in monumental form, nature as green hell having been entrusted with that role. An obvious exception is the Manaus Opera House (and indeed the apparatus associated with the rubber industry), but most of the markers of modernity are represented in a variety of social forms that occupy the uncertain space between the pre-modern *inferno verde* and late-modern national society.

Third, modernity in Amazonia has not been an overt aspect of Amazonia's own — and rather limited—culture industries. Isolated — spatially, historically, politically — from Brazilian centres of metropolitan culture, Amazonian literature, music and plastic arts are overwhelmed by external, received accounts, accounts which invariably highlight an atavistic Amazonia (with native Americans featuring prominently) and/or a turbulent frontier Amazonia courted by civilisation. In terms of cinema, for example, aside from limited distribution ethnographic films, Amazonia is represented by the likes of *Anaconda, Relic, Piranha, Lana, The Lost World, The Emerald Forest* and *The Creature from the Black Lagoon*.

At its weakest, the argument presented here is that Amazonia expresses a passive modernity: it is of the modern world, but not much of a contributor to it. There is a stronger version, however, represented by the chapters in this volume, to wit, Amazonian modernity is not so much absent as unexplored, and one reason for its having been left unexplored is the hegemony of the pair primordialism and modernisation and its numerous surrogates: the Indian and the bulldozer, the swidden and the GM soya plantation, the track in the forest and the Transamazon Highway, the *curare*-user and the goldminer.

The case studies presented below reveal a socially and historically complex Amazonia, but one whose coherence has never been officially ratified. To the degree that anthropologists and others working at the ethnographic level have addressed larger, overarching issues at the regional or national level, they have generally conformed to a simple periodisation that takes the (approximate) form:

- Contact

- Conquest

- Demographic collapse

- Extensive but haphazard extraction of tropical preciosities

- *Cabanagem*

- Rubber boom

- Economic stagnation

- State-led development

● Consolidation of control by techno-managerial state (including NGOs, multinationals)

If these reference points, in an admittedly rough scheme, are widely invoked in ethnographic studies, the sequence does not itself reveal crucial transformations of the social and natural landscapes associated with each point. Doing so, albeit in parsimonious fashion, indicates something about the depth and breadth of an Amazonian modernity far more complex than is customarily acknowledged in the anthropology of the region:

Contact

The foundation myth is: European explorers descend the River and encounter large Amerindian societies. The quest for gold, however, is disappointing, and the tropical preciosities available are not sufficient to displace interest in Andean societies. [*Amazonia is abandoned as centre-piece of Brazilian colonial project.*]

Conquest

Amazonia (and other parts of Brazil) was a potential colony disputed by a number of European powers (Portugal, Spain, France, UK, Netherlands) and religious orders. The rather haphazard economic exploitation should not disguise the fact that various imperial designs were placed on Amazonia from the outset. Indeed, the success of the Jesuits in organising indigenous peoples in line with the Order's interests contributed to their expulsion by Pombal in the mid-eighteenth century. [*Rapid military, religious and commercial incorporation of region within various imperial regimes.*]

Demographic Collapse

Although details of the collapse are poorly documented or understood, it is widely recognised that the absolute decline of indigenous populations was a major event in world history. Disputes about the dimensions of Amazonian populations aside, there is little question that the social landscape of Amazonia was, from the eighteenth century on, largely a colonial construction. This may be the less appealing face of modernity, but it is modernity nonetheless. [*Indigenous societies relegated to margins. Institutionalisation of various extractive-export regimes.*]

Tropical Preciosities

Amazonia was a domain of the so-called *drogas de sertão* (diverse neo-tropical preciosities), sufficient for maintaining active trade, but paling in comparison with the commercial prospects of plantation agriculture implemented elsewhere in Brazil. [*Fragmented, diverse extraction of floral and faunal products. Global market.*]

Cabanagem

The *cabanagem* is variously presented as: 1. A revolt of Amazonian marginals (Indians, *caboclos*, *quilombolas*); 2. A battle between republicans and monarchists; 3. A bid for regional independence. A civil revolt focused around the estuary cities of Belém and Cametá, the uprising was resolved with the intervention of British and French forces and resulted in the death of around a quarter of the metropolitan (estuary) population. [*A local movement informed by main platform modern issues: citizenry, republicanism, state-building, ethnic/class equations.*]

The Rubber Boom

While there was a boom in the last quarter of the nineteenth century, the rubber industry was a significant (and the most prominent) feature of the region from early in the nineteenth century (export records date from early 1820s and in almost each succeeding year — until 1914 — output and prices increased). By virtue of the extractive basis of the industry, the natural monopoly on *hevea* and the remoteness of the region from national political centres, the rubber industry stands outside the cycle of booms and busts which characterise the development of the modern Brazilian state: the market was external; there were few backward linkages; labourers were (in the main) recruited from outside the region (hence little sense of enclave economy primarily dependent on systematic articulation and exploitation of existing labour-providing societies — although Amerindians were hardly unexploited, cf. Putumayo, Mundurucú). While local trading houses (based in Manaus and Belém) were key players, the mercantile apparatus (ships, warehouses, docks, etc.) was largely external in origin. Congealed rubber was exported in unprocessed state directly from Manaus and Belém to New York, London and Lisbon, with no value-added in Amazonia. [*Over a period of around 100 years, the rubber industry established a production-trade system which transformed the economic life of the region. With annually rising prices, the cost of imported food, tools and other material goods could be offset without recourse to structural transformation of local-level agrarian/riperian system.*]

Economic Stagnation

With the introduction of South East Asian rubber onto the world market, modern Amazonia confronted a major rebuff. Not only was it impossible for Amazonian rubber to be produced more cheaply than South East Asian, the extractive (as opposed to plantation/industrial) basis of Amazonian production had resulted in little elaboration of ancillary apparatus. What remained was a credit-system (*aviamento*), some of the physical features (warehouses, trading houses, docks), but not high-volume transport. [Amazonia, having been modernised, was shorn of its modern role. The standard account is that Amazonia fell into an intractable state of economic stagnation. In terms of its position with the rubber industry, this is undeniable, but what happens when you become ex-modern? In the case of Amazonia the answer is certainly not primordialist involution: there was no primordialist position to be regained. In the main, Amazonian rubber-tappers (and associates) were not representatives of anything other than a modern Amazonia, however lacking the overt features of modernity it might have been. Four salient examples (two of which are explicitly addressed by case studies in this volume): a. Japanese colonisation (in Tomé-Açu, for instance, and more generally in relation to market-gardening and jute production); b. the formation of a Jewish community in the lower Amazon; c. the expansion of long-distance *regatão* (small scale trading boat) commerce (McGrath, this volume); d. local development of manufacturing for regional market, e.g. *cachaça* manufacture (Anderson, this volume). The characterisation of economic stagnation addresses more the collapse of Amazonia's position in global trade. In regional terms, by contrast, the period 1915–1960/70, displays consolidation of a regional, circumscribed economy and society.]

State-led Development

In terms of the speed and brutality of the so-called 'national integration' of Amazonia, flagged by the construction of the Belém–Brasilia highway (1960) commenced with vigour following the construction of the Transamazon Highway (1970) and implementation of the associated Plan for National Integration, the heroic/militaristic tropes invoked by the architects (conquest of the tropics, assault on the Amazon, etc.) are accurate, but the notion that Amazonia was a social *tabula rasa* is unsustainable. The effort, for example, to create an independent small-holder peasantry (via colonisation schemes built into the early phase of Transamazon development) was immediately confronted by the reality of an existing, diverse independent small-holder peasantry (not to mention Amerindians), and subsequent efforts to establish large-scale extractive regimes (Carajás, fishing industry, timber extraction, Trombetas bauxite mines) have in all cases revealed the emptiness of *tabula rasa* claims or assumptions. [State-led colonisation, offering various versions of hypothetical integrated Amazonian societies, has been challenged by an already in-place modern Amazonia.]

Techno-managerial Consolidation

The consolidation of federal agencies (SUDAM, INCRA, IBAMA, etc.) and multinational consortia (such as the Greater Carajás Project), as well as the introduction of supervisory apparatus (Tropical Forest Action Plan, SIVAM), has been accompanied by a dramatic increase in NGO activity in the region linked to the demands (realistically addressed or not) of historic Amazonian communities. This co-emergence attests to the differentiation of the social landscape in Amazonia, a differentiation of decidedly modern character. [The engagement of Amazonians in the official development of the region attests not only to the diversity of the constituency, but also the entrenchment of those diverse interests. *Quilombolas, pescadores, sindicalistas, seringueiros, caboclos, ribeirinhos* and *Zé Ninguém* (Joe Nobody) are not epiphenomena of the contemporary 'conquest of the tropics', but legatees of a long history of modern Amazonia.]

This brief outline is intended merely to make one uncontroversial point: the terms of reference for the study of contemporary Amazonian societies have been unreasonably constrained. In part this is due to the parlous position of native Amerindians and the crucial role of anthropology in securing some measure of defence. In part it is due to the historic marginality of the region — even during the rubber era — in relation to the development of Brazil. In part it is due to the dominance of ecologically-focused research in the last quarter of the twentieth century. This is not to say that important and interesting work which combines the ethnographic and the historic has not featured prominently in Amazonianist literature, but it is to say that the priorities have tended not to include ordinary Amazonians to a significant degree.

Aside from the two 'towards a new synthesis' works cited above,[3] two other books should be noted in the context of an amplified view of the Amazonian social landscape, Alcida Ramos's *Indigenism: Ethnic Politics in Brazil* (1998) and the late Warren Dean's *Brazil and the Struggle for Rubber: a Study in Environmental History* (1987), albeit for quite different reasons. Ramos's work bears heavily on the symbolic matrix within which

3.   Roosevelt (1994) and Balée (1999).

Amerindians (and other Amazonians) are articulated by national culture, and in doing so reveals the historic depth of attempts to deal with 'the Indian problem'. Her analysis succeeds, as few others have, in dissolving the crude contrast between traditional Indian society and modern national society, drawing attention to the dynamic qualities of the symbolic capital of Indians and Amazonia and the ways in which exotic Amazonia reflects not only aspects of an original condition, but a durable idiom for differentiation within the national landscape.

Dean's treatment of the rubber industry is noteworthy for its rejection of — for want of a better term — Amazonian social reductionism, namely the assertion that Amazonia 'lost' its industry to South East Asia because of inherent social defects (lazy peasants, cavalier businessmen). The core of his argument rests on environmental obstacles to large-scale plantation agriculture in Amazonia, not on social insufficiency (and after all, the Amazon rubber industry was a great success for almost 100 years, until its natural monopoly was broken). The particulars of the argument aside, *Brazil and the Struggle for Rubber* details, as no other monograph has, a cardinal feature of Amazonian modernism: the integration of peasant production into regional, national and international markets. This integration did not simply take the form of local producers discovering a global market, but a production system created by external industrial demand. .Modern Amazonia arose not from the ashes of collapsed indigenous systems (they had been effectively expunged by the early nineteenth century when the rubber industry commenced), but at the behest of global demand for rubber. Dean's work is of particular interest from the perspective of this volume because of the way in which the intactness of primordial Amazonia (green hell, noble savages) is shown to be untenable.

The work of Ramos and Dean frames key concerns of this volume in drawing attention to the symbolic capital of the notion 'Amazonian society' and empirical material which confounds the coherence of that symbolic capital. The distorted relationship between symbol and fact is a persistent feature of Amazonian discourse (for example, the fraught status of 'sustainable development'), and that fact itself can hardly be ignored. This collection, however, has more modest aims than a complete reconfiguration of Amazonian discourse. The larger issues alluded to certainly have bearing, but for the moment the aims reflect the particular areas of research represented by authors whose work falls outside the official Amazonias represented in the indigenist or modernisationist literature.

CHAPTER 1

'The *Roça* Legacy': Land Use and Kinship Dynamics in Nogueira, an Amazonian Community of the Middle Solimões Region*

Deborah de Magalhães Lima

In various regions of the Brazilian Amazon, the term *comunidade* ('community') refers to a type of settlement where residents have their own political organisation, officers (president, vice president, treasurer, etc.) and a democratic process of discussing their problems.[1] In the Middle Solimões region, the county of Tefé recognises the existence of approximately 63 rural communities in its jurisdiction. Nogueira, a community located on Lake Tefé on the bank opposite the town with the same name, is one of them.[2]

Nogueira is formed by 54 households and, as residents promptly inform visitors, all of them are related through kinship. The link between kinship and locality is not particular to this settlement. On the contrary, the identity of villages as 'communities of kin' extends to all of the Middle Solimões and other Amazonian regions.[3] Since the Middle Solimões is an area of long-term occupation and, unlike frontier regions of Amazonia, does not have intense land conflicts, the existence of social groups deriv-

---

*   Based on the doctoral dissertation 'The Social Category Caboclo – History, Social Organisation, Identity and Outsider's Social Classification of the Rural Population of an Amazonian Region (the Middle Solimões)' (University of Cambridge, Lima Ayres, 1992).

1   The formation of these rural communities was a result of the community empowerment and social work done by the Movimento Eclesiástico de Base (MEB), an organisation associated with the progressive wing of the Catholic Church that began to work in the Amazon in the 1970s. As a result of MEB's work (a combination of mission and outreach), the term *comunidade* has come to define a politically organised locality whose population identifies itself as members of this organisation.

2   Residents of the town of Tefé refer to Nogueira as a *caboclo* community. However, *caboclo* is not used as a reference to one's own identity but to refer to people who, in the regional classification of people, are considered inferior to the speaker. This use originates from the history of the term, initially used to refer to village Indians and afterwards to white and Indian mestizos. It is associated with a negative stereotype that includes attributes such as laziness and craftiness, hence the rural people's refusal to identify with it. For an extensive analysis of the term, see Lima (1992; 1999).

3   Galvão (1955); Wagley (1957); Nugent (1993); Harris (2000).

ing from a stable system of reproduction centred on kinship became a subject of research interest. What is the process of reproduction of these groups, and how did the density of kin that characterises the formation of the *comunidades* in this region come about? The chapter approaches this question by looking at land tenure and economic production in the context of the developmental cycle of households, taking into account marriage patterns and local ways of representing kinship.

Land Tenure and the System of Shifting Cultivation

In Nogueira, as is the case in the majority of the rural settlements in the region, land tenure is based on land use rights held by residents and their relatives. Non-kin can be granted access to land as long as they receive permission from the group to live amongst them. Their traditional model of land tenure is based on a notion of collective 'ownership' of the community's territory that operates in association with the right of exclusive land use rights of plots of cultivated land. Those who have cleared the forest to plant *roças* (patches of cultivated land) are considered the 'owners' (*donos*) of these small areas. The labour that establishes ownership mainly involves the clearing of natural forest. Individual possession of the parcels of land is guaranteed through continuous use. The right to exclusive use is also observed in the *capoeiras,* secondary forests that succeed the *roças* and consist of fallow land for soil recovery and future planting. Thus residents are not bound by the existence of fixed property relations but have to operate in a form of landholding where rights and access are provisional.

This concept of ownership is associated with the agricultural system of shifting cultivation for planting manioc.[4] The right of land use, and not the division of land in fixed plots, gives flexibility to agricultural production.[5] The *roças* and *capoeiras* of different ages make up the patched agricultural landscape common to shifting cultivation.

In Nogueira there are many negotiations and transfers of parcels of land to accommodate the different needs and capacities for cultivation that each family faces, although no one is responsible for the distribution of plots. Since labour establishes exclusive land use rights, in theory, those that can and do invest more work hold larger stretches of land. The sys-

---

4 *Manihot esculenta*, Crantz — a group of several varieties of manioc or cassava tubers which contains poisonous glycosides; only edible after poison is removed.

5 Netting (1993), p. 161. According to Martins (1997, p. 179) it is also related to the Brazilian history of land rights. Many traditional peasant groups retain a conception of land tenure established in colonial times, which based land rights on occupation and use.

Cognatic kinship – no distinction between patri/matri lineal relatives
↳ Promotes survival of family

tem of agricultural production and the definition of land tenure reflect a
collective and egalitarian ideology in which all members of the group (residents, their descendants and close kin) have equal rights of access to the
land.[6] This equality of rights does not prevent economic differentiation in
terms of the size of the area of cultivated land and volume of production.
However, this is not questioned by residents because differentiation is the
outcome of variation of individual labour effort. Ownership based on
labour investment prevents economic inequality from solidifying and creating permanent differences within the group.

Nogueira was maintained as a settlement free from the domain and rule
of bosses (*patrões*) who occupied large stretches of land along the Solimões
River during the nineteenth and the beginning of the twentieth centuries,
principally looking to extract brazil nuts. The ownership of these lands was
established on the basis of the system of *aviamento*.[7] In this system the
owner of the native brazil nut grove, the patron, holds exclusive commercial ties with the tenants. His clients (*fregueses*) are obliged to deliver all
brazil nuts collected on the property to the patron, in exchange for subsistence goods. This form of landholding rests on a commercial relation and
is generally accompanied by the client's debt to the patron; it is a way of
exercising control over labour and perpetuating social inequality in a region
with abundant land. The establishment of ownership through control of
market access is not entirely unrelated to the concept of land holding
based on usufruct since the former is a way of superseding the latter in
order to install economic inequality which could not be justified ideologi-
cally neither in the dominions of the brazil nut groves, since they were
native, nor in explicit forms of slavery, then abolished.

Land conflicts in the Amazon are more frequent in areas where private
property is established. In regions where large cattle ranches and extensive
agricultural farms were implanted, and absolute control over the territory was
imposed, landowners disregarded the traditional land rights and drove the
peasants away by force.[8] Such displacement, extensive and generally violent,

6   In order to keep the traditional model of collective ownership, when residents of
     Nogueira were given the opportunity to legalise land ownership, instead of dividing
     the land among themselves and establishing individual plots they chose to register
     property under an association formed by the residents.

7   *Aviamento* — trade based on barter calculated in terms of monetary values; involves
     an informal credit relationship where manufactured goods are supplied in advance in
     exchange for future payment in extractive products, such as rubber, timber, fish and
     brazil nut; also a noun for the goods supplied on credit.

8   Esterci (1987); Martins (1982).

did not occur in the Middle Solimões. In this region it is common to find traditional peasant communities located within the extractive properties and in these cases the patrons do not charge rent for agricultural production but maintain the commercialisation of brazil nut groves under their control.

In Nogueira there are natural brazil nut trees preserved in the middle of the cultivated fields. They are not owned by anyone, because no one planted them. The gathering of brazil nut shells is done through the system called 'do avança', which means, 'first come-first served'. Residents are not committed to selling the brazil nut to a particular patron, as is the case in the extractive properties. But until the 1950s, when commerce in Tefé was small and the market for non-extractive products was limited, the aviamento system predominated and everyone traded with merchants who supplied goods in exchange for extractive products. Course manioc flour, called farinha, was also traded, though in small quantities. With the growth of the town of Tefé in the 1970s, the demand for manioc flour surged and its production grew considerably to the point where manioc became the main agricultural product of the region. The sale of manioc flour permits a commercial freedom that is not possible with extractive products, such as timber, fish and brazil nuts. These products have to be financed by itinerant merchants (regatões) who, like the old bosses, finance extractive production, but do not maintain the same degree of coercion and exclusive control over the product.

Manioc flour is the principal source of carbohydrates of the Amazon population and, according to Albuquerque (1969), manioc is a 'social crop'.[9] More than just an element in the regional culinary repertoire, manioc flour holds such a significant symbolic value for the population that they cannot conceive of 'eating without farinha'. The various qualities of manioc flour, the different types of manioc plant (the maniva) and the range of other products made from the plant make it a key element of Amazonian cultural tradition.[10] The growth of the market for manioc flour represents a special situation for its producers since they have to manage its destination — for sale or domestic consumption — from a complex chart of necessities and consumer options offered by a market that is more and more accessible and dominant.

In the upland environment of Nogueira (terra firme)[11] the roças are cultivated in continuous sequence. In a specific period of the year the resi-

9   Albuquerque (1969), p. 164.
10   For an analysis of the symbolic representation of food consumption in the lower Amazon, see Murrieta (2001).
11   Terra firme and várzea are the two main habitats of the Solimões. The terra firme is made up of the highest terrains, while the várzea is composed of terrain inundated annually by the waters of the Solimões.

dents can have two or three *roças*: a mature *roça* that is being harvested (planted two years earlier), a 'green' *roça* that is still growing (planted one year earlier) and a *roça* that is under cultivation. The work of opening the garden plot starts between June and August. Land is cleared (*roçagem*), the largest trees are felled and the logs are burned to prepare the fields for cultivation. The planting of the manioc is done from stems cut from the branches that are taken from the mature *roça*.

Contrary to other aspects of agricultural production (such as the size of the *roça* and volume of production), the date of the first harvest is always remembered since it constitutes the reference point in time to administer the volume of each harvest in relation to the estimated duration of the *roça's* *growth*. Many times they refer to this date as the *roça's* birthday, in contrast to the tendency to disregard their own and relatives' date of birth.

Manioc cultivation is critical to the survival and reproduction of rural communities. This dependence is acknowledged by people in various ways. For example, in the middle of a conversation, one woman told me about how she understood the succession of generations: 'When we die, we leave our seed, our children: the legacy of the roça.' I used this testimony as the title for this chapter since it illustrates the strong association between the labour cycles of the *roças* and social reproduction that stand out among all the other characteristics of the developmental cycle of the domestic groups.

The Developmental Cycle of Households and Land Occupation

The domestic economy of Nogueira responds to the evolving composition of households and farm holdings. Parents have authority over their children's labour until they marry. After establishing a conjugal unit, the offspring open their own *roça* and work on it following the same customs of the sexual division of labour. The men cut, clear and burn the trees to open the fields. During planting the men dig and the women plant the stems of the *maniva*; the women weed and, together, men and women pull out the manioc, grate and squeeze it to take out the poisonous juice called *tucupi*, and roast the pulp in the oven to make the flour. Each household works in an area of land which they call *sítio* or site. Here they construct *barracas* — small thatched huts with a griddle for toasting manioc flour — plant orchards and open their *roças*.

The economic autonomy of each household does not translate into lack of collective labour. On the contrary, the *ajuri* — communal work party gathered mainly for agricultural labour — is essential for guaranteeing production beyond the work capacity of the family. They are mainly formed to help in the clearing of the plots and the planting of the *roças*. All forms of labour exchange, whether the work party or the other forms of collaboration, clearly demonstrate the independence of each domestic unit. None of them can interfere, exploit or claim unconditionally the work of another. The reciprocity of the system of work parties is calculated in a commercial manner: the guest participating in someone else's *ajuri* expresses his expectation that he will be rewarded saying that he will 'go earning' ('*vai ganhando*', that is, he joins the work party with the knowledge that by this means he will earn future labour, and is not giving it away) while the owner of *roça* who made the invitation will 'be indebted' ('vai perdendo') for having to repay each of the participants. The respect and reputation of each couple depends on their work and the ability to provide for the households that they head.

New couples very rarely establish their own separate household immediately after marriage, as they will have only just acquired control over their labour. Few unmarried people have individual gardens and, even those who do, do not make use of it in isolation since a large amount of the manioc flour that is produced is for domestic consumption. For this reason recently-formed couples live with the parents of one of the spouses until they accumulate sufficient assets to build their own house and maintain themselves independently.

In Nogueira the majority of households are made up of simple families that consist of a conjugal unit and children. Table 1.1 shows the composition of the domestic groups in Nogueira. For comparative purposes, it also includes the household composition in other settlements in the Middle Solimões: Viola and Vila Alencar, located in the floodplain areas (the *várzeas*).[12] All the data refer to the end of the 1980s.

The family composition of the households in the three settlements is similar and reveals that the common characteristics in the developmental cycle of the domestic groups do not depend on the type of environment. Characterised by Fortes 1958 according to the premises and tension that define its different phases (formation and growth, dispersion and extinction), this development involves demographic aspects of generational succession as well as the social context in which the reproduction of the

12   In Tefé County, the rural settlements of the *terra firme* are the largest and have, on average, 36 households; the *várzea* settlements are smaller, represented by an average of 16 households (data supplied by the Institute of the Development of the Amazon, 1995). This difference comes from the distinct ecological characteristics of the two environments, especially the fact that the areas propitious to habitation in the *várzea* are restricted to the narrow strips of the highest lands — the *restingas*.

group is processed. The locally defined ideal composition of the domestic group is the simple family, as is observed from the statistics of family types and the architecture of the most common houses, which have only one bedroom, in which both parents and children sleep.

Table 1.1: The Household Composition in Nogueira (1988), Viola (1986) and Vila Alencar (1988)

Household Structure	Nogueira	Viola	Vila Alencar	Total
Simple Family	30	8	9	47
(one Conjugal Family Unit)	(68%)	(67%)	(69%)	(67%)
Extended Family	7	3	2	12
(one CFU and a relative)	(16%)	(25%)	(15%)	(17%)
Multiple Family	5	-	-	5
(two related CFUs)	(11%)			(7%)
Complex Families	1	1	1	3
(multiple and extended family)	(2%)	(8%)	(8%)	(4%)
Solitary	2	-	1	3
(lone adult)	(5%)		(8%)	(4%)
TOTAL Households	45	12	13	70

*Definitions based on Laslett (1972).

The cases of multiple and complex families, shown in Table 1.1, represent situations in which new couples live with their parents. This co-habitation does not usually last more than one or two years, as the setting up of a new house is precipitated by, among other factors, the arrival of children to the young couple. The percentage of domestic groups with more than one conjugal unit is relatively low, 11 per cent of all cases, thus reflecting the relative speed with which new couples establish their own household, considering that they only have this period of time to build their first farm holding which, although straightforward, requires effort and commitment.

The instances of extended families reflects the inclusion of relatives from ascending generations — generally a widowed parent of one of the spouses — or from lower generations, usually a grandchild, son of a temporary union left with the grandparents after the mother forms a more lasting union and establishes her own residency. The three solitary cases are adult males who looked after their parents until they died.

While couples establish their own households in a relatively short time, they do not show the same agility in establishing an adequate set of farm holdings and the couples continue to remain connected to their parents. An important aspect of the developmental cycle of the household consists of the allocation of farm plots to a new couple. This is usually made by the parents of the spouse in whose household the couple first lived. A young couple will gradually increase the number of *capoeiras* they have while they progress in their farming activities. The expansion of a household's set of *capoeiras* is related to the length of time the family has been in existence and its capacity to cultivate larger plots. When children move out, the labour force of the household decreases. At the same time, the household's farm holding is likely to be divided among married children.

In this process of partition children occupy farm plots located close to the ones their parents still cultivate. The plots of parents and married children converge on a parental *barraca*. Although they farm separately, parents and married children nevertheless constitute a close cooperative group. The set formed by their separate plots constitutes a joint farm holding. They exchange services and products more casually among themselves than with other households, with whom they interact mainly through the formal labour exchange system of the work parties.

The parental couple heads the joint farm holding until they die or become too infirm to farm. Their children usually remain farming in the parental holding. Over time, siblings are likely to acquire their own *barraca* and separate. The growth of each sibling family might also 'push' a number of them out of the joint farm holding. After the death of the parents the older and more established sibling is likely to remain in the parental holding and the younger ones tend to move out, and he/she will look for another relative for support. The most likely choice is to farm with their spouse's parents. Conversely, when parents are still alive, it is usually the older siblings who move out, leaving the younger and more dependent siblings to farm with the parents.

The system of land claims is flexible and structured so as to allow mobility. If neither parental holding is suitable, the young couple can look for a better site and rebuild their hut there. Residents can open a new site in the forest, take over a site abandoned by an emigrant, or request that a household under less pressure either share its holding or give it out to them. These constitute the seven types of occupancy I observed in Nogueira. I called the sites cultivated by parents and one or more sibling couples a 'parental partition'. In some cases, I found only siblings dividing the parental site and these I called 'sibling partition'. The cases in which one offspring succeeds the parental occupation I simply called 'succession'. These are the three cases of transfer of land holding among close relatives.

Demographic pressure (or the presence of many families in the same site) and exhaustion of soil are some factors that compel the couples to look for areas outside of the immediate circle of relatives. The cases that I called 'take over' refer to the occupation of areas abandoned by some resident in Nogueira without any formal transfer. The 'donation' refers to the concession of an area in favour of a specific resident. Although there is little available land still covered by forest in Nogueira, there are cases of occupation in these areas that I called 'new site'. Finally, there are couples that partition the site of other residents who are not close relatives, dividing the *capoeiras* and the *barraca* with them; this type of occupation I called 'share'.

Table 1.2: Type of Occupancy of 51 Sites of Cultivation in Nogueira and the Spouse Responsible for the Claim

Type of occupancy	Frequency		Claimed through		
	Absolute	Relative	Husband	Wife	Both
Parental Partition	13	25%	6	7	-
Succession	11	21%	8	3	-
Take over	7	14%	1	3	3
New site	7	14%	4	-	3
Share	5	10%	3	-	2
Donation	4	8%	3	1	-
Sibling Partition	4	8%	4	-	-
Total	51	100%	29 (57%)	14 (27%)	8 (16%)

Table 1.2 shows the frequency of each type of occupancy, referring to areas of planting of 51 couples in Nogueira. It also reveals the sex of the spouse who made the claim or succeeded to the area. The occupation of sites that do not involve some type of transfer ('take over' or 'new site') is based on the inalienable right to cultivate areas of communal land that one of the spouses or the couple has, owing to the fact that they are from the place.

The holdings occupied through 'parental partition', 'succession' and 'sibling partition' originate from a parental holding and constitute a little more than half of the total number of farm holdings (54 per cent). Although they resemble 'inheritances' because they were passed down from one generation to the next, the character of the transfer and the temporality of the holdings highlight the comparative 'shallowness' of the linear transfers so central to the reproduction of other peasant societies,[13] despite the fact that new couples initially depend on such occupancy. The categories of occupancy — 'take over', 'new site', 'share' and 'donation' — were established in non-parental holdings and constitute a little under half (46 per cent) of the sample. So, land obtained from a direct transfer made by relatives occurs roughly in the same proportion as access acquired outside the immediate family circle.

In relation to the sex of the spouse who made the claim, the data show that the majority of holdings were claimed through husbands (57 per cent). Only 27 per cent of the claims were made through wives and 16 per cent were based on both spouses. Therefore, one can observe the tendency to have men as successors to parental holdings, not defined by rule but by circumstance: from a young age, boys participate more effectively in farming activities than girls, and so they are likely to be more attached to the family's farm holding. Moreover, girls are 'freer' to move to towns, where they work as domestic servants and study, than the boys whose labour is more valued.

Just as the statistics on family types represent a snapshot of a dynamic process through which a domestic group passes, the same can be said of the types of land holding. The cycles of land occupation are even more diverse and the frequencies presented in Table 1.2 do not allow a common developmental cycle for all cases to be inferred. Only tendencies can be observed, as those mentioned above. The ways to establish a farm holding are diverse, and each couple has to find their own way.

---

13   Segalen (1986).

Economic Performance and Demographic Differentiation

Sometimes families cannot meet their consumption needs of manioc flour because they do not have sufficient productive area at a particular time. In fact, the only explanation that I received regarding how residents determine the size of the *roça*, and consequently their manioc flour production, was that it depended on the area of mature *capoeira* they had at their disposal. This situation in Nogueira — the absence of individual ownership and holding established by usufruct — permits a discussion of the relationship between the volume of production and the family's work capacity, using ideas developed by A.V. Chayanov (1966).

Instead of testing Chayanov's model, the validity of which has been contested,[14] the analysis that follows uses Chayanov's propositions as tools with which to evaluate the importance of the demographic changes associated with the domestic group's developmental cycle in the determination of the volume of domestic production (often referred to as 'demographic differentiation'). There are some aspects in which the Chayanovian model is a useful analytical device, and in these cases the presence of basic characteristics is critical. These include the existence of abundant land to make allowance for the variation in consumer demand of the domestic group (a context that Chayanov called 'repartitional commune areas'),[15] absence of paid work and relative independence from the market.[16] None of these factors is completely observed in Nogueira. Although abundant land exists in the direction of the interior of *terra firme*, the qualification of good land for farming and habitation is its proximity to fluvial routes or, in other words, market access.

However, even with land as a limiting factor, the fact that landholding is defined by labour investment implies that household age and composition has the potential to influence the size of the farmed area and consequently the volume of domestic production. This relationship can be observed in Figure 1.1. The graph shows the mean values of the *roças* of 31 heads of household arranged according to the age group of the household head, used as a reference for the age of the family (data collected in 1986).

It can be seen that the mean value of the *roça* areas tends to present a normal distribution in which heads of households in their forties have the largest cultivated areas, while younger and older male heads have the smallest. Given that the farm holding is established throughout family life, it is

---

14   See for example the reviews in Durrenberger (1984); Harrison (1975); Ennew et al. (1977) and Patnaik (1977).

15   Chayanov (1966), p. 68.

16   Netting (1993), pp. 298; 310.

to be expected that middle-aged individuals would have more *capoeiras* at their disposal since they would have had more time to accumulate than young couples. Older couples tend to have smaller areas for their own use as a result of having started to give away *capoeiras* to their married children.

Figure 1.1: Age of Male Head and Area of Roças

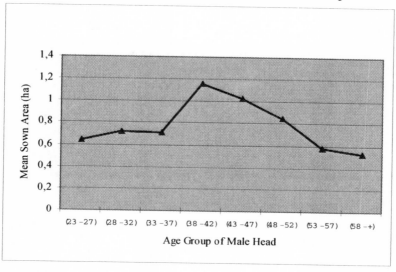

Thus, the values of the sown area reveal a tendency of the household to produce according to family age. It also shows that, in general, the economic differentiation among the residents of Nogueira is influenced by demographic factors associated with the domestic group's developmental cycle. Chayanov's proposition is that the volume of production is determined by the equilibrium point or the intersection between the curves of marginal utility of goods and marginal disutility of labour.[17] This example appears to be confirmed when we take the same rates that he used to measure the relative contribution of the family members for household consumption and production (rate of consumers, producers and consumer/worker ratio).[18]

17   Chayanov (1966), pp. 78–84.
18   *Ibid.*, p. 58. Chayanov claims that the volume of peasant production is determined by consumption needs, and that this is subjectively calculated. In the course of the developmental cycle of a domestic group, when the number of producers starts to increase, the 'drudgery' of work (which was at its peak when children were small), starts to decrease. The volume of production, on the other hand, does not increase

Taking the mean values of the cultivated area by age group of the male head and the sown area, one can observe a statistically significant correlation ($rs=0.87$; $N=33$; $p<0,01$) between the average size of the *roças* and the mean values of the C/W. Figure 1.2 illustrates this correlation.

Figure 1.2: Consumer/Worker Ratio and Sown Area

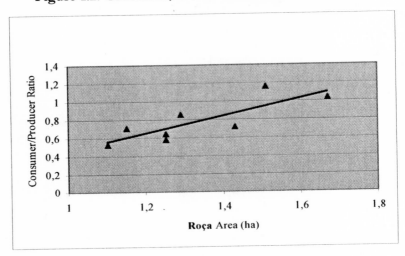

However, analysing individually the values of the cultivated area by each domestic group (and not taking the mean per age group) and calculating their consumer, producer and consumer/producer rates, it is possible to see a statistically significant correlation between the total number of workers and the index W for workers (rs 0.31 and 0.34; $p<0.05$; $N=33$), but neither the total number nor the rate C of consumers, nor the C/W ratio are positively related. The data also show a highly significant correlation with the number of male producers ($rs=0.42$; $p<0.01$), but not female producers.

---

proportionally, but is kept related to the family's consumption needs. In order to weight the relative participation in labour and consumption of household members, Chayanov used rates for consumption (C) and labour (W) to differentiate members according to their ages. In the course of the family developmental cycle, the rate of consumers in relation to the rate of workers (C/W ratio) thus follows a normal curve. The debated aspect of Chayanov's formulations regards not the structural features of the developmental cycle, nor the evolution of the C/W ratio, but the proposed correlation between volume of production and the ratio of C/W.

Following Chayanov's interpretation, the major influence of workers, but not consumers, in defining the areas of cultivation implies the presence of a high utility of goods (to compensate for work exhaustion) or a low level of domestic consumption (the equilibrium point was not reached).

There are two factors that can be pointed to as responsible for these apparently contradictory results: on the one hand, the Chayanovian correlation as a tendency and on the other, the individual variation of the size of *roças*. The first factor is the nature of the relationship between the developmental cycle of the household and the establishment of the farm holding. Since this is circumstantial, for it depends on negotiations over the transfers of *capoeiras*, it is expected that the response to the land needs according to changes in the domestic group will not necessarily be an immediate one. The fit will only show as a trend and not a rule.

The second factor is a family's capacity to obtain extra-household labour. In manioc cultivation, aside from the *ajuri* labour groups organised by strict reciprocity rules, there is also exchange of a day's work (*troca de dia*) and day-labour (or *diária*). The most important phases of manioc cultivation are the clearing and the planting. The size of the *roça* is defined by the labour available to perform these tasks and the people generally assemble work parties to undertake both. An *ajuri* for clearing the fields of brushwood is formed, on average, by groups of nine people, and the one for planting consists, on average, of 21 people.

In fact, there is a correspondence between the size of the work party and the sown area ($r_s = 0.38$; $p<0.05$). In general, the interrelatedness of the planting cycles and the harvest influences the size of the garden to be planted since the cost of a work party is high. Besides the payment in labour exchange, a small meal is offered before the group leaves to work, and a large meal is given after the work is finished, consisting of 'luxury' items: rice, pasta, beans and a fish or meat stew. The cost of these meals is generally covered by the sale of two sacks, or 130 kg., of manioc flour. Only those who have a mature garden to finance the work party can enter the labour exchange circuit. Given that the owners of the largest gardens can pay the expenses of work groups big enough to plant a large *roça*, there is a tendency of the sizes of the gardens to follow a proportional sequence. Large manioc garden owners are able to finance the opening of a large *roça*, and small *roça* owners have limited means to plant a large garden, so they are likely to plant small *roças*, unless exceptional effort is made to overcome such limitation employing only the labour available from the domestic group itself.

In this way, the residents of Nogueira can be distinguished according to a pattern of economic performance, which takes into account the variables of labour availability and size of holding. Such classification is not fixed since exceptional effort can be done to plant a large *roça*. Nevertheless, the size of the garden determines the context in which the individual defines his economic strategy. The possibility of employing extra-household labour and the conditions to have them is the second factor that accounts for the variation of the *roça* sizes. While the definition of the landholding creates an adequate context for the presence of a Chayanovian trend in the determination of the volume of agricultural production, the availability of extra-household labour obtained through work parties and day-labour, makes room for individual choices of economic strategies.

The residents of Nogueira can be classified according to the size of the garden and the economic strategies related to them in three different categories. Table 1.3 shows a classification of 32 residents of Nogueira according to the size of their *roças*.

Table 1.3: Grouped Frequencies of *Roça* Areas Measured in Nogueira (in hectares), and Classification of the *Roça* Owner, 1986 (N=32)

Class of roça area (ha)	Frequency	Classification of the roça owner
(0.20 – 0.59)	31%	Small
(0.60 – 0.99)	44%	Medium
(1.00 - +)	25%	Large

Generally, a small *roça* cannot support a household's consumption needs up to the time of the harvest of the next garden. As a result, owners of small *roças* must look for temporary and complementary sources of income until the harvest of their next garden. The majority of small *roça* owners rely on the possibility of engaging in day-labour for the owners of large *roças* in Nogueira (there is also the option of engaging in temporary wage labour in the nearby town of Tefé). Wages are paid in cash or in kind (manioc tubers or manioc flour).

Owners of the large *roças* (over one hectare) need extra-familiar labour to help them in all the phases of the agricultural cycle, especially to harvest and process the manioc into flour. Besides the resources provided by large *roças* planted the year before, some of the owners of large *roças* use other sources of regular income to finance the extra-familial labour. Such is the case of the local teachers who use their salaries to hire day-labour.

The owners of the medium-sized *roças*, around 0.7 hectares, are able to provide domestic consumption needs with their own labour and do not need to look for sources of complementary income. Normally, these *roças* are opened with the use of medium-sized work parties.

Despite the existence of these differences, I did not observe internal social groupings organised on the basis of economic or consumption differences, neither were individuals in any way distinguished (through prejudice, gossip or alliances) according to economic status. The relationship between day-labourers and the owners of the large *roças* does not show any signs or intentions to assert a difference between the positions of employer and employee. The work of the day-labourer is often called 'help paid with money'. It is preferred by the owners of the large *roças* because it allows them to concentrate work on their own *roça*, without having to contribute to the labour circuit formed by the participants of a work party. There is an interdependent relationship between the owners of the large and small *roças*. The owners of the large *roças* depend on the work provided by those who opened small *roças* and these rely on the labour opportunity provided by the large *roça* owners to get through until their next *roça* matures.

The use of Chayanov's propositions in the analysis of domestic production shows that economic differentiation is based as much on demographic as it is on individual economic choices. 'Demographic differentiation' is expressed in the general trend for economic production to follow the family's developmental cycle. It cannot be said with certainty to what extent this relationship is based upon a subjective calculation of the marginal utility of goods in relation to the drudgery of work, or whether it relates only to the system of household reproduction and land partitioning.

The tendency for a 'Chayanovian slope' to be found in the domestic economy,[19] combined with the existence of demographic-independent household economic differentiation, points to an important characteristic of the domestic economy: the contradiction between the individual autonomy of married adults in decisions concerning all spheres of economic practice and the dependence upon mutual help for these same matters. The household is partially a self-sustaining economic unit. The household supports itself with its own labour and is autonomous in its relationship

19   See Sahlins (1988).

with the market. Market exchanges are, however, disadvantageous for rural peasants. The response to this inequality reveals the communal aspects of the settlement corporativeness, and its main idiom is kinship. The perception of land use, the sharing of transport and instruments of production, reciprocity in consumption (e.g. the idea of a good neighbour is one who regularly gives out food gifts), and the networks of labour assistance show that Nogueira residents conceive economic resources in a collective manner. The community defines the basic collectivity of users of economic resources, although the claims of kin are not restricted to co-residence.

Table 1.4: Frequencies of Different Types of Relationships of the Households to the main Kinship Networks of Five Rural Localities in the Middle Solimões Region

Main Families of the Settlements	2 spouses related	1 spouse related	Affinal Relation	Not related	N houses
S.Fco.	1	2	-	-	3
Santos, Martins	(33%)	(66%)			
Viola	6	7	1	-	14
Medeiros, Cordeiro, Alves	(43%)	(50%)	(7%)		
Catuiri	4	7	4	2	17
Souza	(23%)	(41%)	(24%)	(12%)	
V.Alencar	4	10	-	-	14
Martins	(29%)	(71%)			
Nogueira Araújo, Fogaça,	31	22	1	-	54
Batalha, Quirino da Silva,	(57%)	(41%)	(2%)		
Oliveira, de Pinho					
Total	46	48	6	2	102
	(45%)	(47%)	(6%)	(2%)	(100%)

Kinship and Settlement

The genealogical relationships between couples in five rural communities in Middle Solimões, presented in Table 1.4, is presented in order to illustrate the extensive pattern of kinship density in the rural settlements of the region. These settlements contain one or more families considered dominant, for being the largest and oldest, and these are generally related to one another; a variable number of individuals who have entered the community by marrying into these families, with a number of them being interrelated; some in-married individuals consanguineously related to migrant couples, who are, in this way, related to the dominant families; and a very few totally unrelated migrant couples. In the table, the households classified as '2 spouses related' represent endogamous (with the group) marriages; '1 spouse related' refers to exogamous (out of the settlement) marriages; 'affinal relation' refers to migrant couples related by affinity to one of the dominant families through an in-married relative; and 'not related' are the cases of migrants not consanguineously related to any household in the community.

These data show that, overall, 45 per cent of households in the five communities consist of endogamous marriages, and 47 per cent of exogamous marriages. In other words, in 92 per cent of the households at least one spouse is local. This proves the predominance of ambilocal residence and shows that outsiders enter the communities mainly through marriage. Of the total number of outsiders (56), 86 per cent are in-married. In contrast, the occurrence of migrant couples is low. They constitute only eight per cent of all households and represent only 14 per cent of outsiders.

Another feature of the pattern of local reproduction responsible for the density of kin is the incidence of consanguineous marriages and of repeated family unions (i.e. more than one marriage between the same families). These 'relinking marriages' cause a significant increase in the density of kinship relationships and they occur both among endogamous and exogamous marriages. A number of endogamous marriages are consanguineous, and others repeat the same union between local families. Among exogamous marriages, consanguineous marriages also occur between relatives born in different communities and there are cases of locals married to small groups of in-married relatives.

Table 1.5 shows the frequency of each type of relinking marriages, illustrating that in five localities, 37 per cent of all resident couples represent such relinked marriages. The instances of consanguineous unions are mainly marriages between second cousins, whereas repeated family unions are of various types.[20]

---

20   For example, in the locality of Viola, three couples repeat the same union between the Cordeiro and Medeiros families — three brothers are married to two sisters and one of their cousins, and the marriage between an Alves woman with a Cordeiro man was followed by the marriage of the niece of the Cordeiro man to the son of the Alves woman's cousin. In Vila Alencar one case consists of a brother and a sister married to another sibling couple and another case involves the union of a sibling couple and a couple of cousins.

Table 1.5: Frequency of Cases of Consanguineous Marriages and Repeated Family Unions within Endogamous and Exogamous Marriages of Five Rural Communities of the Middle Solimões

Community	N Couples	Type of Marriage	Endogamous Marriages	Exogamous Marriages	Relative Frequency
S. Francisco	3	Consanguineous	1	-	33%
Viola	14	Repeated unions	5	-	36%
Catuiri	17	Repeated unions	2	-	12%
Vila Alencar	14	Consanguineous	1	-	7%
		Repeated unions	5	6	74%
Nogueira	54	Consanguineous	5	2	13%
		Repeated unions	-	11	24%
Total	102	Total of relinking marriages	19	19	37%

These marriages reproduce and reinforce the intricate network of kinship of the rural communities. The occurrence of relinking marriages is generally interpreted as a strategy to avoid excessive land division and to keep property within the family.[21] Despite of the absence of a formal 'property inheritance', the preference for relinking marriages is still related to land, but only indirectly. The main focus in this case is labour, since it is necessary to keep labour in order to maintain access to land. Relinking marriages strengthen the ties among relatives and thus guarantee the maintenance of a pool of potential cooperative labour.

In relation to the symbolic conception of kinship relatedness, the rural population uses the Brazilian kinship terminology in a special manner, defining with more precision the collateral (i.e. the siblings of lineal relatives such as parents and grandparents) limits of kin to acknowledge a greater number of relatives. The system of Brazilian kinship is cognatic and has an Eskimo terminology.[22] The rural people of the Middle

---

21 Segalen (1986); Woortmann (1995).
22 Eskimo kinship terminology is marked by a bilateral emphasis (no distinction is made between patrilineal and matrilineal relatives) and by a recognition of differences in collateral distance (close relatives are distinguished from more distant ones). Nuclear family members are assigned unique labels that are not extended to other relatives, whereas more distant relatives are grouped together on the basis of collateral distance (a process that is called collateral merging).

Solimões use the same terminology, but extend the range of collateral kin to whom the terms *tio/a* (uncle/aunt) and its reciprocal *sobrinho/a* (nephew/niece) apply. The genealogical basis of this extension is the classification of both cousins' children and nephews' and nieces' children equally as nephews or nieces (which in turn produce the reciprocal categories uncle/aunt as referring to the cousins of one's parents). In Brazilian terminology, nephew/niece and uncle/aunt are terms generally used to refer to ego's siblings' children and ego's parent's siblings, respectively.

This extension of the use of the terms uncle/aunt and nephew/niece to second-degree collaterals produces a distinction between the ascending and descending generations of this collateral level. In general usage, the designate *primo/a* (cousin) is restricted to collaterals of the ego's generation and *tio/a* (uncle/aunt) and its reciprocal *sobrinho/a* (nephew/niece) distinguish between ascending and descending generations of collateral relatives.[23]

From its dynamics, the terminological variation for second-degree collaterals establishes that the filial generation inherits and shares the terminology of its parents' generation for collaterals which belong to generations other than those of the parents and offspring in question. For example, a father classifies an individual who is his nephew's son (BSS) as nephew and this is the same term that the father's son will use (FBSS). Similarly, a father's uncle is his son's uncle. Hence, the terminology has a centripetal dynamic, as it brings relatives of prior generations 'back', by giving them the same terminology they had in the preceding generation.

Figure 1.3 shows the lineal and collateral terms used by Brazilians in general and the local people's terminological variation for second degree collaterals. This variation is not exclusive to the Middle Solimões region. It has been reported in other studies Amazonian peasants,[24] and it is likely to occur in other rural areas of Brazil.

---

23   The terminological rule which defines cousins' children as nephews/nieces is not followed when their age differences are small. In this case, the people use the term cousin as in the general Brazilian terminology. It appears that in the case of collaterals of the second degree, the age difference between ego and alter has priority over the actual generation distinction that may exist between them. This shows that the terminology for second grade collaterals is used in such a way as to symbolise either the equivalence of relatives, if they belong to the same age group, or their distinction, if they belong to different age groups.

24   See Wagley (1957); Maués (1977); Motta-Maués (1977); Nugent (1981); and Harris (2000).

Figure 1.3: General Brazilian Kinship Terminology and the Extended Variant

KINSHIP TERMINOLOGY				
COLLATERAL		LINEAL	COLLATERAL	
EXTENDED			USUAL	
2nd Degree		BISAVÔ(ó) (FFF;…)		**2nd Degree**
		|		
TIO(a)		AVÔ(ó)		TIO-AVÔ(ó)
(FFB;…)	**1st Degree**	(FF;…)	**1st Degree**	(FFB;…)
		|		
TIO (a) (FFBS;…)	**TIO**(a) (FB;…)	PAI; MÃE (F;M)	**TIO**(a) (FB;…)	PRIMO(a) (FFBS;…)
		|		
PRIMO(a)	**PRIMO**(a)	IRMÃO(ã) **EGO** IRMÃO(ã)	**PRIMO**(a)	PRIMO(a)
(FFBSS;…)	(FBS;…)	(B;Z) | (B;Z)	(FBS;…)	(FFBSS;…)
		|		
SOBRINHO (a)	**SOBRINHO**(a)	FILHO(a)	**SOBRINHO**(a)	PRIMO(a)
(FBSS;…)	(BS;…)	(S;D)	(BS;…)	(FBSS;…)
		|		
SOBRINHO(a)		NETO(a)		SOBRINHO-NETO
(BSS;…)		(SS;…)		(BSS;…)
		|		
		BISNETO(a) (SSS;…)		

The terms uncle/aunt and nephew/niece are open terms in terminologies of the Eskimo type which permit regional or idiosyncratic variations. In this terminology uncle/aunt is used for both ego's siblings' parents and the spouses of the ego's parents' siblings. There is no terminological distinction between the two. In this way, the terms uncle/aunt can include affinal partners and make these affines the closest to consanguines in one's kindred. In Brazil, the term for cousin is even more 'open' than uncle/aunt. According to Aurélio B.H. Ferreira's dictionary *primo/a* can refer to a relative without any other special designation.[25] In general, the term cousin is subject to variations since different individuals can reckon degrees of cousinship differently, such as in the USA,[26] where some confine the term for ego's generation, in the same way they do in the Middle Solimões.

Strathern observes that cousin denotes 'a kind of boundary relative', of 'somewhat indeterminate zone, some nearer (e.g. 'real', that is, first cousins) and some more distant (second cousins)'.[27] However, in the case of the Middle Solimões, the variant is a norm rather than an idiosyncratic variation allowed by the Eskimo terminological system itself. Thus, the differentiated terminology for second degree collaterals is a structural characteristic of the region's system of kinship that defines a more extensive kindred than the commonly used Brazilian terminology. In the Eskimo systems, the distance from ego to the relatives that can still be acknowledged as 'kinsman' is uncertain.[28] The intention to define second degree collateral kin with more precision expands the kindred and pushes the ambiguity of the system further away.

The association between kinship and locality is a common feature of rural areas throughout the world, but this association can be made in different ways. The range of relationships can be traced back and emphasised by the residents, but they can equally be restricted and even ignored. In the case of the English village of Elmdon, Strathern (1981: 158-9) notes that the villagers have a 'narrow definition of relatedness' that excludes second degree cousins from the group of kin classified as close relatives and, in some cases, even first cousins.[29] In the settlements in the Middle Solimões, on the contrary, the intention is to maximise these relations. The affirmation *'all is kin'* (or *'the majority here is kin'*), so frequently used in the settlements is the product of the local system of reproduction as much as the people's wide conception of kinship relations which justifies the moral construction of communities as extensive networks of kin.

25   Ferreira (1975).
26   Goodenough (1969), p. 256.
27   Strathern (1981), pp. 145–6.
28   Schneider (1969), p. 290.
29   Strathern (1981), pp. 158–9.

There is still another form in which this construction is done. Residents identify units of kinship in a particular way when they speak of their community. The categories kin and non-kin either refer to houses or to individuals. When the community as a whole was being discussed, the unit of classification was the house. In this classification, the statement 'most of us are kin here' was usually followed by 'only one house is not kin' (*'só uma casa não é parente'*).

For a house to be classified as 'a house of kin' it is only necessary for one of its owners (of either sex) to be related to one of the main kinship networks of the community. Thus, houses with an in-married spouse not consanguineously related to any community resident (i.e., an affine of the main kinship network) were still acknowledged as 'houses of kin'. Granting kinship status to these houses is further evidence of the people's willingness to retain kinship linkages, for the 'adoption' of affines also means that kin are not being lost by marrying outsiders. This can also be interpreted as a sign that affines and consanguines are actually regarded as close relatives.

The only houses that were classified as 'not kin' were those formed by migrant couples who had no consanguineous relationship to the main kinship networks. Even when the owners of these houses became affinally related to the rest of the community when their children married locals (and this was frequent), they were still classified as 'not kin' or 'not from the place'.[30]

In sum, in the combination between kinship and locality, kinship considerations appeared dominant in the conception of the community. In the identification of the links between households, the kinship classification brought people 'in' as one of 'us' (as kinsmen), through its enlarged definition of relatedness and its inclusion of affines. Considerations based on locality (place of birth) were dominant in the conception of individuals, and it distinguished between consanguines. The identification of individuals in terms of community insiders or outsiders however, included both a conception of kinship relatedness and place of birth. Thus, individuals were classified as insiders if they were either born in the locality or could trace a consanguineous link to one of the local families. Although not overtly stated, the people's judgment of rights to residence and land use is informed by this system of classification.

30   In contrast to the system of classification of houses, the classification of individuals clearly distinguishes between consanguines and affines as 'kin' and 'individuals married to kin'. Individuals were further distinguished on the basis of place of birth. Although segments of a kindred which lived in separate communities had their kinship relatedness acknowledged, they were nevertheless differentiated on the basis of their place of birth.

Conclusion

One of the most important aspects of domestic life in traditional Amazonian villages concerns the production of manioc flour. In Nogueira, as in most Amazonian communities, the *roça* is the centre of the household's productive and reproductive system, constituting both its material and symbolic content. The requirements for planting *roças* and for processing the manioc into flour — access to land, to labour, to instruments of work — are a matter of intense negotiation, resulting in arrangements that are temporary and involve economic differentiation. They involve a large network of social relationships, mainly located within the community but not restricted to it. The people's open conception of kinship relatedness reflects the fact that agricultural productivity and land rights are both the result of labour. In this domestic economy where social relations of production are kinship relations, the conditions set by the system of shifting agriculture and land tenure is mirrored in the people's kinship system.

As Bloch (1984) has shown, in shifting agriculture, labour in a sense 'creates land' by clearing the forest. But because labour investment is lost due to fallow requirement, it does not create a permanent asset to be passed down to following generations. In his analysis, Bloch compares two closely related societies from Madagascar, the Zafimaniry, who practice shifting agriculture, and the Merina, irrigated rice cultivators. The Zafimaniry present a situation similar to Nogueira. For them, kinship provides access to labour and land. The kinship system is inclusive and takes affines in, while endogamy is employed as a strategy to keep labour. In the Zafimaniry and the Nogueira situations, property is correctly understood as social relations, and production is represented as the result of labour, not of ancestral property. For the Merina, on the other hand, land suitable for irrigated cultivation is scarce and rice fields constitute highly capitalised land due to heavy labour input. Labour invested by previous generations creates an asset that links people through property relations. The Merina also give preference to endogamous marriages, but as a strategy to prevent loss of land to outsiders. Accordingly, they exclude affines from their conception of kinship relatedness.

This chapter has shown the mechanisms through which Nogueira residents construct an open kinship system: the terminology's recognition of a larger collateral kindred and the incorporation of affines in the construction of the community as a network of kin. The density of kinship results also from a high number of endogamous marriages as well as repeated family unions. The large network of kin is a guarantee for cooperation in labour and provides safe options to obtain access to land.

The lack of fixed property means that in the developmental cycle of domestic groups, parents leave no inheritance of land to their children. Residence in a community of kin and succession of agricultural holdings is what grants right to productive resources. As the lady from Nogueira showed in her particularly perceptive remark ('When we die, we leave our seed, our children, the legacy of the *roça*), instead of parents leaving an inheritance, it is the *roças* that provide the legacy, the children who were raised by means of both the sale and consumption of the manioc flour. The continuity in this system of reproduction is not represented by property passed down (as in a descent based society) but the succession of generations, the continuity of kinship links and the replacement of people by their offspring, in a life provisioned by the *roças*.

Chapter 2

Black Peoples of the Trombetas River: Peasantry and Ethnicity in the Brazilian Amazon[*]

Rosa Elizabeth Acevedo Marin and Edna Maria Ramos de Castro

Anthropological study of Amazonia reveals how different ethnic groups enact and manifest resistance. One such group of men and women in the Trombetas River region (which includes the Erepecuru and Cuminá Rivers) identifies its members as the 'sons of the Trombetas' when dealing with outsiders. These black peasant farmers are engaged in an agricultural-extractivist economy. The motion of the river's flow represents for them both the pulse of their existence and the source of social memory, their livelihood and sense of life. Politically, they take on the identity[1] of *remanescentes de quilombo* (descendants of ancient maroon communities) and cite ancient judicial arguments, legitimated by more than 200 years of effective occupation, to support territorial claims to their communal lands. In response to white society, this political identity has a strong ethnic stress. They are more than peasant/tenants. In the peopling of the waterfalls and of the great river, the Trombetas and its tributaries, they have become complete occupants of their environment sufficiently so to endow them with titles to land.[2] These so-called *quilombo remainder communities*[3] have

[*] This chapter was translated by Adolpho de Oliveiro and edited by Shirley Rhodes. The editors would like to thank the Department of Social Anthropology at the University of St Andrews for providing funds to make this work possible.

[1] Among the political actions pursued by this historical peasantry is proof of their long-term occupation of their lands, a right to legal ownership given to the 'quilombo remainder communities' (*comunidades remanscentes de quilombo*), according to Art. 68 of the transitory dispositions of the Federal Constitution of 1988.

[2] The political agenda of the communities of the Trombetas was formalised through the demarcation of the lands of the Boa Vista community in 1995 and of the Agua Fria community in 1996. Meanwhile, new demarcations are taking place in the middle Trombetas, all based in the article of transitory dispositions in the Federal Constitution of 1988.

[3] *Quilombo*, as a historical category, has the meaning of resistance and self-affirmation of the group against the slave-based order. This meaning, located in time, now has judicial import when deployed to legitimate ancestral territorial claims put forward by the so-called *remanescentes de quilombo*. The updating, or reclaiming, of the term *quilombo*

submitted their history, and their ethnicity, to the legal order of the state. In the quiet waters unbroken by analysis or artificial segmentation flows a time both past and present, the synthesis from the place of the *mocambo* of material and social forms — the river, the fish, the boat, the seeds, the tree — together with images, sensibilities, desires and affects. To the eyes of the outside world, the real and imaginary meanings of existence for this group are grotesquely dilapidated and eroded. But this erosion is the product of another history, another sense of nature, with their differing representations, foreign to the world of the ancient occupants of the Trombetas. The territoriality is the synthesis of their universe. It becomes concrete in everyday practices, in the accomplishment of strategies of life and work, in the performance of actions that create material and social existence.

In this chapter we explore the dual formation in black groups who build their social system within the biosystem of the Trombetas. From their own perspective, we follow the conflicts and tensions of a history of confrontation, beginning with the slave society based in a mercantile economy, moving on to forms of domination created within a network of trade and concluding with the contemporary arrival of actors who represent new forces, those introduced by mining and timber interests supported by public and private bodies. In the local trajectories, what matters most is the conquest and struggle for permanent rights to the land and this struggle brings to the fore the creative features of their history, defined in terms of an ethnic and territorial base, highlighting the political dimension of the *quilombos* of the Trombetas, a testimony to their victories. These creative features have been refined since the ascension of the runaway slaves to the upper reaches of the river at the end of the eighteenth century until achieving demographic and economic stability today. It is estimated that more than 6,000 blacks — descendents of runaway slaves — now occupy the land from the mouth of the Cuminá river to *Cachoeira Porteira* (the gathering rapids) and up the Erepecuru. In characteristic ways, they integrate themselves into the regional economy.

---

occurs from the 1980s onwards as a result of the mobilisation of rural groups, the black movement and organisations that support their struggle for the judicial recognition of lands of ancient occupation, among them those of the *quilombo* remainders. At the heart of this issue are the so-called *terras de preto* (black peoples' lands), *terras de quilombolas* (*quilombo* dweller lands), associated with the sentiment of being part of the history of a specific group.

Black Occupation of the Trombetas River

Slaves of the lower Amazon sought their escape in the direction of the rapids of the Trombetas and Curuá Rivers, across the lakes where few merchant ships, voyagers, *sesmeiros* or religious workers passed. Their histories, unwritten, lived on in their descendants, memories of slavery passed down by those who had escaped from Alenquer, Óbidos or Santarém. The communities of the Trombetas, the *quilombos*, represent the largest areas controlled by runaway slaves, the poor free and detribalised Indians in the province of Pará

At the end of the eighteenth and the beginning of the nineteenth centuries the Portuguese crown distributed a number of *sesmarias* (land concessions) among the inhabitants of the districts of the lower Amazon. Following the example of Santarém, the settlements of Monte Alegre, Alenquer, Óbidos and Faro accelerated territorial occupation under pressure from colonial policy implemented during the administration of the Marquis of Pombal. Some *sesmeiros* began to grow cocoa and raise cattle in the late eighteenth century. Cocoa plantations grew in step with the expanding slave population. In response to the gradual expansion of and fluctuations in the cultivation of the land, cocoa increased in importance in Grão-Pará between 1772 and 1782. In addition, plantations of rice and cotton grew along the riverbanks and in the small commercial towns, but cocoa exports were dependent on uncertain harvests of naturally disturbed cocoa. The unpredictability of weather and market oscillations made extractive production precarious. With this in mind, authorities began the exploration of interior river regions including that of the Trombetas. At the beginning of the nineteenth century the lower Amazon, like the Tocantins valley, became integrated in the cocoa-producing regions of the colonial world. The European market had been earlier supplied by French and Spanish colonies in the Caribbean, in Venezuela and Ecuador. Production in the Dutch colony in Suriname, exporting since 1730, had begun to decline in 1780. The gradual decline in all these colonies then fuelled the search for cocoa in the Portuguese Amazonia. As the importance of the export grew in Grão-Pará, large sums were invested in the acquisition of slaves and in the incorporation of *terra firme* and *varzeas* in the cultivation of cocoa. In 1755 a royal decree freed Indians from slavery and established the *Diretório*. Imported African slaves, on the other hand, were put to work according to the labour systems of the *sesmaria* cocoa-producing plantations. In 1757, the Grão-Pará and Maranhão Trade Company was formed to tackle two of the problems inherent in cocoa

production and trade: transport to the European market and the introduction of African slaves. Cocoa farmers of the lower Amazon were able to
boost their plantations by the acquisition of modest numbers of slaves.
The region amassed some 20 per cent of the slave population of Pará,
with constant flights for escape towards the rapids. The authorities named
their refugees *mocambos*, considered them a threat to property and organised expeditions to destroy them.

With the *Cabanagem* (1834–39) came a hint of liberty, flitting through the
valley, blurring the edges of national frontiers. Slaves, detribalised Indians
and freemen fought, momentarily, not for their masters, but their personal
destinies,[4] until social order was restored, the *quilombos* repressed and alternative forms of land occupation destroyed, in the interests of reclaiming the
labour force. In the decades following the *Cabanagem*, there was an atmos-
phere of mystery and tension around the *mocambos* of the Trombetas region.
In post-*Cabanagem* society, *regatão* tradesmen, who arrived as conquerors of
far-off worlds, began as middlemen to redefine and rearticulate relationships
of dominance between the white and marginal groups.

The *quilombo*, composed of Indians, slaves and freed black men,
exposed the limitations of an order based on slavery and was seen as an
affront. From a positive view, it marked the limit of the old regime of slave
ownership and production, together with the social and political domain
articulated in the social status quo. The wound inflicted on the slave-based
social order then cut deep, and the authorities and owners of the slaves
responded with stigmatisation and repression of the new ethnic boundary.
There followed continuous political exchange, with conflict on both sides
between Cayenne and Pará. Meanwhile, relations grew closer between the
quilombos in the Trombetas and the Bonis, the *Marrons* of the Dutch
Guiana (Suriname), during a phase of relative isolation as they established

---

4   During the 1820s slave runs gave birth to collective forms (thus different from the
     previous individualised ones) of breaking with slave-owners, so they inscribe them-
     selves in a political context of internal ideological emancipationist struggle in Pará.
     The period immediately after Independence revealed significant threats to the politi-
     cal order. The Cabano movement was born, opposing 'natives' and those from the
     metropolis. The movement took the form of a struggle against colonisation, with the
     conflict between slaves and owners apparently pushed to the background.
     Information and recapture were constantly sought. The slaves had the advantage of
     the levels of discontentment and desertion among the troops, as well as their ethnic
     and social origin. The struggle for decolonisation had radical developments, among
     them the creation of a favourable situation for the insurrection of the slaves against
     their owners, but this was not enough to bring them to fight for abolition. The hori-
     zon of their contest of the slave-based social order was restricted.

territorial domains upriver. As communications with the *Marrons* strength-
ened, the *quilombos* assumed a more audacious stance, acquiring the political and cultural traits that would be crucial to empowerment. Among their
gestures of rebellion, they put forward a proposal, more advanced than
any then discussed by partisan elites, for the abolition of slavery.

Despite the strict discipline of the pacification governments (1839–48),
supported by military institutions such as workers' corps, the government
was faced with loss of slave manpower and decreasing traffic in slaves and
military campaigns aiming at the destruction of the *quilombos* became crucial. While accounts of the time reveal aggressive acts of official agents,
nonetheless, the marooned slaves could not isolate themselves completely
from slave-based society. The impulse towards stability functioned in its
most energetic form both in repression and in the increasing movement of
agents of the regional economy. After the suffocation of the *Cabanagem*,
internal networks were rearticulated, together with river and coast navigation. New products emerged for the markets, such as brazil nuts and rubber.

The internal dynamic of *quilombo* empowerment depended on economic production and on the elaboration of new forms of economic support. The natural habitat afforded many and diverse resources for hunting,
fishing and the gathering of forest fruits. Progressively, *quilombos* came to
organise their calendar around production, allowing them to become
established over wider areas, as the natural cycle and concentration of the
produce of the forest was only sufficient for the maintenance of relatively small local communities. This process was accentuated after 1860, when
new territory was added. Contemporary accounts describe a systematic
occupation of the rapids of which Porteira, Campiche, Maravilha, Turuna,
Poana, Trava, Quebra-pote and Espinho were the best known. Along the
river emerged a strategy of occupation reinforced by marriages, linking
families spread through diverse regions. Adopting increasingly more complex levels of organisation, the *quilombos* developed the internal forms of
relationships and structures of government described by Tavares Bastos
(1866–1975), Barbosa Rodrigues (1875) and Ferreira Penna (1867), among
other explorers. Contact between the slave-based society and the *mocambeiros* was governed by the political presuppositions of negative integration. The movement of black peoples in the Trombetas river region
allowed their existence as a separate social collectivity, both independent
of, and in part essential to, the regional slave-based society, a relationship
reflected in their trade with Óbidos. For some, their ability to produce economic surplus allowed them to purchase their freedom.

With cattle-raising and extractive activities, the economy of the lower Amazonas began slowly to recover after the devastation of the *Cabanagem*. Progressively, these activities increased the areas farmed by white men in the *terras devolutas*, state-owned land identified by the imperial government as part of the Land Act of 1850. The Act regulated the purchase of land, allowing room for colonisation projects in the provinces. The lower Trombetas then became engulfed in the conquest of lands rich in timber and brazil nuts. The decree of 26 April 1865 made the banks of the Trombetas reference points in identifying and locating rural estates to be recorded in the registries. Traders old and new, and land-owners from the nearby towns, became the new proprietors, contributing to the alienation and isolation of the territories economically exploited and occupied in the gradual occupation of the rapids by black peoples. The course of the Trombetas represented two opposing spheres: below the rapids, the domain of white men and slave-owners; upriver, the world of the runaway slave. The post-*Cabanagem* changes ended seven decades of relatively insular existence. Steam navigation, extended exploitation of brazil nut and the slave-owners' territorial designs were deployed within the rhythm of migration and the closeness of the groups in the middle and lower Trombetas. Economically, another dynamic emerged, contributing decisively to the involvement of the workers in patron–client relationships. Traders and landowners now presided over the black territory and the uneven integration of the *quilombos* into the regional economy.

Extractive Industries and Patron–Client Relations

Close examination of the period from the 1870s to '90s reveals rapid transformations, especially in Pará. The extractive-agricultural economy recuperated fast. Modernisation, in the form of the introduction of the steam engine in mills, sawmills and more importantly, in navigation, left its mark. Belém and Manaus began to develop an urban infrastructure, incorporating profits from the rubber trade. Such material transformations brought these places to the level of the national debates over the freedom of work and the abolition of slavery, as well as on issues of land, free trade and navigation, as well as options such as agriculture and extractive activities versus agriculture and industry. At the political level, the debate was centred on the choice and transition between different regimes of monarchical or republican government, reflecting pressure on ideals of progress and civilisation. In this way, the decades represented for the Amazon valley, in Tavares Bastos' (1866) phrase, their entry, irreversible and subordinated, into the alternatives then poised at the level of national and international politics. According to the politicians, speaking in terms of division of labour, the slaves were living in small settlements, busy with the production of sugar and in the small-scale cultivation of other consumable produce. This perception is important in our understanding of the contradictions between the slave and slave-property relations against a background of an increasingly dynamic economy, fuelled by extraction, controlled by trade and homogenised by the compulsory work regime.

In Óbidos and Santarém, the most densely populated urban centres of the lower Amazon, the principal products were cocoa, rubber and brazil nuts. According to Tavares Bastos, the whole of the Óbidos region had a population of 11,130, with 1,000 people living in the town. Runaway slaves and army deserters accounted for 2,000, roughly a fifth of the total population, representing a considerable labour force. Bastos warned of the threat the escapees posed even to the marginal territories, such as Trombetas.

By the end of the 1860s, the reorganisation of agriculture and extractive industries was positively reflected in the production statistics of the lower Amazonas. The municipality of Óbidos registered an increase in exports of brazil nuts and fish, particularly *pirarucu*. In 1866, 66,405 *arrobas* of cocoa were produced. The Trombetas was acknowledged as the greatest provider of brazil nuts to the port of Óbidos, its nuts universally renowned for quality and size. Tobacco, Penna notes was produced 'in larger scale than coffee', observing that 'the larger amount and best quality product that comes to the port of Óbidos comes from the *mocambos* of the Trombetas'. Diverse accounts and observations on the Trombetas river region at the time acknowledged the significance of the *quilombo*'s role in the regional economy. In the 1870s the 'people of the *quilombos*' began to come into the town of Óbidos. Had they overcome their fear of those who had once owned them, or had the old slave-based society discovered a new, more open style of social patterns and relationships? Tavares, Bastos and Rodrigues record the laments of slave owners who had seen their slaves escape in groups of 20, 30 or 100. The institutionalisation of the *mocambos* might limit this threat, even though slave-owners lacked the powers to suppress them. But the mechanisms of forced integration, through patron–client relationships, did not immediately succeed in controlling the *mocambo* workers, or homogeneously take root within the group. Some of them intensified their contacts with the traders, as in the case of peoples living in the Porteira rapids, known curiously as *colony*.

Later, family units scattered along the middle Trombetas, from the mouth of the Cuminá up to the upper Trombetas, in the Erepecu and the Acapu rivers, engaged in patron–client relationships as government and economic agents promoted the incorporation of their lands, rich in brazil nut, in private purchase and lease.

The accounts of the descendants of the *quilombos* reveal several fluxes and directions in the distinct phases in their descent of the rapids. The first displacement was towards the mouth of the Cachorro and Mapuera rivers; the second was to the area of the Porteira rapids and the third, towards the lands within the middle Trombetas, closer to Oriximiná. The three movements — to the *rio manso* (calm waters) as opposed to the *aguas bravas* (fierce waters), from the dead river and to the living water, from the large river or Trombetao to the rapids — led to the establishment of relations with the *Kaxuiana* Indians in the rivers Cachorrinho, Cahorro and Trombetas, and with a second group in the Kaxura River. Derby observes that the blacks established commercial links with the 'Ariquinas, Charumans, Tumaianas and Pianacotos',[5] fractions of which left these villages to set up in several places along the banks of the middle and upper Trombetas and in the Cuminá.

The strategy of integration was accomplished by the assimilation of black peoples and did not entail any disintegration of the indigenous social order. The black rebellion represented in the *quilombo* was stifled in the process, turning the very existence of this group of freemen in slave-based society into a problem for white society. During the first two decades of the integrationist movement (1875–1900) they reduced the cultivation of tobacco for sale, inserting themselves into the economy as brazil nut pickers. Prohibitions had already constrained their economic practice, with interdictions on timber extraction and freshwater turtle hunting. Incentives were provided for production more important to the strength of the economy, i.e. for export goods. In the closing decade of the nineteenth century, the movement on the Trombetas river began slowly to polarise between black and white colonisation frontiers. In the middle and upper Trombetas, movement and conflicts between these two ethnic groups sustained a system of patron–client relationships that ended only in the 1960s.

---

5   Derby (1898), p. 370.

From Quilombos to Quilombo Descendent Communities

At the end of the nineteenth century the *quilombolas de fuga*, or *velhos quilombolas*, suffered the hardships of workers and freemen. Their descendants organised their communities both economically and socially around networks of family relationships,[6] moving from an existence dependent on debt to their bosses to subsistence as peasants, picking brazil nuts. Here grew the roots of the *comunidades de quilombo* existing today in the county of Oriximiná.

Sedentism and fixed housing helped to make exploitation of the forest more systematic, and they developed an agricultural-extractive calendar, contributing to the regional economy such products as *copaiba, salsaparrilha*, timber, *cumaru*, brazil nuts and freshwater turtles. As they settled in pursuit of these products, so the areas of harvest and of cultivation grew. Over a dozen new localities appeared, including Arrozal and Nova Amizade close to Cachoeira Porteira, and Tapagem, Tabuleiro, Conceição, Jarananum, Lago do Abui, Sagrado Coração, Sapo des Aguas, Boa Vista, Agua Fria, Sacuri, Palhal and Moura, downriver.

Descending the rapids of the Cuminá, they established Santo Antonio, Livramento, Javary, Formigal, Urucury and Macaco, and Aracua, in the mouth of the Cachorro. The Cachorro, like the Mapuera, was rich in brazil nut trees, though it also harboured plague among its grasslands. The inhabitants of Boa Vista travelled to Jarauaca Lake, Xerepeque and Banda do Rego, places with extensive brazil nut stands. Because of the long distances, they built temporary shacks and depots in the forest to support production. Likewise, blacks from Tapagem travelled to the Macaco and Jacaré lakes, establishing in the latter the localities of Tabuleiro and Ariramba. They made frequent journeys also to the Erepecuru and Acapu rivers, to Lake Janari and to Lake Sucuriju. These places come to stand for the criss-cross of the generations, associated with the names of several pioneers now famous in the history of land occupation. Religion and the family combined to form some place names, as in *Santo* (Antonio) with *Macaxeira*, in Santo Antonio dos Macaxeira. (There is a second Macaxeira, whose inhabitants are related to those living in the lake near Cachoeira Porteira.) Other names come from religious or social authorities. But the act of naming reveals the tissue of familial relationships within the group.

6   The term 'community' is used by the local Catholic Church to identify the forms of organisation of family groups along the banks of the Trombetas and Cuminá rivers. Public institutions such as SUCAM base their work on this spatial configuration. Groups use the word frequently in everyday language, as well as in their political actions. We use the terms descriptively with these meanings.

Kinship is the centre of social relations in the Trombetas river region, and the language of kinship permeates a complex system of magical, religious and political meanings. It forms the basis of alliances and of the constitution and the function of authority within the group. The meanings of such representations of family and power follow rules of great importance to the group, simultaneously informing its ideological structure. In formation, this body of representations in collective and individual life creates a complex field. It runs through the use and distribution of the land, in work and cultural exchange, in celebration and in ceremony, in all the social process, in cohesion and identity. From shared experiences of the past until the present day, a perception is born of the right to the use of the land. The tenants and the titled owners of the areas of brazil nut trees, official regional society, were unable to displace these ancient occupants of the Trombetas, even through the ingenious artifice of Republican agrarian law.

From 1885 until the first quarter of the twentieth century a modest cultivation of cocoa is recorded, with fewer than 2,000 trees. The owners and traders involved in these estates came from urban areas, their accumulated wealth based on trade and transport. Transactions recorded in the Óbidos and Oriximiná registries bring together the participants of new relationships emerging from this new industry: squatters, *agregados, sitiantes* and landowners absent and present, brought together in the circulation of the land as a commodity. The ancient inhabitants of the middle and upper Trombetas appear in the registries of property titles as an almost invisible reference, a mere tangential note on rights acquired through their occupation. The so-called *terras de preto* (black peoples' lands) did not completely disappear under the new system of land identification, though they could achieve anonymity. In 1891, Óbidos resident J.M. de Castro purchased lands below the mouth of the Caxuery, on the bank of the Trombetas that had as upper limit the land of 'the black man João de Mocambique'. By such formulae, documents were registered taking away from the ancient occupants the free use of land and its resources. The presence of the black man is recorded indirectly, in the identification of estates bought and sold, the references confused or incomplete: 'lands of the black man Mocambique and of Geralda de tal'. This followed an official strategy of the appropriation of land parcels. The ancient occupants were unaware of the land law of the bourgeoisie with all its clauses. A juridical order based in private property would not accommodate their claims on land of common use. Because of their collective practices, the blacks of the Trombetas did not assimilate the system of small parcels of land. Their system privileged, as it still does today, communitarian development across a common territory, more appropriate to gathering and gardens.

From a political perspective, patron–client relationships correspond to forms of dependence and oppression established with the landowners and tenants during harvest of brazil nut crops. There are established links between the blacks working in the picking of brazil nuts and the local traders who organise the transport and commercialisation of the product. These links are characterised around the end of the nineteenth and beginning of the twentieth centuries by the monopoly on brazil nut buying practised in Oriximiná and Óbidos by some traders. The relation is defined by the monopoly on acquisition and on transport of the product while the land — up the Trombetas and the Cuminá, its lakes, *igarapés* and rapids — remained *devoluta*.[7] The trader assumed ownership both of the land and of production, since the workers' labour and the selling of the product could only be guaranteed by the control or prohibition of the free picking of the crop. This process of privatisation of the areas with large concentrations of brazil nut trees was supported by agrarian legislation, which favoured, in buying and selling, a particular group of the elite in adjacent municipalities. The legal title to the lands rich in brazil nuts preceded the increase in productivity. From the beginning, legal title was the nodal point of this activity, as the issues of transport and funding of workers were met with the introduction of the *regatão* or travelling tradesman. Small *regatões* were able to sail upriver and in lakes, up to Cachoeira Porteira, serving the *mocambeiros* and opposing prohibitions imposed by the slavery-based social order. The latter, in the form of the *patrão*, found the secret of maintaining control over production through appropriation of land, which led in turn to the subjection of the workers: both producers and consumers were dependent upon him. The tendency to segmentation of such structures, and the lack of interest in funding by the bosses and the owners of brazil nut groves, marginalised the old small *regatões* operating in the Trombetas which were increasingly replaced by steam-powered ships. Market laws set down conditions of subjection for the pickers of brazil nuts, without regard to workers' own ways of production, stipulating where and how hard they should work, quantified in boxes of nuts to be sold to the bosses under unilateral terms.

The picking of brazil nuts, carried out under the traditional form of family labour in the lands considered communal among the blacks, the *cas-*

7   *Terras Devolutas* are lands which, after the Land Law of 1850 (and its regulation in the 1850 Act) were not claimed by anyone as private property, remaining the property of the Union.

tanhais, was transferred to the *castanhais* of the bosses. In 1962, one such proprietor of 40 large boats brought over 400 men to his locality. The supervision of the *castanheiros* and *regatões* in the Trombetas waters brought financial burden for the owners, eased only by the trust and the fidelity of the *castanheiro*, who became the godchild of the boss and bore him moral obligation. The patron–client relationship flowed in this balance between vigilance and trust on the part of the subordinate, between the increase in production and the progressive debt of the blacks, between domination, authoritarianism and paternalist protection. From this was born the encompassing power that emanated from white society. The boss was the godfather, the mayor, the priest's friend, a fluctuating presence overriding all other relationships. The *quilombo* expressed the beginnings of rebellion in the idioms, multifaceted, of words, of scorn, of gestures; in beliefs and prayers, in song and celebration, and even in clandestine sales to other bosses.

Peasantry: Rearticulation of Forms of Autonomous Production

The most ancient segments of Amazonian peasantry originated from the dissociation of slaves from the social and economic structures of the colonial past, represented by the farm or mill. This led to the creation of the older peasant groups, corresponding, in time, to formation of property, by means of distribution of *sesmarias*, and to the 'colonies' of occupation. *Sesmeiros* and colonisers limited the possibilities for the acquisition of slaves to develop agriculture as commercial enterprise. Former slaves became small peasants, rupturing slave-property relations, by defining, within spatial control of the *quilombos*, the conditions for survival based on agrarian-extractivist exploitation of the land. Their dominion had no legal basis until 1988, when the Constitution first acknowledged special occupation.

Currently, their interactions circumscribe interests and values quite specific to the group. The objective and subjective dimensions of identity are in the definition of the limits and the nature of the group, in the acknowledgement of a 'we' that is affirmed in the perception of an other, and in the collisions between them. Strong collisions occur with the expropriatory policies propounded by the dominant society. On the other hand, cooperation and associative practices are instrumental in the unity and permanence of the groups, conforming to a domestic, family-based production in the Trombetas region. This practice has dominated and remained essential for the permanence of blacks since the beginning of the twentieth century in the centres of Cachoeira Porteira, Abui, Abuizinho, Parana do Abui, Tapagem, Sagrado Coração, Macaxeira, Mãe Cue and Boa Vista, and can only be understood through analysis of their complex social and economic systems.

All members of the family engage in different tasks allowing for production, whether or not for trade. Through their participation, children learn productive processes. New generations become socialised within the group. Working as a group provides a way to rationalise productive forces and to maximise results against the limits set by nature on extractive agricultural economies. Despite the use of different methods in their varying activities, the basis of production rests in their techniques for the organisation of work. Those techniques, implemented in agriculture and extraction, go back to the generations who lived in the *quilombos*, when they produced tobacco, cotton, manioc and fruits and gathered *salsaparrilha*, cocoa, wood and brazil nut. Technical difficulties and natural limits — fertility of soil, gestation times of species, access through the rapids or the dense forest trees — certainly had a bearing on the invention of collective practices of production and transport. The timing of this invention, of the production of these systems, is not linear. We can infer a first rupture of groups from ecosystems in the African continent, uprooted by slavery. At other times we find exchanges with indigenous cultures upriver, in a re-invention or renewal of their ecological knowledge. The important point here is to understand how long it took them to produce such knowledge systems, and their fragility; the risk of loss of knowledge to external intervention. The cohesion and solidarity of the group, matured in its constant confrontation with the agents of the slave-based order, reinforced not only the internal network of political and social relations, but also the productive structures. In this way, the essential elements of the collective management of work come through to present times, among them the conception of communal property of land and the unity of nature and society. In relation to narrow technical-economic knowledge, the ideology and politics of the communities in the Trombetas river have remained incomprehensible, obscured by racial prejudice against the blacks.

The *horta* or *roça*, associated with the *verão* (summer) represents the main occupation for the blacks of the Trombetas. It furnishes a considerable diversity of produce such as grains, roots, vegetables and fruits. At the same time, it strengthens links of solidarity, corresponding to the intensification of relations both internal and external to the family, organised in different phases, into work by the family and the *puxirum*. The so-called *puxirum* constitutes a social method of maximising individual energies, collective working exercised as mutual help. As the workers undertake intensely similar tasks, there is another force in action, not reducible to the sum of individual strengths. The form of collaboration is itself a productive force, as the labour force from the collective body augments psychic and physical energy. An area requiring 20 working days to clear is cleared in one day by 12 men within the *puxirum* system. It constitutes a mechanism for the rationalisation of time and individual effort, establishing the rules that define exchange of time and labour. The work is composed of four main phases: felling, cultivation, weeding and harvest. The *puxirum* occurs in the phases that require the greatest intensity of labour. The clearing (or *roçado*) is done by men. In cultivation, where practices are based in family work, several domestic groups collaborate, as previously agreed between them. The workers in the *puxirum* are not related to each other in terms of remuneration of the labour force or partnership. They exchange equal tasks, differing only by prior agreement, and as an exception. One worker, for example, may exchange participation for the search for food (game or fish) to feed workers in another *puxirum*. From this perspective, women also participate in the *puxirum*, mainly through the preparation of food. The conditions and rules established by these customs may exceptionally apply to the breaking open of brazil nuts and their transport from distant areas with large brazil nut groves. These strategies for organising labour and confronting drudgery in the absence of more advanced technologies represent one aspect of the rationality of the productive forces, in which there is a calculus and a comparison between the costs implicit in alternative means of production, under certain technical conditions.

The order of attendance of each family in this practice is prescribed by simple rules, implicit in the formal invitation. Any domestic group can take the initiative. The regulatory principle appears to be as follows. Each family prepares its garden counting on the help of those invited (some 15 men for the felling of trees and an agreed number of families for the cultivation). They commit themselves to reciprocal work in the tree felling phase in the gardens of those who have helped with their own. The blacks of the Trombetas call this relation *troca de dias* (literally, *exchange of days*). A system of customary rules controls commitments to exchange of labour time, ensuring ongoing reciprocal efficiency. Such procedures allow the workers some mobility, moving among several gardens during lengthier tasks involving greater drudgery. The maturing plants reshape the work of the domestic unit. Between neighbours, the exchange of days is increased. The preparation of food by women is perceived not only as productive function, but as an important element in the strengthening of links of collective conviviality and the integration of community relations on several levels, including leisure. The fact that no family remains without a garden affirms the practices of equality, the shared responsibility in reproduction of the group and in its cultural heritage, in order to sustain reciprocal relations.

The peasants' differential relationship with nature manifests itself on other levels too, exposing the rationality behind it. Locations chosen to make gardens are always in a semi-inclined plane, ensuring both organic matter and sufficient rain according to requirements of the different species grown. The choice of place is made by the family group, which also sets the garden's size according to consumer needs, estimating an annual surplus to allow the family group to develop a system of community exchange. Commonly the gardens found are small, around three to five hectares, worked from June to August. The choice of parcel of land reflects an Indian legacy of knowledge of land use. The most common crops are coffee bean and cocoa, cultures well adapted to the places where they grow. Manioc gardens are shifted periodically within a common territory, to compensate for the well known deficiencies of soil. At the same time, the shifts allow for the management and recycling of land, forming the basis of their cultivation techniques. They practice then a form of polyculture, encouraging the balance and recovery of soil. Work in the garden centres on the growth of manioc. Using the concept of *quadra* they identify the areas to be reserved for manioc and other crops including rice, beans, watermelon, pumpkin, cara, sweet potato and sweet manioc. Summer preparation of the garden then involves the selection of the seeds and stems for grafting certain species. At the time of the harvest there is intensification of the preparation of manioc meal.

The summer eases the transit through the forest in search of seeds, wood, fibres and herbs. But summer is also the time of burning and clearing areas for cultivation, and for cultivation too of medicinal and edible species. The backyards of the houses now are cleared, and fruit is grown once more, with herbs like parsley, spring onions and chicory. These are domestic gardens, mainly for culinary and medicinal use. They represent an asset to group heritage, helping in the treatment of disease. Herbs and roots are also grown for use in religious rituals, a plethora of baths and fumigations, and communications with the supernatural world. These communities experience expressive moments of religious syncretism, the mark of their experience, social and collective since the time of their captivity.

The blacks of the Trombetas find it difficult to commercialise their surplus, partly because of distance from the trade centres, but also because of the reduction, in the last ten years, of *regatões* in the Trombetas. The increase of fiscalisation along the river, promoted by the IBAMA

(Brazilian Institute of Renewable Natural Resources) with the support of the federal police against freshwater turtle hunting, has intimidated merchant traffic in the summer months. Only with the harvest of brazil nuts in the winter, do the boats return to traffic in the region's most important commercial crop and at a time when manioc production is restricted to domestic use, the labour force preoccupied with large brazil nut groves.

Nowadays, the land issue in the Trombetas is complex, particularly in areas earmarked for mining projects. These lands are circumscribed by territories occupied by *descendentes de quilombolas* ('*quilombo*-dweller descendants'), who in spite of land titles and conservation units, still may not be able to garner recognition of their absolute established rights since ancient times.

Changes in the Trombetas and Ethnic Reaffirmation

The ethnic identity and territorial control of black communities in the Trombetas are represented in their permanent possession and continued reproduction. Frequently called (and mistaken for) *caboclos* and *ribeirinhos* of the lower Amazonas, they have not significantly changed their place or distribution. Their stability is marked by comparison, for example, with migrant peasants in the town of Santarém. In the Trombetas region, the migratory process began in the 1990s, as a result of occupation of their lands by mining companies and of the barriers created by the Biological Reservation of the Trombetas and the National Forest of Saraca-Taquera. From the cultural perspective, this peasant group is integrated in an intricate network of social relations; the constructions of their history, the deep symbolic structures of the massed *quilombo* memory, now merging in the present as projected social permanence within the conquered lands.

From 1960 onwards relations between the black *castanheiros* and the owners of the *castanhais* have depended on control of trade and transport, consecrated since the beginnings of the extractive regional economy. It is this network of domination, extending to distant *castanhais*, which recently suffered ruptures, marking the decline of the patron–client system. Large traders such as Raimundo da Costa Lima, Cazuza Guerreiro, the Diniz family and the Costa e Picanco families faced increasing competition from *regatões* attracted upriver in search of brazil nuts. With the increasing availability of engine-powered boats, small traders penetrated *furos*, *igarapés* and lakes, selling different products and purchasing brazil nuts from the black workers who picked them. The competition favoured them, opening spaces formerly controlled by exploitative *castanhal* owners known for subtracting hectolitre measures[8] and for paying low prices for the product. Relations with the *regatão* offered other options. *Quilombolas* could identify and reject the personal dependency implicit in relations of *compadrio* and favour, which disguised relations that were socially unequal. Those families in particular without such links asserted their autonomy as they maintained the practice through the decade of picking brazil nuts in the free *castanhais*, found mainly upriver, above the rapids, such as in the rivers Cachorro and Mapuera. Others risked clandestine work within the closed *castanhais*. In both cases, they would sell the nuts in small amounts to the *regatões* who circulated in the Trombetas. Increasingly, they sold to them in preference, ignoring pressure and controls from the *patrões* and their representatives.

The last great harvest of brazil nuts under the direction of the owners' network, in 1963, foretold the imminent decline of their control. The gatherers asserted their autonomy once more — the right to choose the buyers of their product — restructuring their labour time and methods of production. New traders just arrived in Oriximiná joined the small *regatões*, purchasing boats that were better equipped. They followed the same routes, creating new forms of competition. Large owners leased the *castanhais* to families of lesser means as a result. Some gave up the enterprise altogether, according to the registries. At the same time, multinational and South Brazilian companies were looking to become established within the area, following reports of mineral deposits, prepared by official agencies in the mid 1960s. The object of their interest changed from the brazil nut to mineral resources, reflected in the purchases made by Santa Patricia (owned by Jari enterprises) and Rio do Norte mining companies. Some large proprietors began negotiations to this end. On the other side of the network, the black *castanheiros* continued to harvest according to patterns of agricultural-extractivist labour. The fruits of the harvest did not disappear with the decline of the link between patron and client. They recreated strategies of preserving their autonomy, the heritage of generations past, as they expressed communal rights to come and go, exercised for centuries. They recovered their old freedom to go to the *castanhais*, temporarily lost in the patron–client chain. Throughout the river, they reaffirmed the dissolution of the chain, and everything that it stood for. The dichotomy of slave/ex-slave, so pertinent in their history, had entered a new phase.

8   This corresponds to the practice, common in the region, of adopting as measure a 'hectolitre' that does not correspond to the real hectolitre, being some 20 per cent smaller. In this way, the people of the Trombetas sell their picking for considerably less than the market value.

Examination of the history of this group goes far beyond the representations of the dominant white elite, who intervene within the space of
their accomplishments and yet deny them visibility. The Report of
Environmental Impact (RIMA) made by one of the mining companies
(ALCOA S.A.) does not refer to the existence of *quilombos* at all. Before the
end of the 1980s the white world sent other signs that presaged the most
violent forms of domination over labour and lands. These were not mere
alterations in the labour process or the chain of commerce. What was at
stake were radical impositions on their conditions of work. In 1979 the
Brazilian Institute of Forestry Development (IBDF) announced the creation of the Biological Reservation of the Trombetas,[9] on the left bank of
the river. By coincidence or not, the area is acknowledged by the blacks as
rich in groves of brazil nut trees and containing lakes replete with fish, timber, palm thatch, seeds and fibres. In fact, both banks along the Trombetas
river, especially from Boa Vista to Cachoeira Porteira, have these species in
abundance. But the locals, who are experts in collecting, recognise a difference in the quality and density of groves between the banks. The image
of plenty that served to denominate the *castanhais* is presently a cruel idea
of limit, a barrier imposed by the Reservation. The loss of access to the
castanhais has strongly affected the communities, identified too by extractivism, as they are forced to relocate to distant areas in order to collect
brazil nut crops. The intervention of the now extinct IBDF, and afterwards IBAMA, has continued to follow this trail of exclusion. Initially,
access to the *castanhais* was permitted in the wintertime (roughly January to
July), though prohibited in summer.

The creation of the Biological Reservation of the Trombetas overrode
everyone. The action was planned without taking into consideration the levels of power concerned, the black communities or the municipality. There
was general expression of support and indignation, mainly by the politicians,
traders, and the black communities themselves, with representations at
national and international levels. County authorities made summaries of losses incurred as a result of decisions to which they and their legal representatives had not been party. For Oriximiná, the loss is first apparent in the considerable decline in production of brazil nuts, the major source of income
there along with cattle herds. From 1983 to 1987 the county suffered from
increasing loss of nut production and of status in the regional economy.

9   Biological Reservation: one form of conservation unit, of the several defined in
     Brazilian law. It presupposes the total absence of human occupation.

Other losses for the black communities go deeper into the consciousness of the older occupants. The territorial conflict focuses a vision of the loss of native land inhabited for generations *(terras de uso imemorial)*[10] With the creation of reserves, their lands became more limited and smaller, paving the way for new business to take over areas for future enterprise.

Since 1980, new aspects of the conflict have emerged. Twenty-five families living by the Jacaré Lake were threatened with eviction by IBDF if they did not leave of their own accord. This lake is one of the richest in brazil nuts, a factor that gave rise to more complaints about the deprivations previously determined by IBAMA of areas worked by many *castanheiros* during times of harvest. Since the agency installed a fiscalisation post at the mouth of the Erepecu Lake, close to the Jacaré, *quilombolas* have been forbidden to enter an area where in the past they used to gather food.

The *Comunidades Remanescentes de Quilombos* have staged several confrontations with IBAMA, MRN[11] and the federal police. When 90 families were encouraged by the MRN to remove to an area previously occupied by the company, another serious conflict occurred. Apparently, the company did not pay adequate compensation. Consistently, the group has opposed the interventions of the federal police, who are based in the company camp of Porto Trombetas, supported partially by MRN.

The present-day communities establish alliances and discuss the fate of families expelled from the area of the Reservation. In doing so they reaffirm their history of place, the sense of their belonging, of their being there *in place*, in opposition to those who have come from outside, represented by the foreigner, not-being from the place. These discourses are reworked through the memory of slavery and are reborn with each new situation or conflict. They clearly intertwine, particularly when the issue is one of acknowledging their way of preserving the ecosystem and its species, such as the freshwater turtle. The *Remanescentes de Quilombo* recognise and expose what they consider to be the abuses of authority, especially when defined by the sort of one-way control that does not apply to traders or cattle-ranchers. During the IBAMA fiscalisation control, their tools of trade, machetes, shotguns, boats, are confiscated. The material losses such actions inflict aggravate their feelings of discomfort and oppression. In the lands still relatively free from prohibi-

10 *Terras de uso imemorial:* a judicial category in Brazilian legistration, referring to lands used for over five years without such use being contested, even though those use them do not possess land titles. According to Brazilian law, those using them under such conditions become their legitimate owners

11 MRN: Mineração Rio do Norte, mining company on the right bank of the Trombetas.

tion, alongside the Trombetas, the Erepecuru and Cuminá rivers, there is little shortage of food. Here, among communities less affected by restrictions on their habits of work, the discourse is of plenty.

The memory of past brings to the fore a reconstruction of the time of plenty. Currently, the discourse taking place in communities such as Moura, Boa Vista, Juquiri, Juquirizinho, Irepecu and Palhal, is one of restriction, of reduction in food bought with the salaries paid. In their imagery, the place of plenty is displaced. It is symbolised by festivals and visits between kinsmen in communities from Mãe Cue to Abui, places less affected by the changes. They have the conditions there to reproduce, in gardens, fishing, hunting, gathering, even though it means still more distant journeys and harder work. The prohibitions and imperatives occlude the work and reproduction of the peasants, obstructing methods of production to the chosen standards of the group, with their rhythms and movements, and their migrations long and short, patterned according to nature and time.

CHAPTER 3

Social and Economic Change in Amazonia: The Case of Ornamental Fish Collection in the Rio Negro Basin[*]

Gregory Prang

Introduction

In the recent upsurge of interest in Amazonian studies one of the many overlooked topics concerns the intersection of the regional peasantry and the global market in ornamental fish. While there has been a smattering of reports on the region,[1] only Oliveira (1975) has provided more than a passing ethnographic account.

The ornamental fish industry, as I refer to it here, is the totality of producers, commercial agents, scientists, publishers and enthusiasts whose interests, economic or aesthetic, depend on the maintenance of live fish in captivity. Unlike food fish, ornamental fish (aquarium fish, tropical fish and exotic fish) must be kept alive to have value; are generally collected for sale in foreign markets; and are sought and consumed for their symbolic rather than utilitarian value. Ornamental fish collection provides economic opportunities for many commodity producers in Amazonia. Several observers of have commented on the relations of production in the ornamental fishery of the Rio Negro, either employing or implying the term *aviamento*.

Aviamento, fully developed during the rubber boom (1890–1910), is an economic mechanism through which surplus value is appropriated at the point of exchange. According to Santos, *aviamento* appears where: (1) natural resources are dispersed and scarce; (2) technology is simple; (3) eco-

* This chapter is based on fieldwork conducted between 1993 an 1999 as a member of Project Piaba, coordinated by Dr Ning L. Chao. I gratefully acknowledge the following sources of financial support for my fieldwork: Bio-Amazonia Conservation International, the Dr Herbert R. and Ms. Evelyn Axelrod Foundation, the Universidade do Amazonas, the Brazilian Conselho Nacional de Pesquisa (CNPq) and the Associação de Criadores e Exportadores de Peixes Ornamentais do Amazonas (ACEPOAM). I would like to thank Jeff Doan, Lisa Gurr and Paulo Petry for their comments and suggestions on earlier drafts.

1   See Emperaire and Pinton (1993); Lescure and Pinton (1993); Lescure et al. (1992); Galvão (1979a, 1979b and 1979c).

Aviamento!

nomic exchange involves little or no money; (4) presence of a local mercantile elite — native or foreign; (5) local elite has ties to monetised markets and underwrites credit to producers; and (6) there is a significant
external demand for one or more extractive products in a geographical
area.[2] Weinstein (1983) claims *aviamento* appeared as a means to control
labour through coercion and contrived indebtedness, and to extract a surplus where capital was scarce, production seasonal and transport slow.
Generally, *aviamento* is presented as extremely rigid, vertical and exploitative, and therefore the cause of Amazonian underdevelopment.[3]

Oliveira et al. noted that the ornamental fishery of the Rio Negro is
based in 'traditional relations of *aviamento*', referring specifically to contrived indebtedness.[4] The fishery has also been referred to as 'one of the
last strongholds of the traditional indentured labour system of the
Amazon',[5] and 'essentially feudal because it depends on indentured peasants to catch fish'.[6] Such characterisations are, at the very least, over-sim-
plified and assume that history has stood still since the rubber bust.

To understand the relations of production in Amazonia, it is more
appropriate to recognise the historical context from which present-day
peasant societies emerged (Nugent 1993; Harris 1998).[7] Although it can be
argued that the conditions necessary for *aviamento* remain, the 'potential for
coercion which *aviamento* had during the rubber era' (Ayres 1992:110) is
now greatly diminished. Numerous socio-economic and political changes
have taken place since the rubber era: 'With the withdrawal of the apparatus of the rubber industry, tendencies toward centralisation — typified in
[*aviamento*] — were undercut, yet the lower reaches of the mercantile network remained intact'.[8] Alternatives for peasant production increased, but
traditional economic arrangements between petty commodity producers
and smaller merchants ensured that the global marketplace would continue to structure the exploitation of Amazonia's resource base.

2   Santos (1980), p. 155.
3   Ross (1978), p. 194.
4   Oliveira, Pozzobon and Meira (1994), p. 84.
5   Goulding and Smith (1997), p. 23
6   Goulding et al. (1996), p. 111.
7   In order to understand peasant society in contemporary Amazonia there must be
    some 'vision of twentieth-century history and how [the] Amazon caboclo might be
    changing in its new conditions of existence' (Harris, 1998, p. 91).
8   Nugent (1993), pp. 202–3; see Ayres (1992), p. 199.

In order to demonstrate the place of *aviamento* in contemporary commodity production in Amazonia, this chapter explores the global/local linkage between the ornamental fish industry and peasant society of the middle Rio Negro. The approach I take largely historical, in order to provide the context for the present social formations in the ornamental fishery. I will demonstrate how the development of the global ornamental fish industry developed, eventually offering a new possibility for commodity production along the Rio Negro. Ornamental fish collecting began at a time when significant socioeconomic changes were taking place in Amazonia, and, in turn, stimulated other changes. Subsequent political and economic changes provide further context for understanding the social and economic importance of the ornamental fishery today. I describe the basic features of the ornamental fishery, including ecology, fishing methods, and relations of production. I conclude that the patron figure in the ornamental fishery must be understood in his/her own right, and not as a new incarnation of the rubber baron of yore/lore.

Barcelos

Barcelos is located 420 km from Manaus, the capital of the state of Amazonas (see Figure 3.1). The municipality is one of the largest archipelagos in the world, with a total area of 122,573 square kilometres. In 1728 the Carmelite mission of Mariuá, renamed Barcelos during the Pombaline era, was founded. Barcelos would serve as the first capital of the Capitánia de São José do Rio Negro (today the state of Amazonas) from 1758–91 and again between 1798–1803. During the early colonial period (1700–58) Barcelos was an important transshipment point for the Indian slave trade and forest products. Various forest products (including annatto, cacao, vanilla, puxuri and sarsaparilla), collectively known as *drogas do sertão* (backland drugs), were of economic importance. Under the Directorate system (1758–99) the region experienced a brief period of economic growth as the colonial government placed more emphasis on agricultural production (coffee, indigo, cotton, cacao and tobacco). The growth was not sustained however, as slave raiding and extraction continued to be undertaken by colonists in the interior.[9] After the transfer of the capital to Manaus, the region experienced a long period of economic stagnation and the economy shifted to the extraction of a variety of forest products. Principal among these was piassaba (*Leopoldinia piassaba*), a palm

9   MacLachlan (1973), pp. 213–5.

fibre. Piassaba continues to be a key extractive resource in the middle and upper regions of the Rio Negro basin. During the Directorate period it was sought for the production of rope for the maritime industry;[10] today, it is used in the manufacture of brooms and baskets.

Figure 3.1: Rio Negro Basin

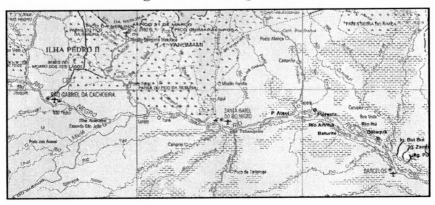

The Rio Negro would experience another period of economic growth during the rubber boom (1880–1910). During the boom, and until about 1940, the rubber trade on the Rio Negro was controlled by the famous *aviador*, J.G. Araújo, known as the emperor of Amazonas.[11] Although the rubber economy crumbled in about 1910, rubber tapping continued to be economically important in the basin until federal subsidies were eliminated in the mid-1980s. From 1923–30 Barcelos experienced another short-lived economic boom with the extraction of *balata* (*Mandilkara bindenata* and *M. huberi*), a white non-slip latex that is useful for machine beltings and golf balls.

Today, the international demand for aquarium fish affords a livelihood, albeit a precarious one, for many people in the Rio Negro basin. Ornamental fish collection in the municipalities of Barcelos and Santa Isabel do Rio Negro is now the principal economic activity, accounting for at least 60 per cent of municipal revenue in Barcelos alone.[12] The remaining 40 per cent is derived from the extraction of piassaba palm fibres and

10   Meira (1993).
11   MacCreagh (1985); Ugarte (1992); Benchimol (1994).
12   Personal communication, Amazonas State Revenue Service in Barcelos (1996).

601 - is Fish !

brazil nuts (*Bertholletia excelsa*), food fisheries, agricultural production for local markets, mining, tourism and other local commercial activities.

The Global Trade in Ornamental Fish

Statistical data on the world trade of ornamental fish are often scant and/or contradictory. The world retail market for aquarium fish, equipment and accessories was estimated at US$4 billion in 1971, US$7.2 billion in 1986[13] and US$15 billion in 1996.[14] The fish themselves represent only a fraction of the overall industry, perhaps as little as 3 per cent of the total retail value.[15] Fitzgerald estimated that 350 million ornamental fish, valued at $600 million, are sold annually,[16] with only ten per cent being wild caught.[17] The Food and Agricultural Organization reports that in 1999 the value of global ornamental fish imports was US$242,470,000, while the value of exports was US$169,430,000.[18] Although the value of ornamental fish exports rose by more than 300 per cent for the period 1985–96, these fell by about 18 per cent during the period 1996–99.[19]

There are many sources of wild-caught ornamental fish. In South America, Colombia is the largest supplier to the world market, followed by Brazil and Peru. In Africa, Nigeria, Zaire and the Great Rift Lakes are the principal sources. In Asia, wild caught ornamental fish originate in Sri Lanka, Malaysia, Indonesia and the Philippines. Additionally, a few of the Caribbean Islands are exporters of ornamental fish. Most ornamental fish, however, are captive bred on fish farms in Singapore, Malaysia, Japan, Israel, Thailand, Hong Kong and the USA. McLarney (1988) writes that 30 per cent of US demand is supplied by US fish farms.[20] In 1985 Florida fish farmers sold ten million ornamental fish, representing 125 species worth US$75 million, providing more than 50 per cent of the total volume of air-freight out of the state. Singapore, however, is the largest exporter of farm-raised ornamental fish, earning ±$40 million in 1992.[21] Over 300

13   Andrews (1992), p. 25.
14   Dawes (2000), p. 110.
15   Watson (2000), p. 7.
16   Fitzgerald (1989), p. 259.
17   Andrews (1990), p. 55.
18   FAO Fishstat Plus (2001) The explanation for the wide discrepancy in export and import value must be attributed to the idiosyncrasies of recording practices of the various countries and the inconsistent reporting of freight costs.
19   I have been unable to ascertain the reason for this decrease.
20   McLarney (1988), p. 50.
21   Fernando and Phang (1994), p. 6.

varieties of 30 species are produced in Singapore, including species indigenous to the Amazon, Mexico and other South-east Asian countries.

A Brief History of Fish Keeping

Humans have fished since the Paleolithic period, but 'it was not until the
development of more leisured societies that the non-alimentary aspects [of
fish] assumed importance in their own right'.[22] The goldfish has been kept
for leisure purposes longer than any other species of fish. The Chinese
kept goldfish from the middle of the fourth century.[23] By at least the
eleventh century, during the Sung Dynasty (960–1279 C.E.), they were
actively being bred, and were considered common home items.[24] Goldfish
were first introduced to Britain in 1691, and to the USA some time during
the eighteenth century.

During the mid-nineteenth century the first home aquarium craze took
hold in Europe and the USA. According to Atz and Faulkner (1971), 'the
intriguing notion of setting up a self-sustaining microcosm in one's parlour
seems to have played almost as important a part in generating the fad's
contagious enthusiasm as did the successful aquaria themselves'.[25] The
introduction of tropical, or exotic, freshwater fish heightened interest in
aquarium keeping during the last quarter of the nineteenth century.[26] By
1893 almost every major city in the eastern USA had at least one dealer in
aquarium supplies.[27]

During the first decades of the twentieth century the number of tropical freshwater fish available in the market grew tremendously. Most of the
first suppliers of wild-caught tropical fish were merchant sailors working
on the various steamship lines; it was they who accounted for nearly all
new imports of exotic fish.[28] As a means of augmenting their incomes
sailors would purchase freshwater fish caught near major ports around the
world. The number of steamship lines serving Amazonia increased greatly during the rubber boom, serving as the economic context in which the
increase in both supply and demand of the tropical fish took place.

22   Banister (1977), p. 9.
23   Atz and Faulkner (1971), p. 11.
24   Banister (1977), p. 9.
25   Atz and Faulkner (1971), p. 15.
26   Banister (1977), p. 21.
27   Klee (1987), p. 45.
28   Socolof (1996), p. 7; Stoye (1936), p. 137.

Specialised publications and aquarium societies devoted to aquariums and ornamental fish contributed further to the growth of the hobby in the early decades of — and throughout — the twentieth century. By 1935 tropical fish had replaced the goldfish in popularity. The 'tropicals' were preferred over goldfish, despite their higher cost, because of their colour, 'finnage', breeding habits and activeness, and because they required less maintenance than goldfish.[29] An increase in both the number of new species and fish available was attributed to direct US imports from Central and South America.[30] The family of fish known as Characins became the most popular. In 1936 the commercial introduction of the 'neon tetra' (*Paracheirodon inessi*), a Characin, initiated a dramatic change in fish keeping. According to Ladiges (1978),

> [The] neon tetra brought a great change to the aquarium hobby. Up to that time there were some people who looked on hobbyists with a pitiful smile and regarded the hobby more or less as a pastime for harmless fools: housewives in particular did not show much empathy. This jewel of a fish brought about a completely new image ... It was through this fish that the genuine 'home aquarium' actually first came into existence.[31]

The commercial introduction of the neon tetra to the global hobby market also initiated a dramatic change in certain regions of Amazonia, expanding the possibilities for petty commodity production. Neon tetras inhabit the streams along the Amazon River between the middle Ucayali in Peru and São Paulo de Olivença in Brazil. Efforts to organise the collection of neon tetras in the region of these tributaries intensified during the late 1930s. During the 1950s the knowledge gained by industry participants in this region was transferred to the Rio Negro with the 'discovery' and commercialisation of the cardinal tetra (*Paracheirodon axelrodi*).

The Cardinal Tetra Boom

The commercialisation of the cardinal tetra occurred at a significant historical moment on the Rio Negro. With the post-war decline in the demand for rubber, economic activity along the Rio Negro slowed. The population of Barcelos and the rest of the Rio Negro basin fell. Many Amerindians returned to the upper Rio Negro or settled along the riverbanks, while much of the rest of the population moved to Manaus. Specialist

---

29 Mellen (1931), p. 287; Coates (1933), p. 18.
30 Chute (1934), p. 96; Coates (1933), p. 18.
31 Ladiges (1978), p. 6.

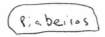

labourers and local industry left the region, and except for the small fixed group of merchants and civil servants, the rest of the population which remained moved according to seasonal extractive activities. The few Portuguese and *caboclo* patrons who remained diversified or began to operate from Manaus. Despite the reduction in population, there still remained a surplus of peasant labour as a result of the lack of viable economic alternatives, a situation that had not been the case in the earlier history of the region.

With World War Two, the monopoly created by J.G. Araújo began to crumble as the war effort brought about the rationalisation of rubber production.[32] His power, and that of other *aviadores*, was greatly reduced by the creation of the Rubber Development Corporation and the Banco de Crédito da Borracha. The US-controlled Rubber Development Corporation began to supply the '*soldados da borracha*' (rubber soldiers) with provisions, skirting the traditional credit arrangements of *aviamento*.[33] By the end of the war, Araújo's Rio Negro empire was being replaced by a number of competitors. In 1949 there were four firms navigating on the Rio Negro as far as Santa Isabel.[34]

A consequence of the increasing competition for shipping revenues was better internal communication throughout the Rio Negro basin. Additionally, battery-powered radios were by then able to pick up stations from Manaus.[35] From at least as early as 1952 Panair, a Brazilian subsidiary of Pan Am airlines, operated weekly flights from Belém to Taraquá on the Rio Uaupés, stopping at the municipal seats along the route. These flights facilitated travel for the larger merchants, state and federal civil servants and local politicians, and improved the postal service in the region. In addition, the introduction of outboard motors and aluminium canoes further improved communication between the towns and the interior.

The collection and sale of ornamental fish offered a degree of freedom from the debt and rigid patron/client relations to which petty commodity producers had become accustomed. In the first few years of the trade, however, those who were in debt to their traditional patron were allowed to enter the fish commerce only when the debts were paid off. The original *piabeiros* (ornamental fish collectors) say that 'traditional' patrons did not care too much for them since they 'did not belong to them; the patrons didn't like the rubber tappers for that matter'. The client class was not very optimistic about the prospects of ornamental fish collecting either. Many had

32   Benchimol (1994), p. 14.
33   Reis (1997), p. 163.
34   Carvalho (1952), p. 12–3.
35   *Ibid.*, p. 88.

no faith in fish collecting and teased the first *piabeiros*: 'Catching small fish is not work, work is brazil nuts and *fantasia* [pelts and skins]; 'it is work for fools and lazy men'. Many extractive producers, however, would eventually find *pegando piaba* (catching fish) much easier and more tolerable than other alternatives. Most producers and their families were accustomed to 'patron time', moving to various locales to extract forest resources or plant gardens.[36] They might stay in one *paragem* (stop), or a series of *paragens*, depending on the season, product abundance and logistical constraints; they might also stay in the same place for several years. When the possibility of ornamental fishing became an option, there were willing recruits. According to one *piabeiro*:

> The opportunity to fish was at least better than being stuck in the jungle. At that time, nobody had ever been to Manaus before. By fishing we would be called upon once and a while by the patron to come to Manaus ... One could now go to Manaus to visit and receive money that could be used to buy products that were much less expensive than those sold by patrons in the interior.

International interest in the cardinal tetra began in 1952, when limnologist Harald Sioli reported the existence of the cardinal tetra in the Rio Içana near São Felipe.[37] It appears that several people were collecting cardinals on the upper Rio Negro by 1955, at least above Santa Isabel.[38] It would take until the end of the decade before those interested in its organised production would realise that the cardinal's natural range extended east to the Rio Branco, and that it could be found in much greater quantities in the region of the middle Rio Negro.

In 1958 Herbert R. Axelrod[39] travelled to Manaus to meet Harald Schultz[40] after hearing of him from industry insiders. Harald Schultz intro-

---

36   Meira (1993).
37   Ladiges (1956); Weitzman (1956), p. 257; Weitzman and Fink (1983), p. 389.
38   One of the first collectors of the cardinal tetra was a Panair pilot, known as Capitão Mauro. He piloted a Catalina aircraft on a weekly flight to Taraquá in São Gabriel da Cachoeira (see Seitz, 1963, p. 67). He learned of the cardinal tetra from Sioli (Géry, 1994, p. 83).
39   In 1952 Axelrod began publishing the *Tropical Fish Hobbyist* magazine, whose current circulation is nearly 60,000. TFH Inc. would become the largest publisher of pet literature in the world, offering more than 1,000 titles.
40   Harald Schultz was a German anthropologist at the University of São Paulo who did ethnographic research among several indigenous Amazonian societies and who was an avid ornamental fish hobbyist. When Schultz came back from the field, he often brought different fish species back to Hans Stegemann, a German ornamental fish and animal dealer in São Paulo. Schultz would later write for Axelrod's *Tropical Fish Hobbyist* as a means to defray his field expenses.

duced him to Hans Willy Schwartz.[41] During that first meeting Axelrod convinced Schwartz to enter the ornamental fish business, an act of persuasion that would have a profound effect on the socioeconomic future of the middle Rio Negro basin. Schwartz soon started an ornamental fish export business called *Aquário Rio Negro*. In 1959, eager to learn of potential sources of cardinal tetras, he asked Dr Roosevelt, a piassaba and caiman skin dealer, to undertake some exploratory research for him. At that time, Louro Fontes, a commodity producer from Barcelos, was working for Dr Roosevelt on Rio Curuduri, near the mouth of the Rio Aracá. Roosevelt had Fontes locate and collect a sample of cardinal tetras. Fontes and his son, Silas, would become the first full-time *piabeiros* on the Rio Negro.

The first organised cardinal tetra production in the Rio Negro was established on the Rio Itú, on the left bank, just above the Rio Demini. In 1960 Padre Estevão, of the Salesian Mission in Barcelos, visited the *Igarapé* (stream) Aduiá, on the Rio Itú, looking for samples of cardinal tetras. Local residents provided him with 2,000 cardinal tetras which he sent to Schwartz. According to informants, Schwartz travelled together with the priest throughout the region for some time.[42] That same year Schwartz led an expedition to the Igarapé Aduiá and organised a group of five collectors among the local residents.[43] Informants say that for the first two years only cardinal tetras were collected, they were not provided with any material to store fish and Schwartz would bring additional collectors to the locale. At the fishing camps fish were stored in plastic-lined baskets, woven by family members of the fish collectors. The fisher collectors would spend three to four days fishing, and then Schwartz's personnel would return to Manaus, transporting the fish in 20-litre kerosene cans. One of Schwartz's boats would stop at the Aduiá every 15 days during the first fishing season, shipping 2–3,000 cans containing 1,000 fish each.

The cardinal tetra was initially transshipped via Georgetown, Guyana, which had the advantage of a regular air service by Pan American Airlines. Ornamental fish exporters established in Georgetown chartered DC3s to

41 Hans Willy Schwartz, originally from Vienna, immigrated to Bolivia in 1938. During WWII, he moved to Manaus where he opened a photography business. In 1955, because of his love for wildlife and some persuasion from Hans Stegemann, Schwartz entered the wild animal trade. Before entering the ornamental fish business, he became well known for capturing and exporting animals to zoos around the world.

42 According to one informant, Padre Estevão once said, 'Mister Willy keeps telling me that piaba is a good business. No matter how many die, the few that survive pay for all of the expenses, for the office, and still there is money left over for him to eat.'

43 Schwartz (1961).

pick up fish from Manaus, shipping them on to destinations in the USA. By 1962 Boeing 707s were making non-stop flights between Manaus and the USA, rendering transshipment from Georgetown unprofitable.

During the next few years Schwartz continued to establish teams of fish collectors (*freguesia* or clientele), probably with the help of Padre Estevão. The second source of fish to be exploited was the Rio Jufarís basin, followed by the Rio Cuiuni, Paraná Atauí near the mouth of the Rio Preto, the *igarapés* on the left bank of the Rio Negro facing Barcelos, and the tributaries (Tea, Aiuanã, Urubaxi) of the Rio Negro near Santa Isabel. Schwartz outfitted the collecting groups well, and balances were paid off with cash. According to one informant, 'Schwartz got us whatever we needed. At the time everything was easy, nothing was lacking. We were paid on delivery; he paid little, but he paid. We never lacked money; we never went hungry under the command [*sob o poder*] of Schwartz.' During the first years, Schwartz followed the economic pattern of *aviamento*, exchanging clothing, radios and other merchandise, and maybe small amounts of currency, for the fish. Informants affirm that Schwartz differed from the traditional patron in that he did not charge a premium on the goods he advanced to his clients. Money as a means of payment, however, only became more common as the fishermen personally transported the fish to Manaus.

After a year Schwartz began buying boats and sending them to fishing areas.[44] He would send employees to take merchandise from Manaus to the fish collectors, and bring the fish back to Manaus, leaving the fishermen to fish. When the collectors had a large number of fish collected, they would send notice to Schwartz who would then dispatch one of the boats to pick them up. After another year fishermen from the various areas transported their own fish directly to Manaus. One individual in each group of fish collectors was provided with a boat for travel.[45] In this way, Schwartz rationalised the transport function of his operation, passing on the responsibility for organising shipment downstream to Manaus to his client fishermen. In many respects Schwartz created a small group of patrons from his clients, in that he selected who would get a boat. The privileged few would then have the responsibility of organising the actual collection process, which generally meant employing close family and kin. Unlike the conventional *aviamento* system, Schwartz removed the credit function, paying cash for the product delivered. After the first *piabeiros* set-

44 Exporters who entered later also furnished boats to their clients.
45 For some time, however, Schwartz continued to send employees to the more remote Santa Isabel to pick up fish.

tled their accounts with Schwartz, a cash balance was still due them and they were able to accumulate some capital.

The possibility of profits from ornamental fish from the Rio Negro did not go unnoticed. Many came to exploit the cardinal rush. According to one veteran fish collector, 'At that time news ran swiftly, "boy, go to the Rio Negro. There they have a type of fish that can earn a person a lot of money quickly." In those days it was really quick. Everybody came running from [neon tetra fishery in] Benjamin Constant and Tabatinga.' The Prefect of Santa Isabel, various dealers from Belém and one Barcelos native, Anildo Macedo, began buying ornamental fish on the Rio Negro. I was told that the Prefect of Santa Isabel was so excited at the economic potential of ornamental fish that he encouraged people to pay off their debts at the *taberneiro* (general store/trading post) and prepare to make some money. By 1964 there were at least six firms exporting ornamental fish from the Rio Negro.

In time, Schwartz and other exporters requested that fishermen bring all types of fish. They began transporting a mixture of fish species. No one really knew what he or she was collecting, only that exporters wanted a variety of species. If they sold well in the world market, fishing effort for the species in question was organised. In this way, the common variety of fish exported from the Rio Negro was established. The *igarapés* that drain the large interfluvial areas between the Rio Demini and the Rio Jufarís, on the left bank of the Rio Negro, became more important by 1963 due to the many varieties of fish found there.

Social Change in the Rio Negro Basin (1965–2000)

During the past 25 years, state presence in the basin has increased dramatically. Various projects were initiated under the military government, with the aims of territorial integration and control of the frontier.[46] In 1967, SUFRAMA (Superintendência da Zona Franca de Manaus) was established, and in 1968, the municipalities of the Rio Negro were designated part of the National Security Area (Área de Segurança Nacional). With financial incentives from SUFRAMA, the Sharp Electronics group opened a palm heart plant in Barcelos, which now employs approximately 40 people. During the mid-1970s, under the banner of the National Integration Plan (Plano de Integração Nacional), a road (Perimetral Norte, BR 307) was planned to link Boa Vista and São Gabriel. In 1985 Project Calha

46   Oliveira (1995).

Norte was created to promote the occupation and development of the Northern Amazon Region.

These projects transformed the upper Rio Negro by increasing the number of migrants and military personnel,[47] but also by allowing an influx of capital and a restructuring of transport services in the region. Commercial activity in the state of Amazonas increased, leading to a fall in the price of many common products in the interior, as well as luxuries such as televisions and radios. The shipment of merchandise, building materials and passengers to São Gabriel allowed for the regularisation of transport services along the Rio Negro and increased the number of shippers. Unlike in the rubber period, when the *aviadores* consolidated purchasing, shipping and credit functions, the new shipping concerns only provided transport services. By 1985 most exporters of ornamental fish utilised *recreios* (regional transport boats) to handle weekly shipments.

With the implementation of the Calha Norte, mining, particularly for gold, by large mining companies and by independent *garimpeiros* (prospectors), increased in the upper Rio Negro basin.[48] This new economic activity was accompanied by numerous conflicts related to environmental damage, social disruption and indigenous land rights. Mining was principally concentrated in the Içana and Cauburis rivers, but *garimpeiros* worked throughout the basin, including the Rio Negro above Santa Isabel, and the Aracá and Padauiri rivers in Barcelos. Most of the *garimpeiros* involved had formerly operated on the Rio Tapajós or Rio Madeira. In order to mitigate the environmental hazards and social disruption caused by unregulated prospecting, the federal government ordered the removal of all mining concerns from the basin in 1993.[49] Although gold mining has been banned, there has been an increase in the mining of tantalite. Tantalite has a low radioactivity content and is used in the manufacture of capacitors, circuitry, nuclear reactors, jet engines and cellular phones. Some of the more prominent merchants, and the municipal government of Barcelos, have shown a keen interest in the mining of tantalite in the basins of the Padauiri and Aracá. Tantalite prospecting has offered yet another commodity production alternative for some individuals in the region. Several of my informants in the ornamental fishery shifted to tantalite extraction, prospecting or providing transport.

47   *Ibid.*
48   Oliveira et al. (1994); Oliveira (1995).
49   Oliveira et al. (1994), pp. :27–32.

During the 1970s, the latex of sorva (*Couma* sp.), used to make chewing gum, varnishes and paint, became an important extractive product in the Rio Negro. There are two types of sorva: *sorvinha* (*Couma utilis*) and *sorvão* (*Couma macrocarpa*). They are found on the *terra firme* (high ground), and are obtained by either tapping or felling trees. Exports of sorva began in 1970, reaching a peak in 1976 and were almost nonexistent by 1990. Many of the former patrons of sorva (*sorveiros*) went on to become buyers of ornamental fish. Although rubber production still has some importance in certain regions of Amazonia like the Juruá basin and Acre, production ceased in the middle Rio Negro with the elimination of federal subsidies in the mid-1980s. Interestingly, with the decline of rubber and sorva prices, the *regatão* (urban-based itinerant trader) is no longer a fixture in the socioeconomic landscape of the Rio Negro, leaving the patrons of the extraction minerals, piassaba and ornamental fish as the principal sources of merchandise for many in the interior of the region.

There are few other agricultural activities, except manioc for family consumption,[50] and no agro-forestry projects in the region. Recently, the municipal government, with sponsorship by the State of Amazonas ('Terceiro Ciclo'), has offered producers incentives for the cultivation of sugar-cane (for use by Coca-Cola in Manaus), as well as *pupunha* trees (peach palm, *Bactris gassipaes*) for sale to the Sharp Group. Until recently, palm hearts were extracted from the *jauarí* palm (*Astrocaryum jauarí*), ubiquitous along the many islands of the Mariuá Archipelago. Sharp is also planting peach palm trees in order to reduce environmental pressure on jauarí species.

As in other regions of the Amazon, urban growth in the interior of the Rio Negro has been significant.[51] Brazilian census data indicate that the population of the municipality of Barcelos has more than doubled in the last ten years, from 11,035 in 1991 to 24,121 in 2000.[52] Much of the increase can be attributed to the increase in commercial activity and government employment in the city,[53] as well as the availablity of healthcare and education. Many of the current residents in the city migrated from São

---

50   During my fieldwork I only met one family that planted more than two hectares, producing a surplus for sale or barter; generally traded to the intermediaries of piassaba and ornamental fish. Most families produce '*so para nosso próprio consumo*' (only for our own consumption). — Manioc

51   Ayres (1992); Cleary (1993); Nugent (1993).

52   IBGE (2000).

53   The largest employer in Barcelos is now the municipal government, employing as many as 400 people, depending on state and federal grants.

Gabriel, Santa Isabel and the riverine communities within Barcelos. Migrants from São Gabriel came because of population pressure and the difficulties associated with subsistence production, and those from Santa Isabel came in search of economic opportunities and *movimento* (social activities). Out-migration, however, is as significant as in-migration. Given the lack of opportunities for gainful employment in Barcelos, many migrants eventually move on to Manaus. Despite the growth in population, and the increasing presence of the state in Barcelos, 1991 census data (IBGE 1991) reveal that the literacy rate continues to be quite low, less than 50 per cent, and lower for women, older and rural residents. In addition, healthcare is a continual problem as equipment, medicine and health professionals are in short supply.

It is in this context that the importance of ornamental fishery must be understood. An eventual bust of the fishery would compound already difficult socioeconomic problems. In 1998 ornamental fish exports from the state of Amazonas were US$2,216,509.[54] While exports represent only a small fraction of total exports, valued at US$138 million in 1996,[55] they provide the municipality of Barcelos with at least 500,000 Reais (US$200,000) per year.[56] Given the lack of economic alternatives and the relative lack of capital in circulation, the ornamental fishery plays a key role in the local economy. In town and the interior, *piabeiros* often assist members of their large kin networks. Additionally, the collectors and intermediaries patronise many of the local merchants. The cardinal tetra is central to these exchanges, since it represents more than 80 per cent of annual exports.

Ornamental Fish Collection in the Rio Negro Basin

Cardinal tetras occur naturally throughout the middle to upper Rio Negro basin and parts of the Rio Orinoco basin, and depend on the presence of wetlands.[57] Cardinal habitats are found in the shallow areas near the fringe of the floodplain where there is sufficient shade. The seasonal variation in water levels determines the rhythm of life for the cardinal tetra. As the water level rises, the cardinal tetras migrate upstream (*arribação*) and towards the edge of the flooding zones to spawn, and as it falls, they return downstream (*arriação*). According to *piabeiros*, when water neither rises nor

54 IBAMA (1999).
55 Benchimol (1997).
56 Based on discussions with state revenue service employees, and calculations of production data from Chao (2001), p. 171.
57 Harris and Petry (2001), 213–4.

falls, the fish stay put. When the water level begins dropping precipitously, cardinals begin migrating downstream in small schools of 12 to 30 fish. The breeding season of the cardinal tetra, which coincides with the annual flood cycle, begins in late March/early April and ends around the end of June. Breeding can also occur during *repiquetes*, when the water level rises during interpluvial periods.

There are two basic methods of collecting the cardinal tetra: *cacurís* or traps, and *rapichés* or dip nets, both made of polyester mosquito netting. The *cacurí* is used principally in the *chavascais* (low marshy woodlands), and is the principal means of capture in the floodplains of the major tributaries of the right bank of the Rio Negro. The *rapiché* is employed when fish are found along the water edge of the igarapés, particularly in *tributaries* of the left bank. Both methods require that the fish be first located by sight. In addition, the amount of time spent paddling to and from the fishing areas may account for half of the time spent in the collection process.

There may be over 1,000 *piabeiros* involved in the capture and sale of ornamental fish in the region during the fishing season (August–April). The number of intermediaries varies over time, but there are roughly 60 to 70. Each intermediary maintains a *freguêsia* (personnel, a group of clients) ranging between two and fifteen full-time collectors. The maximum number of collectors (1,050) would only be possible during peak production periods. I estimate that there are no more than 500 full-time fish collectors. This does not include those who provide auxiliary labour in the fishery, however, who are usually family members. Eisenstadt (1992) estimates that possibly 80 per cent of the local population have some relation to the trade.[58] Although the exact number of participants, as well as the number of indirect jobs involved, is still unknown, Eisenstadt's estimate is probably too high.

The patron in the ornamental fishery of the Rio Negro is, by definition, a boat owner. They are variously known as *piabeiros*, *atravessadores* (referring to one who profits by traversing the rivers to buy commodities), *intermediários* (intermediaries) and *compradores* (buyers). The term *piabeiro* is ambiguous, however, as it may describe both the patron and the client: 'we're all piabeiros because even the patrons fish'. Some patrons only buy fish from client/collectors, while others buy fish and fish themselves as well. There is no terminology for the patron/client dyad comparable to that of the rubber trade: *seringalista* (rubber stand owner)/*seringueiro* (tapper).[59] While the terms *patrão* (patron) and *freguês* (client) are ubiquitous in discur-

58   Eisenstadt (1992), p. 2.
59   Prang (2001), pp. 57–8.

sive practices along the Rio Negro, the term *piabalista*, seemingly a fitting term for the ornamental fish patron, is absent. The absence of the patron/client dichotomy may reflect the lack of a clear-cut distinction between patron and client, since clients sometimes become patrons themselves.[60]

Most patrons are children of Nordestino (generally from Ceará) or Portuguese fathers born in the region; fewer than 20 are from outside the region. Kinship, family, marriage and *compadrio* relations[61] mediate the organisation of production in the Rio Negro fishery, in terms of both patrons and clients. At least 15 of the intermediaries are the sons of current or former intermediaries. Some were given boats by their fathers, while others assumed responsibility for their fathers' operations. There are a large number of marriage alliances among the intermediaries, increasing the density of kinship relationships in the fishery, both endogamously and exogamously. Seventeen of the 60 to 70 intermediaries are linked through kinship and marriage, across three generations, and at least seven more linked by *compadrio* relations. This core group of intermediaries makes up roughly 30 per cent of the total number of patrons. *Piabeiros* in this core group do a lot of swapping of species on the river to meet the requests of the exporters. One exporter asked me why he was unable to obtain quantities of a certain fish with which other exporters had no difficulty. I discovered that the fish was most abundant in the region of the Rio Itú, and that his personnel did not possess any kin or fictive-kin affiliations there. It seems, then, that within a system of usufruct and community rights (discussed below), exporters must, at some level, strategise in order to maintain stable sources of supply.

Not infrequently, the patron/client arrangement operates within family and kin relations, but in all cases, production is conceived of as corporate. Much must be done to maintain and transport live fish: boats maintained, water changed, handling equipment cleaned, unwanted and dead fish removed from *viveiros* and tubs, etc. Who performs what tasks depends on the composition of the work groups, and whether or not they are working from permanent or temporary residences.

60   Nugent (1993, p. 203) has stressed that with the decentralisation of *aviamento* following the decline of rubber prices, differentiation between direct producers and merchants became more ambiguous: 'small-scale traders, for example, frequently being producers themselves as well as functioning as merchants. The living standards of such traders are in many respects equivalent to those of their debtors.'

61   Relationships created among parents and godparents (*compadres*) in the Catholic ritual of baptism.

Where the relations of production are not explained in terms of family and kinship, fictive kin relations (*compadrio*) are a ready substitute. Relations among *compadres* can be either hierarchical or egalitarian. Hierarchical *compadrio* relations of a nature serve to manipulate the 'impersonal structure [of patronage] in terms of person-to-person relationships'.[62] Through both spiritual and commercial relationships, the patron is often able to form a large labour force, securing a steady supply of commodities, while the client obtains economic and moral security. According to Wagley (1976), 'the number of godchildren and co-fathers which an individual can claim is an index of social position'.[63] One of the largest ornamental fish patrons, for example, claims to have more godchildren than he can remember, 'probably more than 300'.

Compadrio relations are not, however, confined to vertical socio-economic relations. Most client fish collectors have many *compadres*, serving various social, political and economic objectives, including simple friendship. There are two varieties of *compadre: legítimo* (legitimate) and *de fogueira* (campfire), the former resulting from a church baptism and the latter from a pledge of solidarity between consenting colleagues. The latter have a special significance in the fishery, particularly for those who spend much of the year at temporary fishing campsites. Based on the Brazilian tradition in which large bonfires are built for the festivities in honour of São João and on São Pedro in late June, friends can pledge solidarity by pronouncing themselves *compadres de fogueira*.[64] These ties, although not as binding as those established at baptism, do increase one's web of secure personal relations.[65] In the ornamental fishery of the Rio Negro, however, colleagues do not necessarily wait for these religious holidays to become *compadres*, consummating bonds whenever two parties consent. This type of *compadrio* relation is almost exclusively maintained between status equals.

Patrons generally procure fish in several traditional fishing areas to hedge against low production. Although ownership of inland waterways is not permitted under Brazilian law, *piabeiros* generally respect traditional fishing areas. Most patrons have fixed fishing areas that are defended according to traditional usufruct rights. Some patrons are considered *ambulantes*, or itinerant *piabeiros*. The *ambulantes* move from fishing area to fishing area, depending on the type of fish requested by the exporter, or on the availability of fish in a

62 Mintz and Wolf (1950), p. 346.
63 Wagley (1976), p. 157,
64 *Ibid.*, p. 153.
65 *Ibid.* pp. 153–4.

particular stream or river. If a patron leaves the trade, his area is up for contention, and for this reason most fishing areas are rarely vacated during the fishing season, except to prevent over-fishing of an area.

There are three basic forms of usufruct rights found in the fishery of the Rio Negro, associated with riverine communities and indigenous lands, private ownership of land in which smaller streams are located and open resources. Riverine peasant communities that are dependent upon certain natural resources are granted special legal status in Brazil, which gives them stewardship over those resources. They regulate the access of outsiders to those resources for economic purposes. Communities like those at Baturité, Samauma and Daraquá — which control access to the Rio Arirahá, Lago do Rei (Deminí) and Igarapé Daraquá respectively — generally prevent fishing without their express permission. The Indian affairs agency (FUNAI) requires permission to collect within indigenous territories. Frequently, if an amicable deal can be arranged between the *piabeiro* and the community, collecting is done informally, either with or without community members. However, conflict is not uncommon. Ricardo (2000) reports that in October 1999, a *piabeiro* arrived in the indigenous community of Castanheiro in Santa Isabel and asked for permission from the *capitão* (community leader) to collect.[66] The *capitão* proposed that the community members do the collecting and then sell him the production. The *piabeiro* rejected the counterproposal and said he would collect anyway. The *capitão* insisted that he had the legal right to refuse him. The *piabeiro* argued that if the *capitão* wanted to pursue his rights, 'he would never find them, not even in hell'.[67] Most *piabeiros*, collectors and intermediaries alike, claim that incidents like this are rare, and many protest at such behaviour by their colleagues. They claim that if outsiders act as gentlemen, and treat their counterparts with respect, everyone benefits.

There are several *piabeiros* who own title to the lands in which productive fishing grounds are located, mostly in the stretch of the Rio Negro between the Rio Deminí and Rio Jufarís. According to Brazilian law, inland waterways are national property, and property titles only apply to the land that is a certain number of metres beyond the water's edge. Fishing in Brazilian inland waterways is open to all who possess a fishing licence. Thus, land titles do not prevent others from fishing within the boundaries of private property, except in the case of community property or indige-

66 Ricardo (2000), p. 284.
67 *Ibid.*

nous lands. There have been several cases in which more itinerant patrons have fished within privately-owned lands. In one case, the property owners went to court to demand that the individual desist. The judge in Barcelos sympathised with the complainants, but explained that the invader was within his rights. In another case, an interior resident without a property title has been more successful in keeping outsiders from fishing in 'his' *igarapé*. He negotiates with prospective *piabeiros* in the same way that the communities do, upsetting those who are unable to strike a deal with him. Despite the lack of legal backing for the defence of 'his' *igarapé*, those who are refused honour his refusal, most likely for fear of reprisals. It should be emphasised, however, that most *piabeiros* honour land titles as being accompanied by the right of the owner to allow or deny outsiders to fish within property boundaries.

Most tributaries of the middle Rio Negro are open to anyone who desires to fish, but, particularly along the larger river courses where many patrons control production or have fished for many years, the general rule is that others may fish anywhere they please, as long as they do not utilise the *paragens* (stops or campsites) or the *caminhos* (trails) through the *igapós* that patrons have painstakingly cut.[68] Although conflict can arise when a non-traditional (without usufruct rights) patron fishes within a traditional (with usufruct rights) patron's fishing areas, even more is generated if he competes for established clients (*mexe com pessoal*, or mess with personnel). In 1998, one family left its traditional fishing areas on the Rio Jufarís to fish on the Rio Aiuanã. I do not know the reason for the change or expansion in fishing areas, but conflict ensued between the family and two traditional patrons who had been organising production in the river for more than ten years. It may be that the conflict was responsible for a fire that burned at least 40 hectares of *igapó* and *terra firme* on the right bank of the Rio Aiuanã.[69] One of the parties involved called the incident a *besteira* (foolishness): 'The area that was burned was a spawning ground which produced over 600 tubs [roughly worth US\$3,600] of cardinals per year.' Asked whether the fire was intentional, he would not comment. At the time of my departure from the field the Federal

68   The only exception to this rule seems to be the Paraná Atauí, where patrons from all areas rush to send their clients when the cardinal tetras migrate downstream in large numbers. The lack of 'traditional' patrons on the Atauí is probably due to a large fire that was accidentally sparked by some *piabeiros* about 1980. *Piabeiros* relate that production in the area was negligible for about ten years, thus precluding the establishment, or maintenance, of usufruct fishing rights.

69   See also Ricardo (2000), p. 284.

Environmental Protection Agency (IBAMA), FUNAI and the federal police were investigating the case, forcing the patriarch of the invading family to hire a lawyer for his defence.

There are two categories of clients in the ornamental fishery:[70] rural and urban. In the interior, most producers live in one of the communities or *sítios* (isolated rural domiciles) near productive fishing areas. These can be divided into two groups based on the degree to which they depend on commodity production to meet subsistence needs; peasants and commodity producers.[71] Peasants are part-time agriculturalists, fish and hunt for food, collect ornamental fish during the low water season and cut piassaba during the high water season. Fish collection is a supplement to subsistence production and a part of overall household economic strategies. Many such producers only fish when they need money, perhaps for a specific household item. Typically, younger men and adolescent boys collect, while other family members tend to manioc gardens (*roças*) and other domestic chores, but entire families may leave their homes to help in fish collection when migrating ornamental fish are abundant. The economic proceeds from the collection of ornamental fish may be corporate or individual in nature.

In the communities of Santa Rita and Floresta, near the mouth of the Rio Ereré, all males between ten and 50 can be categorised as either current or ex-*piabeiros*. The actual number of client/collectors fluctuates monthly, but averages about 25. These communities are regularly visited by two *piabeiro*/patrons. In the interior, the merchandise that the patron brings is very desirable because there is no commerce, and the distance to town (150km) makes shopping prohibitive. In Santa Rita and Floresta most exchanges are based in barter. If fishing is good, however, the collector will receive cash in addition to merchandise. When fishing productivity is low, many collectors turn to other economic activities. Additionally, if fish collecting is undertaken to obtain specific items, such as radios, ovens, boat motors, etc., the collector may cease fishing once the debt is paid.

Those I define as 'commodity producers' are from the interior and travel to the fishing areas of his patron, and might be considered full-time collectors. Most often, a commodity producer travels without his family and can be called upon by the patron with little or no notice. Patrons commonly recruit commodity producers for their knowledge of the waterways

---

70 Prang (2001).
71 These are analytic categories employed by Ayres (1992), p. 132: 'Whereas petty commodity producers are more independent from each other, the peasantry is characterised by strong communal bonds, particularly in relation to land.'

and forest. In addition to fish collecting, many also guide the patrons' boats and hunt and fish for food for the patron and other collectors, in which case they are referred to as *ajudantes* (helpers). Like other producers from the interior, commodity producers may be involved in barter (*troca*) negotiations, but more often receive cash and credit. According to some patrons, barter is the conventional arrangement during the *safra* (harvest, dry season), but at the end of the season they pay their clients in cash so they can ride out the *entresafra* (rainy season).

Other collectors live in town — Barcelos or Santa Isabel. It is this group of collectors that exemplifies the blurring of the distinction between town and country.[72] Urban-based collectors either accompany the patron to the fishing areas on a regular basis or set up camp in one or another *paragem* to fish for some period, generally one to two months. *Ajudantes* are not infrequently urban-based as well. These collectors can be distinguished from those from the interior by their more intense interest in cash remuneration. Although many may be considered full-time collectors, most have wide experience, shifting productive activities (wage labour, food fishing and so on) frequently. Most are young and unmarried, are often related to the patron, or friends of close family members of the patron. One sub-group of the urban-based collectors is the food fishermen, who collect ornamental fish during the first months of the season (August–September) but fish for the local food market when the water level falls.

Aviamento: Fighting over Crumbs in a Peripheral Economy or Indentured Servitude?

The relations of production in the ornamental fishery are transformations of those of the rubber era. The ornamental fish trade has much in common with *aviamento*; it is another manifestation of merchant capitalism. Local-level production is unquestionably disciplined by the international demand for aquarium fish, and the relations of production of the hobbyist do not resemble those of the collector: the former capitalist, and the latter, kin-based. If we bear in mind, however, that all participants in Amazonian extractive economies 'are under the same pressures to combine income-earning strategies ... in order to survive in a marginal economy',[73] the social relations of production in the ornamental fishery of the Rio Negro can be better understood.

72   Nugent (1993), p. 124.
73   Whitesell (1993), p. 130.

The application of *aviamento* to the ornamental fishery implies the presence of debt bondage. Debt bondage entails an advance payment, in some form or another, together with the prohibition on working for other employers so long as the debt remains.[74] In contemporary Amazonia, however, *aviamento* is 'less binding, as the debt no longer defines exclusive relationships'.[75] Further, there is no prohibition on working for others in the ornamental fishery. Patrons allow their clients to partake in other economic activities so long as the outstanding debt is paid, and many debts are never repaid. Although free wage labour does not exist in the fishery, there are more structural categories of both patron and client than during the rubber boom, and cash has become as common as barter.

During the rubber era the patron's goal was more to avoid the loss of labour, rather than to increase production; client debt was the means to achieve this. In the ornamental fishery of the Rio Negro, however, labour is not an issue and is readily available, given the lack of economic opportunities in the region. With a surplus of labour, patrons can be selective, and are. If collectors cannot produce, or they jeopardise the patron, or are irresponsible in their habits, they are released. Further, clients can be selective, switching patrons as often as they switch extractive activities. Just as Ayres (1992) found in Tefé, producers in the Rio Negro now have 'more freedom to choose patrons, and there are more patrons to choose from'.[76]

The patrons of the ornamental fishery do advance goods to their clients, but at the request of the clients.[77] Monies still owed the producer are frequently paid in cash so that the producer may make purchases from other passers-by, or kept against some future delivery of merchandise. The so-called 'traditional' debt situation arises when clients request more valuable items. The clients are advanced the goods, translated by the patron into thousands of fish to be delivered. The riverine peasants of the Rio Negro, as well as some Amerindians,[78] have strong desires for consumer goods. Riverine societies are regularly exposed to the dream worlds of television, as well as the consumption patterns of the national society. I have

---

74   Brass (1986), pp. :51–52.
75   Ayres (1992), p. 122.
76   *Ibid.*
77   The average markup on advanced goods is about 40 per cent. According to most patrons, this markup reflects the risk of bad debts, transport and time spent searching for the items requested, especially consumer durables such as stoves, etc. Most patrons treat the delivery of merchandise as a form of courtesy to their clients; claiming it is on the fish delivered that they earn their living.
78   Hughes-Jones (1992).

witnessed collectors going into debt at the beginning of the fishing season, requesting high-priced items (such as hi-fi stereos) before production begins. Credit purchases and debt are not confined to the ornamental fishery; a visit to any merchant in Barcelos will confirm this. High rates of interest on transactions in the extractive economies of Amazonia are found in all of Brazil. For example, if one buys a freezer on credit (*parcelado*) at an appliance store in Manaus, the effective price of the item over a twelve-month period may be double the original price, or more.

I argue that producer relations with patrons are more collaborative and legitimate than exploitative, even though producers invariably criticise various fishery participants. Where peasant societies are 'fighting over crumbs', so to speak, in an extreme peripheral economy, jealousies and intrigues abound. I have heard many complaints about the patrons of the fishery, but when pressed for details, when asked whether a particular patron was good or bad, producers consistently described him as 'not bad'. The real issue, for clients as well as patrons, is that external processes shape the socioeconomic reality along the Rio Negro. The nature of the relations of production in the ornamental fishery is 'as much a reflection of the specific kinds of linkage created between local producers and external markets as it is an intrinsic feature of a reified "Amazonia"'.[79]

---

79   Nugent (1993), p. 207.

CHAPTER 4

Peasants on the Floodplain:
Some Elements of the 'Agrarian Question' in Riverine Amazonia[*]

Mark Harris

Prologue

In recent years the Amazon floodplain has become the object of scholarly scrutiny and developmentalist concern.[1] Although it accounts for about two per cent of the land area of the Amazon, the historical, economic and ecological significance of the floodplain is much greater than this small proportion indicates. And it is not difficult to understand why. The rivers have for the past 12,000 years of recorded occupation been the means of movement, communication, trade and sustenance, as well as a source for the symbolic life of the imagination.[2] Living near rivers has been an integral part of human settlement of the region from pre-conquest to colonial to post-colonial and contemporary societies.[3] How does

[*]   The chapter is based on fieldwork in 1992–94, funded by a doctoral award by the Economic and Social Research Council, and in 2001, with money from the British Academy, who also awarded me a postdoctoral fellowship. I am grateful to these institutions. I also thank Richard Pace for inviting me to participate on a panel at the 1996 AAA meetings in San Francisco, where a draft of this chapter was presented; James Carrier for an e-mailed comment on the survival of peasantries; and Maia Green for providing suggestions and stylistic improvements all those years ago.

1   See Goulding et al (1996). and Padoch et al. (1999). One of the first studies to focus on the floodplain was Sternberg's unpublished thesis (1956), based on research in the 1950s in a village a few miles downstream of Manaus. Sternberg's prime interest was in the physical geography and how erosion and sedimentation takes place over time and how this affects land use, but he does include data on cattle raising and social organisation. One of the significant themes in his work (see also 1975) is the constant flux of the floodplain environment, the rising and falling of river and the negotiation of economic activities surrounding these changes. More specifically, Michael Chibnik (1994) has analysed the political ecology of farming on the Peruvian floodplain. His main concern was with the everyday strategies involved in securing a living, labour organisation, food and income sources and unionisation.

2   Roosevelt (1999).

3   Porro (1996).

this 'continuity' sit with the area's turbulent history? I have in mind a Braudelian type of longue durée which frames the shorter term ruptures. The point is to avoid a presentist orientation when looking to the past.

The possibility of a kind of Braudelian approach is complicated by the violent break occasioned by the European conquest. The history of Brazil starts in 1500, but as an anthropologist of indigenous peoples the history is largely unknowable because little evidence of pre-historical soicieities survived. Some work, however, is beginning to bridge the gap and trace the histories of indigenous peoples from pre- to post-conquest by looking at linguistic features, archaeological remains and travellers' and missionary accounts.[4] With respect to the non-indigenous peoples of the Amazon it would seem that their history did start with the creation of a new category of mixed bloods.[5] It is precisely this formulation that needs to be questioned, not because it is wrong but because it closes down many interesting matters crucial for understanding the reconstituted peasantries of the Amazon, particularly those which grew up as a result of colonial policies.[6]

One major problem is that the '*caboclo*isation thesis' fails to give sufficient importance to the encounter between Portuguese colonists (poor and rich) and the Indians who were rounded up in the mission stations and subsequently the export producing villages of the eighteenth century.[7] These encounters were promoted by the Portuguese crown through a series of laws, which gave financial benefits to mixed marriage couples. Essentially it was the children of these unions that formed the new category peopling the lower and middle Amazon. How did they negotiate the influences of their parents? What did their parents know and what did they pass on? Was this older knowledge from renaissance Iberia and Aboriginal Amazonia irrelevant to surviving in this context? Did new kinds of knowledge need to be invented, as Mintz (1989) says was the case with the slaves transferred from their homeland to the Caribbean plantations? Were some practices and ideas privileged over others, such as aboriginal ecological knowledge and forms of classification?[8] What

4   See Porro (1996); Roosevelt (1994); Balée (2000); and Whitehead 1999.
5   See Parker (1985) for this view of the emergence of the *caboclo* — the '*caboclo*isation thesis'.
6   As Parker (1985) and others have so well demonstrated.
7   See Maclachlan (1973).
8   For example, Balée (2000) argues that ethnobotanical knowledge is resistant to change since it is grounded in survival and everyday life and would therefore have had a high degree of continuity from pre to post conquest. I see no reason why there may not be other areas of social and economic life which may also be similarly resilient, possibly because they are so divorced from daily work, such as death rituals (see, for example, Brown, 1981, on the cult of the saints).

ideological constraints were there on the kinds of knowledge that could be passed on? What was the role of the Church here and the elites who engaged slave and free labour?

A small part of this field is investigated here (socioeconomic transformations on the floodplain). What I am suggesting is that mixed blood peoples of Amazonia may have formed a new category,[9] but that the actual human beings were not simply created out of thin air. They merged several histories, which had come from distant places and times; the structures and knowledges came from somewhere. This longer time depth to, and larger framework for, contemporary Amazonian social life has been proposed by other authors, but rarely is it located in political contexts: the werewolf stories come from Europe;[10] the dolphin is distinctly indigenous in origin; some farming techniques resemble contemporary indigenous ones and so on.[11] My concern here is to understand the myriad of forces, the moments of fusion and fission, which have shaped the different presents in the lower and middle Amazon. It is proposed that it is only by having a sense of what Portuguese colonists brought to the region and how their discourses were transformed by local influences can we fully appreciate the complicated ethnographic and historical realities.[12] All meetings and combinations take place under the sign of one or more fields of power, so mere homogenisation is out of the question. What spaces do these fields leave for people to enact, repudiate or negotiate relations of power in different contexts and circumstances?

Caboclos in the conventional portrayals are beyond otherness, but not in the sense of being an underclass or simply milling around in the state of permanent subalternism. They are beyond otherness because they are Amazonians made over in the image of Europe in a way which reflects badly on the influence of civilisation.[13]

This 'beyond otherness' thesis is a powerful, and neat, way of putting an anthropological problem. What frameworks do we need to recognise peasants, *caboclos*? Amazonian anthropology has offered cultural ecological and structuralist account, a robust alternative to which this chapter is inspired by the work of Wolf and Mintz, and later Roseberry, who provided a more dynamic account.

9   See Saloman and Shwartz (eds.) (1999).
10   See Maués in this volume.
11   See, for example, Moran (1974).
12   Cleary (1993; 1999).
13   Nugent (1993), p. 45.

Characteristic of each of these projects [Wolf's and Mintz's] was an attempt to understand the constitution of particular anthropological subjects at the confluence of global, regional and local currents of state making, empire building, market expansion and contraction, migration and so on. In his study of peasant rebellion, Wolf suggested that 'the decisive factor in making a peasant rebellion possible lies in the relation of the peasantry to the field of power which surrounds it.'[14]

This 'field of power' creates a web of connections between various times, places and people. My intention here is to examine one place in the rhythm of these connections. Far from being a resting place, it is but one continuing expression of the flow of forces which have come to be felt in the region. This portrait is community based, since it focuses on one floodplain area. This ethnographic indulgence, I hope, is justified in my attempt to concentrate on larger and wider historical and contemporary characteristics as they occur in one location.

What is more, the focus here is on the agrarian question as a way of thinking about the specificity of the historical peasantries who live in riverine areas. Mostly, the floodplain has been discussed in terms of its resources and their management, possibilities for conservation and community control.[15] By casting the floodplain in terms of a longer history of land and peasant economy and identity my aim is to throw into sharp relief the social, rather than natural, aspects of Amazonia.

Agrarian Change on the Lower Middle Amazon Floodplain

In essence, the agrarian question refers to the 'development' of rural and agricultural non-capitalist formations (i.e. peasantries) into fully capitalised ones.[16] This transformation has been considered to be dependent historically on the emergence of a generalised commodity production and exchange following the differentiation of the peasantry into large-scale farmers owning the means of production and a depeasantised proletariat. With the possible exception of Argentina, the European expression of this transition has not neatly prevailed in any Latin American country.

---

14   Roseberry (1995), p. 56.
15   See, for example, Hiraoka (1992); McGrath et al. (1993a and b); Maybury-Lewis (1996); and Furtado et al. (1993).
16   For Latin American versions of the agrarian question see Duncan and Rutledge (1977); Goodman and Redclift (1981); and for a recent revisit see Goodman and Watts (1997).

With respect to Brazil, Forman has written that the 'agrarian problem [there] reflects the unequal patterns of land distribution and the favoured position of *latifundia* in the competition for land and labour among different sectors of the rural economy'.[17] Land conflicts in the Amazon, especially those of the last 30 years of the National Integration Programme mirror those elsewhere in Brazil. However, a separate casting is necessary for the agrarian question on the floodplain, which does not parallel its counterpart on the *terra firme*.[18] The floodplain issue is about the very control and access to lakes, rivers, streams, rather than their uneven distribution in the first place. Neither does the 'water/land issue' involve any competition for labour, since plantation agriculture never occurred on a significant scale and nor are labour markets significantly developed in the Amazon. Like the wider agrarian crisis however, it is an economic problem concerning ownership and supply of basic foodstuffs and other commodities and it is a social and political problem, expressing a conflict between people with different interests.[19] And what is of interest here are the dynamics between richer and poorer peasants as they adapt to new demands for products and the allocation of their labour. What is the role of merchant capital, which dominates economic production in riverine areas, in the transition from partly capitalised to fully capitalised relations?

A recent interpretation of some of these matters has been formulated by David McGrath and his colleagues. They have analysed conflicts in the access to the productive lake fisheries in the Lower Amazon.[20] McGrath and his team describe a 'jute based system of resource management', which was organised around the seasonal and diverse exploitation of floodplain areas: growing jute, raising cattle, fishing and hunting. This economic complex developed in the mid-twentieth century and depended on the local appropriation of land and water, where residential proximity offered usufruct rights and communal 'ownership'. Outsiders had no right, in this view, to use the waters and lands of another community. This understanding is at odds with the legal ownership of water, and indeed the land of the floodplain, which belong to the nation-state and therefore should entail public access and use.

---

17 Forman (1975), p. 39.
18 For example Schmink and Wood (1992); and on the *Movimento dos Sem Terra* (landless peoples movement) see Stedile (2002).
19 Forman (1975), p. 38.
20 McGrath et al. (1993a, 1993b).

The pattern outlined by McGrath, however, has collapsed since the 1980s for two reasons: the decline in the sale of jute and the intensification of the fishing industry. These factors have contributed to a change in economic orientation of not just peasants but also town dwellers, ready to cash in on a lucrative market. This has resulted in outsiders 'invading' the so-called public waterways with their large boats capable of holding scores of tonnes of fish. Peasant producers have complained that their very livelihoods are at stake, they neither have fish to eat nor sell, and that these outsiders have no right to enter in their communal spaces. The result is a conflict based on entirely different perceptions of responsibility and ownership, though still one between people with differing scales of commercial interests; one which is part of the nation-state's legal code and one which is oral and 'traditional'. Given the new conditions riverine dwellers find themselves in, the authors suggest that people are looking for new ways of managing their environment. Blocking off the lake and community organised development is one such solution. Ecologically this raises its own problems since some species of fish migrate long distances when they spawn and therefore cannot be contained.

McGrath and his colleagues end by arguing for a two-way model for the future of the region, which bears some similarity to a classic European depiction of the differentiation of the peasantry. On one hand, peasants could be successful and defend their communal resources, depending on a diverse and seasonal economic complex for their livelihoods. The second possibility is where resources of the floodplain are depleted to such an extent that people can no longer support themselves. Such areas get taken over by large-scale commercial fishing boats and the cattle owners who make use of the extensive pasture areas for grazing, forcing others into the slums in large Amazonian cities. Explicit in McGrath et al.'s account then is the casting of the problem in terms of a successful management strategy, and those outcomes are dependent on finding the 'right' sets of resource practices.

With the floodplain issue, we are dealing with a specifically Amazonian problem that highlights the isolation of the Amazon from national Brazilian agrarian development. Moreover, it presents a rather different picture of 'land' ownership than that of other peasant populations in the Amazon, such as those recent migrants living on the 'frontier' of the Amazon. Perhaps most importantly, it signals the emergence of a revised account of Brazilian Amazonia, traditionally represented as a vast and hostile resource domain, peopled by adaptable mixed bloods and indigenous 'exotics'. In the past, the water issue may have been portrayed as a conflict over scarce protein resources, which happened to be between a peasant and a merchant-elite class. Now, such an explanation is totally unsatisfactory.

The specificity of the floodplain is set up in overlapping layers: the longue durée of environmental history, the post-conquest peasant societies that came to settle in and around riverine colonial towns and more recently these peasants' continued occupation of the floodplain-based locally-managed economic strategies. The aim in the rest of this chapter is to continue to provide empirical evidence that complicates neat models of agrarian development and peasant differentiation, and, at the same time, to connect with other peasant societies, and the questions raised from their study, in other parts of Latin America.

An Economic and Social History of a Floodplain Area

The area which is the focus of the empirical material of this chapter lies near the mouth of the Trombetas river, about five hours journey upstream from the town of Óbidos, state of Pará. It is known locally as '*a costa do Parú*', a stretch of alluvial land alongside the Amazon river. Behind the levee lies a vast network of waterways, ponds and lakes. Parú is a locally recognised as geographically bounded area, since the Trombetas and Cachoerri rivers separate it from other areas. At the lowest point of the river in the dry season the landscape is land and water, but in the wet season, the whole area is inundated, the floors of the houses and the trees' branches just above water level. The annual changes in the height of the river produce an inescapable rhythm of existence for the people who live there. They have to gauge their economic and social strategies in terms of these changes, when to plant or reap, where to fish, what to fish, when to move the cattle and so forth. Other changes result as well. The massive increase in water both deposits the soils from the weathered Andes and erodes tracts of land. What was land one year may not appear the next. This creates a certain amount of speculation and anxiety on behalf of people who live in Parú. On the other hand, new land can appear, which means it can be used for building houses, planting or raising cattle.

Seasonality, in the form of the dynamically changing river height, and its associated social and natural effects, is the most basic condition of life on the floodplain. The ambiguity between what is water and what is land is perhaps one factor to have contributed to the invisibility of the floodplain in state-sponsored programmes for development (though there have been some attempts to increase production of cocoa and rice, for example).

Parú is a stretch of land which continues for about 32 kilometres along the Amazon river. No land is unused or not lived upon. This means that unlike the *terra firme* areas, people neither practise shifting cultivation (they do slash and burn agriculture, but in the same place year after year), nor do they decide to pack up and build a house on some piece of land elsewhere (unless it is some newly appeared land). Roughly 1,000 people lived in Parú in the early 1990s in a long line of houses following the riverbank (and the number was about the same in 2001). In order to distinguish themselves from people who live elsewhere they call themselves Parúaros, expressing a geographical, and not ethnic, identity. The houses are generally clustered together in sibling sets focused on a parental house. There are dense links between clusters through repeated interlinking marriage, in some cases a sibling set marrying another one from a neighbouring area, i.e. two to five brothers and sisters marrying the same number from elsewhere. This creates repeated endogamous links between people in Parú. There are also a number of cousin marriages, from first to fourth grades, with no distinction between parallel and cross cousins, as with typical Eskimo terminology.

By marrying geographically and genealogically close to home, people maintain their claims to land and resources on the basis of continuous use and residence. This prevents competing claims by outsiders and is further reinforced by a number of other factors, among which the most important are residential preferences. There is an explicit desire to continue living with parents, siblings and children. Obviously, marriage decisions make it impossible in some situations, but the construction of closely knit clusters means that the preference can often be realised, particularly if fellow siblings marry into the cluster as well. There does not seem to be strong evidence for either uxorilocal or virilocal residence. However, the statistics are confounded by the fact that people over the life cycle are constantly moving from one parental cluster to another and then to establishing their own. Very briefly then, these are the dynamics of social organisation. The point of outlining them here is to underline their effect, primarily to maintain, for the community as whole, continuity of residence, use of and access to resources. Despite their constant internal movements, so long as they keep it within themselves, outsiders cannot get in and destroy the very fabric of their lives. This continued residence is of supreme importance given the context of their lives. And, as such, kinship is one of the keys to understanding floodplain life.

Having provided a brief overview of aspects of contemporary social organisation in Parú, as far as could be ascertained — and like many

Amazonian settlements — there is no origin story to Parú: no first family to settle, no story to commemorate its inception (apart from the ones to mark the building of the two chapels in 1954 and 1977). Nor is there a tracing of a relationship to a boss, who is said to have brought people to the area, as is common in the upper Amazon, especially in Peru.[21] There are, however, a number of large families that are said to have been living in Parú for a long time.

Many people do state that their great-grandparents and grandparents were born and lived in Parú. In support of these claims, they recall the stories their grandparents told them of former lives, economic and social. In particular, people cite the existence of farms with small numbers of slaves. They say that the slaves used to prepare cocoa for export and chop down trees for firewood to sell to passing steamboats. When slavery was abolished in 1888 the slaves apparently just left and, like the Indians who were the first inhabitants,[22] it is not known where they went. The *cabanagem* rebellion of the late 1830s is another historic event which is recalled frequently. Stories have been passed down about the existence of buried treasure in Parú, as well as the cruel maltreatment of slaves and peasants which led to the attempted revolution.

A number of processes of migration and settlement gave rise to the current situation. Firstly, there were two missions very near Parú: Pauxis (nowadays Óbidos) and Muruapig (Oriximiná). Óbidos then became a directorate village in 1757. It seems likely that people would have spilled out from the town from about this time; possibly there were others who wanted to live near a town for trading purposes and had come down river having gone up river escaping the Portuguese slave raiding parties of the early eighteenth century. At the very least we know that the floodplain has provided commodities since the mid-eighteenth century,[23] and the legacy of the directorate was to have connected virtually the whole of the riverine system of the Amazon in trading networks of debt.[24] Second, waves of Portuguese and Italian migration in the nineteenth and twentieth centuries could have given rise to residence in Parú, as they did elsewhere in the region. Indeed some people claim to have grandparents born in Italy.

---

21 Fernando Santos Granero (personal communication).
22 People say the Amerindians were the original dwellers on Parú, a fact they are constantly reminded of when they find pieces of pottery.
23 See Maclachlan (1973); Alden (1976); Ross (1978).
24 See McGrath in this volume and Leonardi (1999) for an example in the lower Rio Negro.

Finally, internal migrations prior to the twentieth century seem likely to have contributed to the expansion of the settlement, when land was available. In fact some people claim their grandparents told them their parents or grandparents came from down or upstream.

Some historical depth is indicated by the first land registration programme (for tax purposes), which began in the last decade of the nineteenth century when there were about 35 people who recorded themselves as owners of land in Parú, but not necessarily occupiers.[25] This number is further supported by the first Brazilian census by the national statistical office, IBGE. In 1920, about 50 heads of houses were resident in Parú.[26] In 1993 there were 191 houses.[27] These data demonstrate a large increase in population in the early to mid-twentieth century. This can be verified with life histories and genealogies. Without exception, all residents claim to have a kinship link to Parú, affinal or consanguineal.

At the beginning of the twentieth century, economic activities were highly diverse and complex. The bulk of trade was done with the *regatões*, since the journey to town would have had to be done in a canoe, involving two days' journey there and back. It is worth pointing out that the older *Paríaros* say that money has only been used in the last 30 or so years as a means of exchange. Before then, they claim, money never came into their hands, with one product being exchanged for another. These same people associate the introduction of money with current problems of high prices, inflation and poverty.

In the nineteenth century the largest export crop was cocoa, and it is likely that most of the high ground in Parú was covered in cocoa trees. These cocoa trees have now mostly gone, having either been drowned in a series of high floods or been cut down to plant jute. There were also a few rubber stands, with one man remembering exactly how the rubber was prepared for sale to the passing trading boats. Firewood was another crucial resource, produced for the steam boats going up and down the river until diesel boats were introduced after the Second World War. This wood was exchanged for goods that were not locally produced. There were about four firewood deposits in Parú and most deforestation on the floodplain was probably caused by demand for firewood (commencing mid-century). Cayman skins, salted Pirarucu, turtles, their eggs, kapok cotton, feathers and many other preciosities were also important products which made up the repertoire of floodplain commodities.

25 See Muniz (1907) for a full list in the state of Pará.
26 IBGE (1922).
27 SUCAM (1993), personal communication.

Cattle have been raised on the floodplain areas of Óbidos since the eighteenth century.[28] Inglês de Souza in his novel *O cacualista*, written in the 1850s, describes a floodplain area opposite Parú, where cattle roamed freely under the cocoa trees. Cattle have historically been a relatively safe and lucrative form of investment: their meat can always be sold for consumption in urban centres. In Parú cattle meat was salted for export to large towns in wooden boxes and then sold to the *regatões*. Nowadays, cattle have become the single most important sign of wealth. Money not spent on necessities and house building or maintenance is used to buy cattle. 'Cattle are', according to a *parúaro*, 'like a peasant's bank.'

From the 1930s there was a boom in the production of jute on the floodplain. In Parú, this meant that most, if not all, people were involved in the clearing of ground, planting, reaping and bundling jute for sale. As noted, McGrath et al. (1993) claim that the economic pattern surrounding jute growing gave rise to system of traditional resource management on floodplain. Research in Parú has provided little evidence of this being 'traditional'. The point they also make is that the system was relatively stable, in that there was little conflict in demands on time and energy between different activities. It should be added that jute was also a relatively lucrative crop: many people in Parú told me that they had built their fine houses, bought fishing nets and diesel powered boats with jute money. Jute demand fell following cheaper imports from South Asia into Brazil and the introduction of plastics from the 1970s.

This decline coincided with the growth of the fishing industry (improved technology, building of ice and fish exporting factories) and so *parúaros* turned to the sale of fish as their primary source of revenue. This was not a traumatic change, since they had always fished for subsistence purposes. Nowadays, this has led to another increase in the income of the area. An eight tonne capacity boat owner in Parú could in 1993 earn up to ten times the minimum salary from the total of a good month's sale of fish (which he would then have to share amongst his crew). With what *parúaros* see as dwindling stocks, they say that 'fish should be for eating not for selling'. A few people in Parú have done well out of selling fish and now own diesel powered boats, with a number of nets and canoes (for more on economic differences see below). Thus, they control significantly more resources than most people and so they attract young men — typically their younger siblings or cousins, or nephews — to work on their boats. In

28   Reis (1979).

sum, small-scale commercial fishing is dependent on accessing local resources, unlike that of larger-scale exploitation which has the advantage of being able to access a number of areas. It is clear then that the mobility of large-scale commercial fishing prevents them from taking seriously diminishing stocks: they go where there are fish, whereas localised riverine dwellers such as *paruaros* have no choice but to rely on proximate resources.

This is a sketchy summary of the economic history as it has been recounted to me by *paruaros*. It is interesting to note the flexibility of cycles of exploitation, from one product to another (almost to the point of extinction of each commodity, from turtles to firewood). The ease with which people have moved from one activity to another is remarkable. Despite the historic upheavals in the region they have been able to reproduce themselves without compromising their position (for example, by migrating, converting in significant numbers to Protestantism,[29] relying more on bosses for credit, and so on). Instead, it appears that at each stage the continuity of floodplain life has been re-affirmed. It shows, therefore, that despite being ostensibly marginal to the economic and political system, they have been able to adapt to its demands and yet remain relatively 'autonomous' as a community on the floodplain. In other words, there is a thought-provoking contradiction. On the one hand, the communal economy in Parú has been integrated into, and constituted by, larger influences since the eighteenth century. On the other hand, *Paruaros* give the impression of a separation between the communal and the regional, and that they are more or less in control of this situation. Crucially, then, the peasant economy generated on the floodplain and its constitution by external forces, is able to reproduce itself somewhat outside the dominant commodity economy.

This is a fundamental point in understanding the socio-economic transformations of the region. The impression one has from reading about the economic history is of stagnation after the rubber boom. This came about because there were few high-earning exports. From a local perspective, however, the picture is somewhat different: that the twentieth century has been a time of growth and strengthening of the peasant floodplain economy. It is also a picture (and reality) that has remained largely outside the military government's attempts to 'develop' the region.

From the perspective of locals, Parú is a desirable place to live and work. It has a good fisheries area and extensive pasture for cattle in the dry season, and good land for crops. These factors are linked to the preference

---

29   Though there have been individual conversions, which has meant moving out of the community to avoid conflict with Catholic neighbours.

to live near and work with kinsfolk. This is reinforced by a dislike of city ways, the violence it breeds, the need for money and the selling of labour to earn that money. It is perhaps this last factor that *parúaros* are most clear about, the intention to remain one's own boss. Before looking at this concept of labour, I shall turn to the dynamic of the economic differences between kinsfolk.

Differentiation and the Kinship Idiom

There is a degree of economic inequality amongst the kinsfolk who live in Parú, and indeed these differences are both embedded in and masked by the fact that most people are related. Kinship networks can act as a way of redistributing resources, but they can also distant that distribution. The age hierarchy can be exploited to the disadvantage of the younger people who have little or no right to challenge their elders. Kinship, in one of its many forms, acts as an idiom to organise labour. And in any case the resources which are accumulated by parents are ultimately distributed to their children.

Parúaros engage in a wide variety of economic activities, which in turn engage them in different kinds of relations with each other, including labour exchange, wage labour and family organised work groups. Here the concept of petty commodity production adds analytical precision.[30] The term refers to economic activities in which there is a low capital investment and little dependence on hired labour. Petty commodity production is economic activity oriented to generate income from market sales. It brings clarity to the idea of the peasant economy because it reveals more precisely the economic relations involved. It shows that peasants can be both capitalists (own the means of production, land, capital and technology) and workers (put their labour to work for themselves). Bernstein says: 'as capitalists, they employ — and therefore exploit —themselves'.[31] It would appear that richer peasants are better able to employ their poorer kinsfolk, and this sustains economics difference. But it may be more complicated than this, given that there has been a large degree of continuity in the families that have lived in Parú. The key economic difference between poorer and richer kinsfolk in Parú concerns their ability to move from one activity to another.

It is interesting to put this claim alongside wider economic cycles. With regard to the general economic role of peasants in Amazonia Nugent has written, 'the peasant system [in Amazonia] is not wholly contingent, thus its specificity includes conditions for social reproduction which are main-

30   Friedman (1980), Nugent (1993).
31   Bernstein (1990), p. 73.

tainable even in the absence of a rationale by periodic "integration"'.[32] In times when peasants can get a good return for their products (such as in the time of jute) their economy will expand, and the diversity of economic activities may diminish as they converge on producing one crop. But when the market collapses the economy contracts and they return to a more diverse exploitation of economic options.

This expansion and contraction phenomenon must be seen more specifically, which in turn reveals how internal differentiation occurs. To give an example: Antonio, who is married to Nazaré, is one of seven children, five of whom stayed on the parcel of land of their parents, which was divided equally between the remaining siblings on their father's death. In the 1950s and 1960s Antonio said that he and Nazaré worked very hard planting jute, which is intensive work in the run up to the flood season (March to May). When he was not planting jute he was fishing (in the low water period of September to December) and they also grew a few subsistence crops. Over time the fishing, and to a lesser extent jute, proved to be profitable. They were able to buy a small motorised boat which then allowed them to transport and store more fish. The price for jute declined and they devoted all their efforts to commercial fishing, any profits being used to buy cattle. Antonio and Nazaré have 13 children, all of whom have stayed living near their parents, partly because they have a relatively secure economic base, but without their children's diverse contributions the couple would not be able to maintain the range of economic activities, which are dominated by petty commodity production, rather than wage work or peasant farming.

Antonio's brothers were not able to transform their productive forms and technology so easily from a jute-based to a fishing-dominated economy. They had not built up the same level of resources as Antonio and Nazaré, nor had they access to the same pool of labour. Nowadays, the brothers and their families have to rely on a greater diversity of strategies and decrease their consumption. The economic transformations over the 30 or so years have been accommodated better by some and not so well by others. Antonio and Nazaré are so-called middle peasants, and are in a good position to adapt. The danger is that a concentration on a few activities in a petty commodity repertoire might mean the loss of some skills which are vital to surviving at times of contraction. This would make a return to some kind of peasant baseline extremely difficult and force outward migration.

32 Nugent (1993), p. 124.

In communal terms, Antonio and Nazaré are accused of 'only selling fish'. This accusation comes from a special understanding of labour as a process which creates a product. Fishing, in this view, is an extractive activity, which does not involve creating something new, as will be seen below. Fishing is associated traditionally with the subsistence rather than the commodity economy. More pertinently, Antonio and Nazaré do not engage in the physical effort of work, but get their children and nephews to catch the fish. All they do, it is claimed, is sell the fish once it is stored on ice and ready for sale. One of the consequences of this differentiation is conflict between local folk. It should be noted that the differentiation does not lead to a fully capitalised economy, as is predicted in some models; petty commodity production in fishing would decline with lower market demand. It is an open question as to whether the prominence of peasantries in Amazonia is functional for the kind of capitalist accumulation there, namely merchant capital in conjunction with a patron–clientilistic state,[33] or whether it is precisely because capitalism has not been able to develop enough, and that peasants are a residue of both precapitalist collapse and capitalist failure.[34]

Conflict over Resources

There are a number of characteristic conflicts on the floodplain. The nature of these conflicts concerns rights over and access to resources. There are two principal types of strife in Parú: use of waterways and lakes for fishing and 'fence politics'. The latter is an older problem and is relatively minor compared to the possibility of dramatically reduced stocks of fish.

'Fence politics' refers to the problems of grazing animals in cultivable areas. As *parúaros* say, cattle, pigs, goats, horses and buffalo 'do not have a law', they wander around eating grass and plants or digging up earth for roots and such anywhere and everywhere. This suits the floodplain extremely well, because unlike the *terra firme*, in the dry season there are vast areas of land which are not used for agriculture.

The understanding in Parú is that anybody who grows crops should fence off the areas being cultivated, thus preventing animals from getting in. It is then the responsibility of the farmer to build the fence, rather the owner of crops. This is because Parú is locally assigned as a *terra de criação* (and not *terra de plantação*), that is principally an animal raising area. In reality many of the people who have gardens also have a few or more head of

33   As, say, Taussig (1982) has argued for the Colombia's Cauca valley.
34   Mintz (1989); Nugent (1993).

cattle and so the conflict is not only between people with completely different interests, but between competing economic activities.

Disputes arise when cattle break down fences and eat crops belonging to other people. Neighbours normally manage to sort things between themselves. But conflict arises when cattle from an area some distance away continually break into the same garden. In such cases, the owner of the garden should complain to the animal owner. If by the fourth time the cattle are still disrespecting the fence, the garden owner has the right to slaughter the invading animal/s and to take half of the carcass. The fact that animals can roam freely on the land neatly expresses the traditional pattern of land use in Amazonia, based on collective access and rights. Outsiders have no basis for land claims, since they do not live there and therefore cannot use the land.

The second type of dispute is much more recent. In Parú I was told by many people that in the past fishing was a very 'easy activity', all you needed to do was choose which type of fish you wanted and go and get it. Nowadays, however, people complain of the difficulty in getting certain types of fish and the diminished range of choice. This has meant people have to eat previously undesired species of cat fish, which are also taboo for the ill or for women in menses or who are pregnant. *Parúaros* point to two different causes of the decline in fish stocks. The first is the growth in fishing within the community itself. Due to the fall in the price in jute, people turned to the next best option, which was selling fish. People started using techniques which increased the size of the catch, and so sold more fish and made more money. The second is the 'invasion' (*invasão*) of large-scale fishing boats into the waterways of Parú. *Invasão* is the word people use, meaning that people come in without permission to fish using highly predatory techniques. It is recognised that outsiders from other communities have always fished on Parú, but not with such predatory methods.

In Parú a number of incidents have occurred over the past five years which indicate the extent of the conflict being generated by the intrusion of large-scale fishing in the area. The first was the commandeering of an ice boat from Santarém. This involved the men and women from upper Parú climbing onto the boat at night and tearing up the nets with knives. The boat owner reported the damage to the police and the people who were alleged to have done it were ordered to pay costs. The second is internal to Parú. Despite the degree of equality and homogeneity, there was a dispute between the owner of an eight tonne capacity boat who lives in middle Parú and a number of people who live on upper Parú (where the previous incident took place). The latter say that the boat owner has no right to fish in the areas near their houses. They point to diminishing fish stocks and the need to preserve them for their basic survival. The fisher-people's union (*colonia dos pescadores*) has become involved in this dispute and there is currently a general agreement between the parties as to the need to respect each other's territory and not to use small mesh gill nets or catch undersize fish, or to eat or sell fish during their spawning season. In other words, the intensification of the fishing industry has led not only to conflicts of scale between large- and small-scale commercial interests, but also more divisively to local disputes over rights of access.

The point is that there is a highly divisive problem over rights to and ownership of resources and the political economy aggravates it. At the root of this conflict lie notions of resource ownership and responsibility. Proximity and residence are said to concede usufruct rights, but how near do you need to live? What are people's interests: money to buy food (and other things), or food for now and the future? And how can we understand the perception of resource ownership in Parú? What about the connections between labour and ownership? I shall now turn to two conditions which are at the heart of the continuity of floodplain life.

Ownership and Perception of Water and Land

As outlined by other authors in this book, land rights are the source of much conflict. Title deeds to land are granted by INCRA (on the *terra firme*) or ITERPA (for the floodplain titles are extremely costly and difficult to get).[35] Nevertheless, as far as *Parúaros* are concerned, plots of land with houses are considered individually owned and everybody recognises the borders of another's land, whether or not they are demarcated by fences or paths. In support of this claim they produce a certificate of purchase detailing the sale of land. In legal terms, however, this document is worthless, it only shows that the land was bought from so and so. However, as long as people are using the land on a constant basis, they can claim *posse da terra*.

---

35 Nevertheless, whenever there is a redrawing of land maps for tax purposes (*recadraste-mento rural das terras*, organised by INCRA) people flock to registry office because they think that they will get legitimate title to land at last. If someone wants to have '*domínio*' over a floodplain plot of land ITERPA (Instituto das Terras do Pará) is the place to go. There he has to make a claim, has to employ a lawyer, has to appear per-sonally himself there (or get another to be in person for him), employ a team to demarcate the land and so on. The process can take up to ten years to go through, and is obviously rather expensive, so it means only the rich get land ownership.

Posse da terra is an old Brazilian land rights custom, giving an occupant of
more than five years' standing a sort of squatter ownership. The occupant
can then sell the land at a price worked out through a combination of its
potential productivity (the current crop grown and what has been grown on
it previously, and the minimum salary). Although *posse da terra* has a legal
basis, no title deed is actually issued and, given the anomalous nature of the
floodplain, if the land were to disappear no compensation could ever be
claimed. In other words, *posse da terra* is not a form of private land ownership. It is rather a form of land tenure which started with the 'frontier' and
colonisation of the Brazilian hinterlands, but which also has a remarkable
continuity with Amerindian notions of land use. *Posse da terra*, then, is most
importantly part of the non-capitalist relations of production embedded in
a 'domestic economy',[36] where land per se has no value, only what is done
with it. Instead, property is created by living on it or applying labour to it,
and as such does not mask the real value of land and water in Parú as relations between people, rather than between people and things.[37]

   This non-capitalist nature of the relations of production is further reinforced by notions of usufruct rights to resources outside these personal
tenures. These areas are regarded as being communally owned. These
include the river that passes in front of the community, the lake behind it,
all the waterways in between and the beach areas of the lake in the dry season. Ideally, all people resident in Parú have equal and communal access to
the flora and fauna resources in these spaces. But as seen in the last sec-
tion those in the more immediate area argue that ultimately they are
responsible for its 'stewardship'. Such rights are conferred by residential
proximity, continued use and knowledge of the area.

   Communally owned areas then are not a form of 'group or corporate
property'. They do not 'belong' to *parúaros*, because they are neither passed
down from one generation to another, nor are rights to it exclusive —
there are no ancestral connections to a place. They are not exclusive for
two reasons. First, as we have seen, outsiders also gain access in differing
degrees and, second, in the local view these 'undomesticated' areas cannot
be strictly 'owned', individually or communally. Residential proximity gives
access to an area, but this does not equal ownership of the place itself.
Instead, the undomesticated territory of the lakes, rivers and hunting
grounds is the realm of the malevolent spirits who protect animals and fish

36   In Gudeman and Rivera's sense (1990).
37   See Bloch (1975).

from humans, and as such no one can own these areas. These 'un-domesticated realms' outside the community are not there to be dominated or conquered, rather 'used responsibly'.[38]

The knowledge of the environment, its processes and relations, about which we have heard so much recently, is a result of the constant movement in and experience of the environment. Thus, the floodplain landscape becomes a lived one, born of the interaction of people and places, which is reflected in the temporal dimension of kinship and social reproduction. Thus, land and water, their use and access, cannot be represented in the abstract or with an external reality acted upon by human agents but should more accurately be represented through lived human experience and interaction with them.

In Parú it is a surprise to recognise the vagueness of people's references to places in the vicinity. If I asked a man where he had been fishing or a woman where she had been visiting, the answers would go something like this: 'there up river' or 'there on the igarapé do curuaçu'. I was forever confused by such statements because they told me nothing I could relate to. I had no mental map of the area, and nor did I know where up stream was or who was there. But this is exactly the point — I was not part of the process of kinship and series of movements that would have informed me that so and so has a cousin up river or that curuaçu is a stream just behind so and so's house. In other words, the superficial obscurity of their representations was not due to some cultural idiosyncrasy, but due to the vast wealth of knowledge that lay behind what was being said, available only to insiders.

In sum, the notion of lived space is extended to include the whole of the environment in which *parúaros* daily interact. The way in which *parúaros* live in their surroundings arises within the history of specific types of activity among specific types of relationship, meaning that knowledge and practice cannot be 'de-environmentalised'.[39]

Obviously, there are limits to this practical knowledge. This is where the dominant market economy intrudes into the daily lives of floodplain dwellers, but what is described here is an outline of the representation peo-

---

38 See Slater (1994, pp. 74–8) on the notion of the dolphin as the 'owner of the waters'. This conception of the environment is complemented by the view that animals and fish have their own 'intelligence'. Fishermen say that fish often play games in order to outwit the pursuer. Game are aided by their 'spirit mothers' to avoid being hunted down. It is the skill and cunning of the hunter/fishermen to be able to come home with a catch. The sense then is of intelligent beings pitted against each other in a battle of wits.

39 As structuralists would have it, see Ingold's reading of Heidegger (1995).

ple on the Parú floodplain have of their surroundings, how they come to
own or use it and how they perceive their part in it. The reason for doing
so is to emphasise what is at stake when riverine dwellers block off their
lakes from outside intruders, to contextualise the response. In short, the
creation of the floodplain as a lived in space allows *parúaros* the conditions
of their own social reproduction.

Concepts and Allocation of Work

Physical labour has been a constant theme running through this chapter. It
has been shown that work creates not only value but also social relations
in the domestic economy. Another underlying theme has been the distinction *parúaros* make between living in the town and on the floodplain. I shall
now draw together these two issues by looking at the meaning of work.

Parúaros prefer to produce items for sale independently since this is most
compatible with their preference for living and working with kin and for
remaining in control over their own deployment of labour. Given that
parúaros depend on the market for obtaining certain necessary goods, it is not
the extent of the dependence or integration that is in question. Instead, what
is at issue is the nature of the integration of people in Parú into the world
outside their community and their rejection and embracing of this fact.

Labour costs of people in Parú are reproduced outside the market system. The reason that *parúaros* can put up with escalating prices and lower
returns for products is because they produce most of the food they consume. This security is embedded in a local communal and kin-based economy, which is fundamentally seasonal and diverse. Thus, there are at least
three factors which prevent the full transformation of labour into a commodity: the existence of the subsistence sphere; the extra earning power
possible with the periodic sale of produce; and personal preference, such
as the desire to live near and work with kin. In common with other rural
producers, exploitation is restricted to the point of exchange between producer and buyer and not from the sale of labour. The main way the buyer
can exploit the producer is to buy the primary product cheaply and sell the
item in return for a higher price, the underpricing and overpricing of
commodities. Since *parúaros* produce most of the food they consume this
form of exploitation can continue as long as the subsistence economy is
strong enough to reproduce itself. In other words the bosses and traders have
just as much interest in maintaining the communal economy as those
involved in it. And here we can link up with the agrarian debates in general
because we have a classic contradiction: peasants produce commodities for

sale which are central to the regional economy, but at the same time the basis of these livelihoods is being destroyed by the class who depend on peasant production.

Throughout my conversations in Parú, I was told definitively that everything a person does is work, from the sewing that women do, to the rearing of children, to the planting of seeds and hunting of game. This is very similar to the notion of work as any type of physical or mental exertion which involves purposive activity.[40] It also indicates a weak division of labour by either age or gender. There is, however, a hierarchy whereby activities are classed as heavier or lighter depending on how much physical effort they involve (measured in the amount of sweat produced). Thus, agriculture is seen as the hardest type of work (and even then some crops require differing amounts of effort), with fishing and sewing fairly low down the order.

This importance of physical effort stems from the understanding of work as a force or a strength. *Parúaros* say that each person is the owner of their strength of work, *dono/a da força de trabalho*. Ideally, everybody should work on their own behalf coming and going as they please and without being ordered around by anybody else. This strength to work is kind of an embodied attribute, and as such it should be nurtured by eating and living well. One man told me that work is health, without doing it everyday he would lose his desire to live. Each person can apply this force to create products using their acquired skills.

A key aspect of *parúaro* livelihoods then is their resistance to selling their labour and living far away from close kin. This is not to claim that *parúaros* never live in towns or never sell their labour; but the realisation of the ideals of living with kin and remaining the owner of the strength of work over people's lifetimes signifies an attempt to create their own autonomous 'space'. Indeed it is precisely because when they do sell their labour or live in towns they do so as young single men and women (i.e. marginal adults) to give an extra dimension to their lives and not out of desperation and for survival. For example, no remittances are made when these young people temporarily migrate, all money is spent as quickly as it comes in.

The resistance to selling labour power demonstrates that *parúaros* also have a notion that labour can be separated from the person in contexts outside their domestic economy. And indeed this is taken to a logical extreme in their discourses because the selling of labour power is associated with slavery, where the person has no meaning or purpose outside his or her capacity to work.

40   Marx (1976), p. 284.

Such a strong association of wage labour with slavery is in total contrast with the autonomy and freedom of work that obtains on the floodplain. According to *paruáros*, when you work for someone else, by selling your labour to a boss, you lose a vital sense of freedom and do not get just rewards for the work put in. You cannot come and go as you please, or stop to talk or think, or just lie in a hammock if you feel like it. You have to obey and take orders from another man, since it is he who owns the force of work of the paid employee, because the boss is giving money in return for work.

It is this ability to decide when and how to do things that is one of the key factors for people wanting to stay on the floodplain. I often asked where people prefer to live, in Óbidos or in Parú. The answers I was given expressed an unambiguous wish to stay on the floodplain of Parú and remain the owner of one's own labour and its products; even though they may spend periods of time in the town or go there frequently. In the town there is violence and a person has to pay bills just to have water, or to watch television. For *paruáros* there is a set of logical contingencies between living on the floodplain, residing with kin, being one's own boss and being the owner of the products which a person's work creates. The rhetorical opposition by *paruáros* between ways of life is a construct which valorises their practices and relations, in opposition to the prejudice stacked upon them from city dwellers. This amounts to an inversion of their imputed marginality to the market economy and national society that we have to take seriously.[41]

Conclusion

Why use the 'agrarian question' as a frame for this chapter if, following Cleary (1993), the classic concepts of political economy are too crude to comprehend the Amazon? A rather general response might be to point out that Amazonia has generally been left out of discussions of Latin American peasantries. By exposing Amazonia in the way this chapter and volume attempt both to connect with other peasantries and to signal empirical realities. Furthermore, land and labour remain critically important whatever local variations they have.

The floodplain question is less about the unequal distribution of land, than rights to natural resources. Different perceptions of these rights have brought peasants and outsiders into conflict and those who live on the

41   See Harris (2000).

floodplain with each other. The outcome of such conflict is not entirely predictable and depends on factors such as the location of the area, near a city or a lake, the ability of the community to act together, and the pattern of economic activities. The survival of these floodplain peasantries ultimately depends on the success of capitalist forces in the development of precapitalist formations. The failure to transform, as has been the case, is not straightforward, as the blockage can be a result of weakness (the desire to transform those peasants, but the apparent inability to do so) or other factors (the satisfaction at having those peasants available as subsidisers of the cheap products and labour force).

It has been suggested here that a series of contradictory characteristics find expression in the peasants on the floodplain. Differentiation occurs, but appears to be a temporary inequality and is flattened out after a generation or two; hence the need for recognising different presents or beginnings in the past. Kinship relations enable continued access to natural resources, as well as organising labour, masking some exploitation of junior kinspeople. Petty commodity production is essentially capitalist, but is only one kind of economic activity. The ability to work is the source of freedom, but also the peasant organisation of such work enables the production of cheap goods for market sale and thus is a source of self-exploitation. Land tenure amongst locals is informal and is held onto through marriage and use in order to maintain rights of residence. This contrasts with the formal basis of land ownership in Brazilian law, where title grants inalienable rights. This mixture of non-capitalist and capitalist in becoming appears to express, from the peasants' perspective, something viable and historically resilient.

The extent to which the constitution of a riverine peasantry or peasantries has been a success or a failure is an open question, and ultimately a moral one. From the perspective of a commodity export economy the current situation can be seen in quite positive terms: a self-supporting peasantry, which produces goods cheaply for sale. What more could be asked of a peripheral economy? On the other hand, what I have tried to reveal in this chapter is just as important: the existence of sets of processes and practices which are fundamentally opposed to agrarian capitalism. In this sense the peasantries of Amazonia are as much 'beyond otherness' as becoming other.

CHAPTER 5

(Some) Other Amazonians:
Jewish Communities in the Lower Amazon

Stephen Nugent

This chapter has three themes. The first concerns representations of Brazilian Amazonia — scholarly and journalistic — that pay little heed to the diversity of societies, peoples and communities of the region. The second concerns one such community, that of Sephardic Jews, resident in Brazilian Amazonia since the 1820s. The third concerns some of the ways in which anthropological communities — an unbounded set — come to attention or remain invisible. The second is the focus, but the first and third provide crucial ancillary contexts.

The naming and identification of peoples of Brazilian Amazonia has long been an uncertain project. So-called Amazon women warriors themselves, of course, were speculatively compared with figures from ancient Greek, Libyan and Turkish sources,[1] and in recent years publications emanating from developmental enterprises are often satisfied with designations such as 'populations', 'inhabitants' and 'peoples'. Setting aside Amerindian Amazonians, potentially hyphenate Amazonians (Lebanese-Amazonians, Dutch-Amazonians, etc.) seem to constitute an empty set, as though the overwhelming naturalness of Amazonia precludes differentiation of this sort. The one significant exception is neo-Amazonian, a term common since the developmentalist assault (c. 1970), and generally used to indicate frontier colonist.

With regard to Amerindians, the anthropological convention[2] has been to use tribal names despite the fact that such usages are not widely adopted by Amerindians themselves (for whom, often, 'we the people' typically suffices; other 'tribes' are often regarded as *tapuios*, not-quite-Indians). Such well-known markers as 'the Yanomami' and 'the Kayapo' are not

---

1   Curiously, in view of the number of novels and feature films based in Amazonia, warrior women have little prominence. An exception is *Lana: Queen of the Amazons* (Von Cziffra, 1964).

2   Amazonian anthropology has focused almost exclusively on Amerindian peoples. For studies of neo-Amazonian peasantries, the term *caboclo* is widely — if not uncontroversially — used as a generic.

often used by subjects themselves (except in special circumstances, in national/international political arenas, say, when representing Amerindian interests in idioms demanded by Northern discourse). At a higher level of abstraction there are superordinate linguistic families (Gê-Bororo, Tupí, Arawak, Carib), but these systems of classification are largely archaic from the point of view of contemporary ethnographic research,[3] evocative artefacts of earlier episodes of anthropological inquiry.

The uncertainty of the labelling process is not surprising given the scale and speed of the demise of Amerindian peoples following conquest. Systematic anthropological work in the region commenced several hundred years after 90+ per cent of the original Amazonian populations had disappeared.

In the chronicling of the celebrated descents of the River by the Spaniards Orellana (1542) and Aguirre (1561), Luis Aranha de Vasconcelos' mapping of the lower reaches of the River (1616), and Pedro Teixeira's ascent of the River to Quito (1637-8), named Amerindian groups feature prominently and maps of the period depict extensive 'indigenous provinces'.[4] The subsequent slave-raiding in the name of private, imperial and religious aims, as well as the devastating effects of introduced diseases, led to the complete disappearance of what a significant group of scholars[5] regard as the typical and dominant kind of pre-conquest Amazonian society: sedentary, riverine, proto-state, no examples of which have been available for ethnographic examination. The decline of population was not prevented by the implementation of the so-called Directorate — a system for rationalising the integration of Amerindians into the colonial project — and amidst the recommendations of the subsequent Pompaline reforms (1757) was a proposal to institutionalise miscegenation, creating — amongst others — the category *mameluco* (offspring of Portuguese and Amerindian).

While the historical origins of raciological (and other) classifications of Amazonians since conquest have been the subject of a number of insightful investigations,[6] it would be fair to say that most work in this area has taken place at the national level, indeed as part of Brazil's nation-building programme, one from which Amazonia was — until recently — largely excluded. A central — if contested — agenda has been that closely associated with Gilberto Freyre and his attempts to define the Brazilian national char-

---

3   But see Dennis Moore for a significant departure.

4   For example, the Omagua, the Tapajós, the Tupinamba, etc; see Porro (1996), pp. 172–80.

5   Lathrap (1968); Roosevelt (1994).

6   See Motta Maués (1989).

acter as a combination of European mental outlook, African physical
strength and Amerindian fecundity, an agenda extensively deconstructed by
Lilia Schwarcz in *The Spectacle of the Races* (1999) and, earlier, in Skidmore
(1976), whose observations about 'whitening' (*branqueamento*) also reflect the
long-standing comparative work on slavery in North and South America.

In the narrower Amazonian context, this version of the 'race' issue has
had less prominence. In the major Amazonian civil conflict of the mid-
nineteenth century (the *cabanagem*) the main sub-sets of Amazonian cited
in analysis are Portuguese/white, Amerindian, *caboclo* and African/black,
but it could be argued that the racial idiom was less significant than that of
a struggle among elite interests — monarchists, republicans and
Amazonian separatists.

In the contemporary setting, not all of these racial/ethnic designations
have the same currency, while there are two notable additions: *nordestino* (generally a reference to immigrants from Ceará and Pernumbuco, but not exclusively so) and *sulista* (someone from the South, generally with connotations of
whiteness). Two categories refer to enclave communities — remote
Amerindians or descendents of runaway African slaves living in *quilombos*.
White, *caboclo* and — in modified form, African and Amerindian — are now
represented in a vast national, racial typology that, according a survey carried
out in 1976 by the Brazilian Institute of Geography and Statistics, includes 136
terms.[7] These include terms that hark back to the Freyrean tripartite division
(for example, *Bugrezinha-escura*=Indian appearance; *Bem-branca*=very white;
Cabocla=mixture of white, Negro and Indian; *Negrota*=Negro with a corpulent
body) as well as obscure idiomatic designations (for example, *Polaca*=Polish features; prostitute; *burro-quando-foge*='burro running away', implying racial mixture
of unknown origin, opposite of *cor-firma*='no doubt about it').

Anthropological Codes

To the degree that Brazilian Amazonia has been regarded as a significant
anthropological landscape, rather than the green hell of folklore and
Hollywood — tolerating modest and largely obscure human intervention
— two broad social types have held sway in the literature: indigenous
Amerindian societies and outsiders.[8] The former have been closely linked
with intense and revealing anthropological investigation and express a coherence which endures despite the absence of a pan-Amazonian anthropologi-

7   Schwarcz (1996).
8   There is a pre-historic Amazonia, but its scholarly profile is in its infancy by compar-
     ison with the ethnographic record. For discussion see Roosevelt (ed.) (1994).

cal overview.[9] The latter have a decidedly more vague profile, one that reflects not only the historic uncertainties of the Amazon region's relationship with the colony and — later — state,[10] and its unusual stop-and-start colonisation, but also the view — typically most forcefully put by the military —[11] that Amazonia is fundamentally a natural resource domain lacking a significant social presence. While the profusion of research activity since the 1970s has vastly increased knowledge of the region, the construction of an accurate portrait of the social landscapes has been deferred.

From the perspective of most anthropological research in the region the Amerindian versus outsider distinction has considerable potency: Amerindians are beleaguered and there is little question that incursions by representatives of national society — whether these be federal agents or small-holder frontier colonists or large-scale extractive enterprises — provoke an understandable temerity ranging from distrust to overt hostility. From the perspective of non-Amerindian Amazonia, however, the distinction between Amazonian and outsider/Amazonian neophyte is less clear cut, and this is not surprising given that peasant Amazonia (glossed here as *caboclo*) does not represent an elaboration/degradation of Amerindian societies as much as a complex immigrant society, and an immigrant society that is highly inclusive. Provenance may count in some circles (suitable candidate for the Yacht Club?; entry into regional or national level politics; 'old commercial family') and there is no doubting the existence and power of that familiar class architecture, but on a quotidian level such considerations do not necessarily extend very far in terms of eligibility as a generic Amazonian. Despite the existence of all the material necessary to construct a multicultural political assemblage that would produce the kinds of hyphenate ethnic identities so prominent in the USA, for example, that kind of configuration is suppressed in Amazonia. This is not to say that Amazonia has achieved the kind of racial democracy so long fought over at the national level, but it is to say that competing racial, ethnic, foreign, immigrant identity claims are significantly mollified, or perhaps simply poorly or obscurely articulated.

9   See Jackson (1975); Overing (1981); Viveiros de Castro (1996). This is not to say that the condition of indigenous Amazonians is not extremely precarious, only that the anthropological gaze has mainly fallen on them.

10   During the mid-nineteenth century *cabanagem* revolt, for example, Amazonia was claimed by monarchists, republicans and autonomists.

11   In an article published in *Low Intensity Conflict and Law Enforcement* (1994), Colonel Alvaro de Souza Pinheiro of the Brazilian Army writes that 'Forest, Indians and ecology are a kind of mask to avoid the development of a region everybody knows is rich in minerals and other biodiverse resources ... Brazil is not a 'pollution country' and the preservation of the envrionment is tied to development'.

One explanation for this state of affairs represents a long-standing conceit about the dominance of nature over culture in Amazonia to the effect that tropicalism has been the great leveller: although occupied by Dutch, French, Portuguese, English, Japanese, Lebanese, US Confederates and others, Amazonia-the-humid-neo-tropical-forest-river-system has rendered such multiple and varied cultural imprints relatively benign. Faced with the enormity of the natural apparatus, the argument seems to go, the cultural apparatus has made do with what little is on offer,[12] with the result that the significance of cultural difference is significantly attenuated.

This is not to ignore clearly bounded immigrant communities in Amazonia that manage to maintain identities outside the 'neo-Amazonian' or *caboclo* cover terms[13] — the Japanese colony at Tomé-Açu, the *quilombos*[14] on the Trombetas River for example — but generally speaking, immigrants seem to have become Amazonian rather than maintaining ethnic hyphenate identities (such as Italian-Amazonian), and acknowledgment of extra-Amazonian antecedents is generally only casually registered in phrases such as 'my grandfather was Lebanese', 'my mother's uncle was French' etc. Even in recent years (since the construction of the Transamazon Highway and a highly interventionist programme of modernisation), the once potent contrast between *nordestino* colonist Amazonians and in-place — traditional, *caboclo, ribeirinho* — Amazonians has shown signs of erosion. Amazonians who are Amazonian + something else, are so according to diverse and transitory rules defining inclusion, exclusion and transgression. Maintaining *nordestino* + Amazonian identity is quite a different matter from being Amazonian + Moroccan Jew or Amazonian + Japanese, but these hyphenate possibilities are largely subsumed under the generic Amazonian.

A corollary is that the notion of 'community' in Amazonia is vaguely defined, not withstanding its wide usage. The term may be employed with reference to co-residents with no implication beyond spatial propinquity (*'nosso communidade, aqui na beira do rio'*/'our community, we who live on the river bank'); to religious affiliates ('the Pentecostal community'); to the previously mentioned ethnic enclaves (such as 'the Japanese community'); to political groupings (such as independent squatter agriculturalists allied against local authorities); to occupational groups ('the fishing community'); and so on.

12 In a different context, Blaut (1993) has introduced the notion of 'the Doctrine of Tropical Nastiness' as invoked to explain the antinomy between civilisation and the tropics.

13 'Neo-Amazonian' is imprecise, but in the main refers to non-indigenous Amazonians.

14 *Quilombo*=runaway slave settlement.

In part, this denial of the coherence of the notion of community in Amazonia as more than a shorthand for people who happen to live there is little more than a reflection of the special status granted the region as a last frontier as well as a green hell, constructions highly compatible with the aims of a Brazilian state and external allies keen to emphasise the gross resource potential of the region without paying too much attention to the history of the region and the histories of its occupants. Amazonia is not a social blank-slate, but for some it is useful to present it in such terms.

The Jewish community of the Lower Amazon provides an example of a group whose cohesion is shaped by a simultaneous denial and acceptance of generic Amazonian identity, and its fragile — but durable — intactness is registered in different ways both within and beyond the community itself. In the former there is content, but not much category; for the latter is category with little content. Formal religious life, for example, is almost completely absent, yet for non-Jewish Amazonians it is precisely religion that sets Jews apart.

The Jewish Amazonian community of the Lower Amazon[15] is a network that includes (and sometimes excludes) Jews resident in the cities/towns of Belém, Santarém, Obidos, Alenquer (and other peripheral towns). In fact, the network extends much further nationally and internationally — to Rio, São Paulo, New York, Tel Aviv, Rabat, Houston — and regionally — Manaus, Paratins, Itaituba, Boim, Monte Alegre — in local terms of inclusion. The focus here, however, is on relations within a regional network, effectively that of the cities of Santarém and Belém, the former whose Jewish community is described by one member as 'Jews lost in the forest', the latter regarded (both in Santarém and Belém) as the only actual community. The material is primarily drawn from a series of interviews conducted in Santarém, Alenquer and Belém in 2000,[16] as well as earlier fieldwork.

Belém is far and away the largest of the cities (and the largest in Amazonia) and the only one that has an official religious community (as well as a Jewish community centre, the *Centro Israelita do Pará*, which publishes a newsletter distributed throughout Para). Relations between Belém, on the one hand, and Santarém and Alenquer, on the other, are complicated, and this complexity reveals something about the dynamic qualities of the community overall. For one thing, many Jews of Santarém and

---

15   The Lower Amazon generally refers to the region between Manaus /Santarem — in the interior — and Belém, near the Atlantic coast.

16   Most of the interview material was gathered in the course of a film production — *Where's the Rabbi: Jewish Communities of the Lower Amazon* — in collaboration with Renato Athias of the Federal University of Pernambuco.

Alenquer are kin of *belenenses* and are regarded by such *belenenses* as extensions of the Belém community, yet those same *santarenos* and *alenquerenses*
regard themselves as severely isolated from that community. One *santareno*
(30 years of age), for example, observed that Jews in Santarém were more
highly regarded by *paulista* Jews than they were by *belenense* Jews: 'People in
Belém look down on us. From their point of view we are just out here'.
Another *santareno* (64 years of age) is a bit more pointed: 'The people in
Belém act as though they are Orthodox and as such don't recognise us as
Jews of their type', a view clearly articulated by a young *belenense* woman:
'There is nothing there, just a residue'.

Although dismissive of the 'part of the community' claims of interior-
dwelling Jews, the same informant is unabashed in admitting that many of
the regular attendees at her synagogue don't understand a word of Hebrew.
'Ok, they have the prayerbooks and they know the lines, but they don't
understand what they're saying. They've learned it by rote and that's it'.[17]
She finds this comical, but hardly damaging (and it is hardly unique to this
community). 'That's the way it is here'. Her mother, 70-year old daughter
of a Moroccan who first settled in Alenquer — one of the now dismissed
interior communities — comments that, 'It's always been like that. We
came from far away. We've lived here a long time. That's just the way it is,
as far as I'm concerned'.

Background

Jews of the Lower Amazon — with few exceptions —[18] are Sephardim
from Morocco, mainly from the cities of Tetuan, Rabat, Casablanca and
Fez. Events leading up to expulsion from Luso-Iberia (Spain, 1492, and
Portugal, 1496–97) are not much part of the local narrative, which — if
Roth is correct — is just as well. 'It is necessary to stress,' he writes in the
conclusion to *Conversos, Inquisition and the Expulsion of the Jews from Spain*,[19]
'in the remote possibility that the point has been missed, that almost everything previously written concerning the expulsion of the Jews from Spain
is incorrect (the single exception is the extremely valuable study by Motis
of the expulsion from Aragón)'. What he is referring to in particular is the
protracted debate about *marranos* and *anusims* (real converts versus forced

17   Not that this relationship between the text and understanding is necessarily different
     in more cosmopolitan settings.
18   There are Ashkenazi in Belém, but they regard themselves as extensions of Rio or
     São Paulo networks, not Amazonian.
19   Roth (1995), p. 313.

converts; there are many sub-plots), a matter which arises in Amazonian conversation only in relation to other Brazilian communities — especially those of Recife and Olinda of the sixteenth century. The community in Amazonia does not regard itself as part of a general Brazilian diaspora except in the sense that many (perhaps the majority) of Amazonian Jews subsequently moved to the centre-south.

Moroccan Jewish emigration to Amazonia did not commence until the early nineteenth century and took place under circumstances very different from those of the first Jewish migration to Brazil. Although Jews accompanied the Portuguese Cabral's voyage to Brazil in 1500,[20] and his claiming of it on behalf of Portugal, Jews in Brazil appear not to have achieved recognition as a community per se until the Dutch successfully contested Portuguese claims in the north-east of Brazil (1624) — what is now Pernambuco, and specifically Recife/Olinda —where they ruled until 1654. According to Keller (1971) 'Their rule meant freedom for the New Christians of Brazil'.[21] The designation 'New Christians' is the subject of much scholarly debate,[22] the implications of which, as noted above, are not galvanising issues for contemporary Amazonian Jews. In discussions with Amazonians, Pernambucano/Dutch Jewish issues were invoked only in discussions of the Brazil-US connection (contribution of Jews to the formation of New Amsterdam/New York), and only by seniors.

In 1821, a year before Brazilian independence, the Inquisition was declared at an end in Portugal and its colonial territories. In 1823 occurred the first Jewish emigration to Amazonia.

With the advent of the exploitation of rubber, Jewish emigration to the Amazon region grew significantly with Jews of Hispano-Portuguese origin who had fled to Morocco arriving in large numbers in the states of Pará and Amazonas, establishing themselves in the capitals of those two states.[23]

Although the early nineteenth century is still cited by Amazonian Jews as marking the beginning of the Amazonian community in the region (and Benchimol's recent *Eretz Amazonia: Os Judeos na Amazonia* (1999) underlines this), most contemporary Jews in the Lower Amazon date the appearance of their effective community from the early twentieth century.[24]

---

20 See Seed (1995) for discussion of Jews and Portuguese conquest of Brazil.
21 Keller (1971), p. 315.
22 See in particular Roth's withering treatment of Baer and Netanyahu (1995).
23 Bentes (1987), p. 347.
24 The most recent immigrant arrived in 1951, although his father had been involved in Amazonian commerce since the 1920s.

Immigrants during this period were single (or unaccompanied, married) men whose passage was paid by relations or associates in Morocco on the understanding that they would share the proceeds of their fortunes with their sponsors. In some cases these men were shortly followed by their families, but more typically, those who stayed married non-Jewish women — a continuing source of uncertainty within the community and between the Amazonian and metropolitan Brazilian Jewish communities. Arriving just as the rubber industry was collapsing, most became traders in extractive produce (*cumaru* — a type of wood, brazil nuts, skins, as well as rubber and other tropical, extractive produce), buyers and sellers of agricultural produce (jute, *cacão*), ranchers, owners of trading establishments or itinerant river-boat traders (*regatões*). Contemporary residents of Santarém, Alenquer and Belém lived in — or had relations in — a much wider variety of Amazonian settlements than is characteristic today. These include, as well as the major cities of Santarém, Manaus and Belém: Obidos, Oriximina, Boim, Parintins, Monte Alegre, Aveiro, Itaituba and Cameta.

While Samuel Benchimol (1966, 1999) is the pre-eminent authority on the history of the Amazonian Jewish community, his version of events may apply better to a Jewish Amazonia that has Manaus as its core than it does to Lower Amazonia. He writes, for example, that:

> The principal characteristic of this movement [Jewish emigration to Amazonia] resides in the fact that, in contrast to the majority of other immigrants, this was a migration of family groups — men accompanied by women and children. This provided the features of gregariousness and domesticity of Jewish life, capturing the religious and cultural values in the grip of the family and community, assuring the survival of the characteristic culture and tradition.[25]

Contemporary Jews of the Lower Amazon (excluding, perhaps, some of the more prominent families in Belém) describe entry into Amazonia somewhat differently. For one thing, most of their antecedents came at the end of the rubber period and encountered a declining rather than booming economy. Second — as noted above — many came not in family groups, but as single males. Third, they are both recognised as linked with the founding community (by name, by tombstone), and detached from it by virtue of marrying out while still not repudiating their antecedents (even if others do). While acknowledging official determinations of Jewishness, they simultaneously deny that their various degrees of assimilation deny them Jewish identity.

25   Benchimol (1966), p. 137, my translation.

Diffusion/Diaspora

There is widespread agreement (among Jews; this is not an Amazonian issue) that the state of the Jewish community in the Amazon is precarious, and widespread agreement that it has been so for some time — perhaps from the outset — but despite the absence of overt indications of a religious community (there are no synagogues outside Belém, and even those two are without rabbis; there are few Jews in Santarém and Alenquer who claim to be practising Jews) or evidence that the situation is changing for the better, there is no hesitancy about being identified as Jewish or unwillingness to explore the implications of that declaration. Typically, people say it is hard to be a Jew because of the lack of 'conditions' (*condições*) (no rabbis, no synagogues, no kosher food), but the main obstacle — characteristic from the outset: lack of Jewish women — is not regarded as fatal. At one end, there is excessive attention to conversion as a normal part of the process of maintaining the Jewish community, and at the other end there is a sort of resignation ('we have mixed marriages, but there is no pressure to conform. We have a double religion, and there is no problem. There is only one god after all'.)

While conversion was previously more widely available, with the absolute decline in the Jewish population in Amazonia and the need to go further afield for conversion (typically, São Paulo or Rio), mixed marriages are the norm. As one man explains, the nature of work in Amazonia militates against proper marriage:

> I work in the forest,[26] hundreds of kilometres away from anywhere. Where my mother lives, in São Paulo, it's different. You go to synagogue, you meet lots of people, and everyone there marries this cousin or that cousin. It's nothing like that here. It's impossible (C. Chocron).

He himself is married to a Catholic woman. Their two daughters are baptised, attend mass occasionally, and identify themselves as 'Catholics with a Jewish father'. The father does not attend church, but does not object to his children's doing so. Twenty years ago, his father's house in Obidos served, in the absence of a synagogue, as the *shul*. His is not an angst-ridden, soul-bearing narrative. The condition of the Jew in Amazonia has always been such. 'We have no leadership. What community we have is what we make.'

This is a theme repeated by many men of his generation (grandsons of Moroccan immigrants): 'we are not actually a Jewish community in the

---

26 He works for the Federal Environmental Agency (IBAMA).

sense we would prefer, but we remember such a community, even if it was still uncertain — given the conditions of immigration. Despite the fact that the community we imagine is not realised, what else can we be but Jews?'

Não Ha Condicões

While the condition of 'being Jewish in Amazonia' is not a preoccupation of Amazonian Jews, nor is the condition of 'being Jewish' ignored. Confronted by researchers (both, by the way, similarly *mestiço*-Jewish), all the interviewees displayed 'what's-the-big-deal?' attitudes. Where there is divergence about allegiance to a larger Jewish community, it focuses on matters of authority/authenticity. For example, *belenenses* — who have religious infrastructure — are disparaging about those in the interior who are even more compromised than they are, despite the fact that the conditions in Belém hardly differ.

A 70-year old man of Belém — a former trader in skins and brazil nuts — recounts the pressure he was placed under when, in the early 1950s, he wanted to marry a non-Jewish woman:

> In those days there was lots of pressure — family pressure — not to marry a non-Jew. So I was deported to Rio for a year. And I forgot about her and married another (I. Serruya).

The issue of who is a Jew by virtue of correct marriage, however, is by no means clear. Almost all Jewish families in Santarém and Alenquer, for example, have mixed marriages and while this leads some to say that the 'Xs are not really Jewish anymore — all the sons married Catholics' — those who are non-Jewish in the eyes of some still regard themselves as Jewish by descent. As explained by a man whose father was regarded as an outstanding religious adept — but took a non-Jewish wife:

> It's usually put this way: how do you manage to maintain this Jewish tradition — it's more or less extinct. But descendants of Jewish families still assume that's what they are — Jewish (G. Serique).

Even amongst the first settler families, the possibility for pursuing a more or less rigorous religious life depended on the absolute size of the local/regional Jewish population such that the houses of seniors could be used on Saturdays in lieu of a synagogue. Most second and third generation Jews in Santarém, for example, remember such in-house *shabbat* observance as the last — and now lost — phase of religious observance that exceeded the boundaries of their immediate families, but today, even those few families in Santarém that regard themselves as the standard bearers only cite a few high holidays as occasions for such observance.

The degree to which religious observance is regarded definitively as a thing of the past increases directly with distance from Belém, and in Santarém and Alenquer, for example, those who regard themselves as Jews have occasion to define themselves religiously as Jews only in a few circumstances, mainly involving pressure put on their children to be baptised. Typically, men assent to the baptism of their children with the proviso that they themselves shall retain their Jewish identity and offer that to their children should they want it (Catholic officials, it is said, use the pressure for baptism to try to diminish the Jewish presence). In Belém, the existence of synagogues and a more or less continous (in the twentieth century) religious officialdom, means that a higher degree of religious orthodoxy is on offer, although many Jews in the interior (i.e. outside Belém) are somewhat dismissive of such claims. Several commentaries on the differences between the Belém community and those of the interior reveal the range of opinion about who is still regarded as Jewish in the Lower Amazon. One synagogue-attending Belenense lawyer — now married to an evangelical Christian — has sent his children to Israel to learn how to be Jews. It has, he reports, been painful: they speak neither English nor Hebrew, and like another *santarena* veteran of a roots search in Israel, they are regarded as strange ('...they expect Indians in Amazonia, not Jews').[27]

For most Jews of the interior, the durable features of Jewish identity have never depended heavily on consistent religious observance. In the 'old days' (reference here is to pre-World War II period), according to an Alenquer baker — non-Jewish father, non-Jewish wife, two children baptised as Catholics):

> ...it would be very unusual for a Jew to be left to get by on his own in Amazonia. If anyone got into trouble, people would go to his aid, find out what was needed and provide it. This is not just a matter of people you knew, but anyone who was known to be Jewish. Life then had this kind of solidarity. Today, I'm not so sure. It might be a bit difficult (M. Mendes).

By contrast, a Belenense pharmacist of the same generation describes the activities of his father who, encountering two Jews:

> ...who were dying without medical assistance, without religious assistance, without food ... he founded a Hebrew Centre in order to provide aid to all Jews (I. Israel).

The enduring contrast between a Jewishness supported institutionally and

---

27   This response is not limited to Israelis. Many people find the idea of Jews in the Amazon astonishing.

informally underlines a rift between *belenense* and interior Jewish communities, one commented on frequently by members of both communities. The son of a Jewish woman (Catholic father) whose father entered Amazonia in 1922, notes with some bitterness the attitude of Belenense Jews towards those of the interior:

> We are better acknowledged by, and have greater respect from, Jews in São Paulo and places like that than we have from the people in Belém ... as far as they are concerned we are just people lost in the forest (A. Malheiros).

In interviews with Belenenses, such views were by no means universal, but were well represented and bluntly articulated:

> As to the question of people in the interior, it's really a question of tradition ... in Obidos [her birth place], there used to be a centre, in a house, where everyone would go on Saturday. Today, it just doesn't exist. Anyone wanting that today has to come to Belém. You no longer have 'that house of the Jewish woman who does all the *pascoas* and so on',[28] where everyone can go. You have to come to Belém. Those who still live in the interior only have family links, they have to come to Belém because there they don't have any kind of communion. What they have is maybe a father-in-law, a cemetery, a couple of families, lots of intermarriage. They have to come to Belém, that's the point of reference these days (E. Cany).

This woman is not herself a 'traditional Belenense', but a migrant from the interior, and is well aware of some of the contradictions residing in claims of the superiority of the Belenense community.

Discussion

Religious, national, ethnic and racial affiliations in Amazonia are no less relevant markers than they are elsewhere. The potency of such affiliations in Amazonia, however, is conditioned by sociohistorically specific constraints that are poorly understood, not least because of a durable belief that the Amazonian environment is intrinsically inhospitable and presents an absolute limit on the emergence of social complexity. Blaut (1993) has named this belief 'the Doctrine of Tropical Nastiness', and although his argument focuses on the way the Doctrine reinforces a notion of the

---

28   *Pascoa* = Passover, but is also a generic for religious holidays.

uncivilised (and uncivilisable) tropical African, his observations are appo-site in the neo-humid tropical context. In that context, and strongly and persistently influenced by some of the more mechanical and reductionist versions of cultural ecology that have shaped modern anthropological research in Amazonia (i.e. post-Nimuendajú), Amazonian society is a sequestered society: small groups of hunter-gather/horticulturalists, tech-nologically rudimentary, symbolically profligate. That such a society is typical of the region prior to conquest is a notion slowly being refuted (Lathrap, Roosevelt, Whitehead), yet while that compelling debate over the development/retrogression of social formations in Amazonia unfolds, the actual colonial, post-colonial and modern societies of Amazonia are pushed outside the frame established by cultural ecological discourse. This is not say that they are unacknowledged, but it is to say that they have not — generally speaking — emerged as worthy subjects of serious inquiry. Hence, the condition of the Jewish communities is both singular (there is a dynamic exclusive to the Luso-Iberian diaspora) and generalised (there are lots of immigrant Amazonian peoples, assimi-lated as 'Amazonians' to greater or lesser degrees). Jewishness in Amazonia informed by local, regional, national and international configura-tions that have shifting bearing on the perceptions of Amazonian Jews as to the cohesiveness of their community, while for other immigrant Amazonians, the external terms of reference are more limited (regional, national). For some, the cohesion is of the past — in Morocco, in the found-ing immigrant communities of nineteenth and twentieth centuries, in the now abandoned *shuls*. For others, the cohesion is renewable through reli-gious observance and fealty to Israel. For others, it is the struggle to acknowledge the preoccupations of the ascending generation that provides focus (such as the non-Hebrew reading *alenquerense* who hoards his father's extensive collection of religious texts). For others, the claim is founded on asserting a cultural identity based on religious affiliation despite the absence of formal religious apparatus. For others, it is a memory occasionally renewed by association with others who similarly mark the passing of time with sombre reflection on what might have been.

An older Belenense speaks for many when he says:

> I'm a Jew, but I don't feel — how do you say ... religious, yes, but what's the right word? It's not in the language. Tradition? Yes, that's understood. What I don't feel is ... a devotee. Let's say that. There may be other expressions, but I don't feel pious. I lead a normal life. Go to synagogue on Saturdays, but I follow my own path.

CHAPTER 6

Malineza (Evil): An Amazonian Concept [*]

Raymundo Heraldo Maues

Evil (*mal*), malign (*maligno, malina*), maleficent (*maleficio*) and evil-doings (*malfeito*). The concepts are loose and approximate and they can be found in the popular and elite culture of Brazil and Portugal.[1] But the Portuguese term *malineza*, or evil in English, composed of *malino* and *eza*, is defined in dictionaries as a special idiom of Pará state in Brazil. It constitutes a concept of major importance in rural Amazonian areas, where anthropologists interested in the religion of the historical peasantries (*caboclos*) have worked: Itá (Gurupá) in the Lower Amazon, and Itapuá, in the coastal Salgado region of Pará and in a variety of other places in the eastern Amazonia.[2]

Malina (badness), a possible corruption of *maligna* (malign) according to Câmara Cascudo, refers to a strong fever of diverse origins, and can be serious or fatal. *Maleficio* or *malefiço* can mean witchcraft, enchantment or a deathly state; to do witchcraft means 'to cause harm (*mal*), to do sorcery (*enfeitiçar*), to damage (*prejudicar*), to violate (*deflorar*), to rape (*estuprar*)'.[3] Malevolence (*malfeito*), in the sense of sorcery (*feitiçaria*), in connection to 'love magic' (practised by women) and 'business magic' (performed by men), was found by Alceu M. Araújo, in his research conducted in Piaçabuçu, in the interior state of Alagoas in northeastern Brazil.[4]

How can the concept of *malineza* be understood? We can begin by relating it to the concepts mentioned above. In a general sense it is the practice of evil, which would include malefaction (*maleficio*), evil-doing (*mal-feito*) and sorcery (*feitiçaria*) in general. In some cases, it could also refer to the

[*] This chapter was translated from the Portuguese by Mark Harris. The article first appeared in *O mal à Brasileira*, edited by P. Birman, R. Novaes and S. Crespo (1997), pp 32–44, in Rio de Janeiro by EDUERJ and was included (pp. 237–249) in a collection of essays by the author entitled, *Uma outra 'invenção' da Amazônia: religiões, histórias, identidades*, published by Cejup, Belém, in 1999.

1   See Camara Cascudo (n.d.) and Araújo (1979).
2   Galvão (1955); Maués (1990, 1992 and 1995).
3   Camara Cascudo (n.d.), p. 538.
4   Araújo (1979), pp. 185–6.

mischievousness (*maldades*) of children. Despite this, a more accurate observation is that the concept can be more suitably applied to intentional actions of a magical, or supernatural, nature, which are provoked by human and non-human (or not fully human) agents against other humans, plants, animals and material objects, especially personal possessions.

The term *malineza* is used by Eduardo Galvão (1955) in his book *Santos e Visagens*.[5] It was then employed by Roberto da Matta in his structuralist-inspired analysis (1973) of *panema* (bad luck in hunting and fishing). More inclusive than *panema*, the concept of *malineza* came to my attention in fieldwork undertaken in Itapuá, a fishing village in the Vigia municipality, on the Paraense coast in the mid-1970s. My later studies elsewhere in the Salgado region, which includes Vigia municipality, allowed a deeper understanding of *malineza*, its importance to the rural people, and those in urban areas who came from the countryside.

In a similar (though not identical) way to the kind of witchcraft (*bruxaria*) occurring amongst the Azande,[6] *malineza* can be thought as a way of explaining unfortunate events. In this category one could include 'sufferings' or illnesses, that can be called, following local ideas: evil eye; another form of evil eye that affects only children (*quebranto*); persecution or haunting by spirits (*mal-assombrado*); incorporation or possession by spirits (*ataque de espirito*); darts of enchanted animals (*flechada-de-bicho*); currents of the deep (*corrente-do-fundo*); attack by enchanted dolphin (*ataque de boto*); magic spells cast by witchcraft or sorcery (*feitiço*). These sufferings belong to a category of illness of non-natural origin. This is opposed to natural or normal ailments, which are considered to be 'sent by God': flu; fever; malaria; ailments or pains in the chest (popularly supposed to be caused by a falling of the breastbone, *espinhela caida*; shingles (supposedly caused by contact with a cobra or snake, *cobrelo*); hernia (*mola*); irregular menses; tuberculosis; measles; smallpox; mumps; and many others. The occurrence of an illness of a non-natural origin is generally associated with *malineza*, however, as we will see, there are exceptions to this rule. These anomalies are thought of as 'non-normal', which excludes them from the scope of western medicine, since the treatment can only be exercised by local specialists, such as blessers (*benzedores*), experts and curers (*curadores*) or shamans (*pajés*).

As is clear, some of these illnesses are quite generalised and part of a wider phenomenon. Specifically, the evil eye and *quebranto* occur in various

---

5   This book is a translation of Galvão's 1952 Columbia University thesis based on fieldwork with Wagley at various times in 1940s.

6   Evans-Pritchard (1937).

parts of the world.[7] In the Salgado region of Pará, we find that the evil eye is distinguished from *quebranto* since it is caused by the 'staring eye' of humans. People with this particular look, who have the evil eye, or 'the mad eye', can touch others of either sex and any age, as well as plants and animals. While *quebranto* is caused by 'admiration' and only affects young children, it arises from the declarations of praise concerning the beauty or the health of the child, which are not accompanied by the phrase 'God bless' (*benza Deus*). Apart from this, there are various types of evil eye, which are designated according to the causal agent of the illness: the evil eye of a person, of an animal (*bicho*), of the sun and the moon. The evil eye is not just a human phenomenon, but can also be conceived as a property of stars, and can be provoked by '*bichos*' (as discussed below), an expression which actually designates enchanted beings which live in the forests, river bottoms, beaches and swamps.

In reference to the haunting of ghosts and spirit possession, we are also in the presence of quite widespread notions.[8] This is not separate from the human world, since these spirits are thought to belong to dead people, those with bad or penitent souls, who thus haunt their human victims or possess them in unexpected circumstances (or occasions).

More particularly Amazonian are the beliefs relating to the wounds caused by the darts of enchanted animals (*flechada-de-bicho*), currents of the deep (*corrente-do- fundo*), attack by dolphin (*ataque de boto*). These conceptions, which are sometimes known by other names, are found in various anthropological studies.[9] Although these concepts are thought to have an indigenous origin, as Galvão 1955 mentions, it is clear that there is also a European influence. This presence transpires in the particular terms used to classify the enchanted beings that provoke these harms.

The *encantados* are seen as human beings who do not die, but pass into another realm of being, the enchanted kingdom (*encante*). They live in the forest, in river depths, in the swamps and on the beaches. The *encantados* of the forest, who are less obviously human, are the *curupira* and the *anhanga*. Their relevance is diminishing in the Salgado region where the forest is becoming less important, owing to the long period of colonisation starting from the seventeenth century, and to the higher population density in

7   See Adams (1952); Araújo (1979); Câmara Cascudo (n.d.); Foster (1953); Galvão (1955); Reminick (1974); Rubel (1960); Spooner (1970); Wagley (1976), among others.
8   Câmara Cascudo (n.d.).
9   See Galvão (1955); Wagley (1976); Figueiredo (1976); Figueiredo and Vergolino e Silva (1972); Gabriel (1980); Salles (n.d. and 1976).

relation to other areas in the Amazon. The *encantados* of the deep, however, occupy a central role, in this area (near to the Atlantic Ocean and to the mouth of the Amazon River) where fishing is the primary economic activity. They are known as the 'beasts of the deep', and appear in different forms of aquatic animal, such as dolphins, fish, snakes, crocodiles and so on. They are also known as *oiaras*, when they take human form in the swamps or beaches. They are also termed *caruanas* (a sort of spirit helper), as they manifest themselves, even though they are invisible, in the body of the shaman during the curing sessions.

Another widespread concept in Amazonia is the belief that each element of the natural world has a guardian mother. So there is the mother of the forest and mother of the river. A hunter who abuses his work, by taking too many animals, especially of one particular species, can be punished by the mother of the forest. The hunter could be attacked by the evil eye or by invisible darts from animals (*flechada-de-bicho*), or could be bewitched (*mundiado*). The evil eye of an animal, as in other forms of evil eye, causes a very bad headache. The invisible darts inflict pain in a specific part of the body, and unless correctly treated can lead to death. If the hunter is bewitched, on the other hand, he could get lost in the forest, with dire results.

In the same way, if a person crosses a river or stream without asking permission or, even worse, urinates or washes his bloodied hands in running water, the anger of the mother of the river could be provoked. As a result of the misdeed the enchanted being of the deep will put the evil eye on the miscreant, or pierce him or her with a dart.

It is also thought that, occasionally, enchanted beings of the deep become 'friendly' with humans. In this case, they can provoke the currents of the deep (*corrente do fundo*) or a dolphin attack. The symptoms of the currents of the deep become part of an assault on a person's spirit. Two illnesses can result. The victim is subject to involuntary possessions, at unexpected times and places; and is made to run into the forest, or leap into the river, at the risk of drowning, or to sing strange songs (from the deep) and dance. It requires a lot of strength to control a possessed person, even a young girl; many men are often needed to hold down the victim. It is believed that the enchanted beings, when friendly with someone, want to appear as *caruanas*, using the body as a vessel to hold them. An evil or penitent spirit will also take advantage of the weakness of the victim to seize their hosts' body.

Those who suffer from the 'currents of the deep' (*corrente do fundo*), or who are attacked by an evil spirit, should be treated by a shaman. If the victim has the shamanic gift (that is, a gift to incorporate the good *caruanas*, in shamanistic sessions, that are held specially as healing meetings), the bad spirits and bad *caruanas* must be sent away, while the good *caruanas* will be kept and tamed, to be recalled on other more suitable occasions. If the treatment succeeds, the person will become a new shaman. But if the person does not have the shamanic vocation, the gift, all the spirits must be expelled in order for the person to be fully cured. The process is quite complex; it includes the obligation, for those who have the gift, to submit themselves to the will of the *caruanas*, while also controlling them, under pain of punishment, such as when the person refuses to train his special ability. Moreover, the novice shaman, especially if a woman, will always be suspected of also being a sorcerer or a witch, since it is thought that those who know how to heal also know how to cause harm (illness, or other misfortunes).

A more dreaded form of 'friendliness' on the part of enchanted beings is when they take the form of a 'dolphin attack'. Only women are subject to the evil influence of the enchanted dolphin, especially if they are menstruating. The dolphin is attracted by blood and tries to seduce the woman, appearing in a human form, often as a lover or her husband, and engaging in sexual relations and sucking her blood. Thus the dolphin acts like a demon or a vampire. Successive sexual relations will weaken the woman, who will become anaemic, possibly leading to death.

In some areas of Amazonia, people say that a woman can conceive a child of a dolphin (*um filho do boto*) as a result of the sexual relations.[10] The figure of the dolphin, an aquatic mammal, with the form of a fish, but not a fish, is always highly ambiguous. Feared for the harm it can do, it is also a friend of fishermen, helping them in fishing expeditions, and protecting and saving people who have capsized.

We have come, finally, to the last two unnatural illnesses, sorcery (*feitiço*) and *panema*, whose causes are linked, exclusively, to the action of ordinary living human beings. Sorcery (*feitiço*) is thought as having three distinct forms: evil magic (*feitiço*) proper, anger (*aborrecimento*) and parauá. *Panema*, which could also derive from sorcery (*feitiçaria*) possesses however a complex aetiology, as well as illustrating one of the most interesting forms of *malineza*.

Panema has been excellently described by Galvão (1955) and Wagley (1976), and also by da Matta in his brilliant analysis (1973). Nevertheless, it is present in the Salgado region, except for a small variation in detail, with precisely the same characteristics as when was studied by Galvão and Wagley in the mid-1940s in the lower Amazon.

10   Câmara Cascudo (n.d.); Galvão (1955); Wagley (1976).

In the Salgado region *panema* is conceived as fundamentally a product of jealousy over the success of the fisherman or hunter (although hunting has less importance, for reasons mentioned earlier). It can also be directed against good fortune in any other economic activity (especially in trading). For this reason, *panema* can be defined as a negative state, which affects the successful outcome of productive activities, principally fishing. As in the lower Amazon, *panema* does not affect horticulture. Gardens can be attacked by the jealousy of the evil eye, particularly if it is accompanied by admiration and praise. The plants will dry out very quickly, but not from the force of *panema*.

Panema can also be caused in other ways. This includes the contact of a menstruating woman with fishing or hunting equipment, the consumption of the spoils of fishing or hunting by a pregnant woman, 'distrust' (that is, if food is refused when given as a gift), the eating of leftovers and entrails of fish and game by domestic animals (chickens, ducks, turkeys and so on), as well from sorcery (*feitiçaria*).   *S = Purposeful   P = accidental*

Sorcery (*feitiço*) is always the result of a deliberate action by a sorcerer or witch, who is generally a woman, against the victim. *Panema*, for example, can be caused by mixing meat or fish with excrement, strongest if human, or else by putting a concoction of smelly (urine or faeces), itchy (the aninga plant) and hot substances (chili pepper) over the fishing or hunting equipment. But the black magic (*feitiço*), in its diverse forms, does not just cause *panema*. It results in the manipulation of external substances and can manifest itself in a variety of apparently natural illnesses; making a successful diagnosis and treatment difficult. As such, a leg-wound, for example, resistant to treatment with local or pharmaceutical remedies, could be the result of sorcery (*feitiço*). This possibility can only be ascertained by the shaman, who with the help of his spirits (*caruanas*) will try to undo the harm and return it (or not) to the aggressor. Nevertheless, the shaman may still be unable to cure the wound. This theme, as is clear, has a universal relevance and has also been studied in the urban areas of the Amazon.[11]

Alternatively, anger (*aborrecimento*) is a problem that can be caused by a handful of ash thrown by the sorcerer (*feitiçeiro*) against the back of his victim. This produces a terrible and intense itching all over the body, as well as a lack of desire to work. This differs from *panema*, which also has the effect of incapacitating productive activities, but does not affect the will to work.

And finally, *parauá*, a form of black magic (*feitiço*) which leads us to a special category of sorcerers, the so-called *fadistas* (restless beings). There are two types: a kind of werewolf, *labisônio* (which in Portuguese is obvi-

---

11   Boyer-Araujo (1994).

ously a corruption of *lobisomem*), a man who turns himself into a pig at night and attacks passers-by; and the *matintaperera*, who is the worse type of sorcerer, and should properly be called a witch. The *matintaperera* is always a woman. She has extraordinary powers and can fly and transform herself into various kinds of animal, most commonly the bat and the pig.

These restless beings are believed to have a pact with the devil, because they are obliged to carry out their 'fate' (*fado*): to wander around at night in non-human form. In the case of the *matintaperera* (something like an owl), whose understanding is the most pronounced, its wanderings are said to be accompanied by a *xerimbabo* (a wild animal raised as a pet, a familiar), a bird of the same name (*matintaperera*), which makes a strange whistling noise that betrays its presence to those in the vicinity. According to some versions, the *matintaperera*, despite being a living entity, is said to be capable of sending its own spirit to possess the victims it wants to belabour.

Furthermore, it is believed that the *matintaperera* can transmit its 'fate' to her own grand-daughter. It approaches the young person and asks, while knocking on her back, 'my grandchild, would you like a present?'. Following the positive reply, a 'parrot' (the *parauá* sorcery) is left on the back of the child, which will develop wings, conferring on the owner the power to fly (as a witch). However, the 'fate' can, if discovered in time, be averted by a shaman, who with the proper treatment takes out the *parauá* from the victim's body.

All the situations described above are, or can be conceived, as cases of *malineza*. In these cases it is necessary to distinguish between intentionality and non-intentionality (or involuntary action), that is between a *malineza* which is caused by an agent's intrinsic power and that which is produced by the manipulation of external substances.

In principle, an evil provoked without the intention of the causal agent is not seen as *malineza*. Thus, for example, a person, who admires a beautiful child and causes *quebranto*, does not act out of wickedness, but is giving way to an interior force. This force is the quality of someone who is considered a *quebranteiro*, a person who is born with this attribute and cannot help its manifestation. In the same way, someone who has the mad eye (*olho doído*) cannot be aware of the fact that looking at a garden, or a person, will unwittingly cast the evil eye. Nevertheless, it is also said that once a person begins to be aware of his powers, he may come to use them intentionally, and this produces *malineza*.

In the same way, it is problematic to talk of *malineza*, with reference to the evil eye, when it is caused by an enchanted being, or his invisible darts, if the victim, because he had abused 'nature', was guilty of attracting the evil eye or the arrow to himself. Nor can the evil eye of sun and moon, despite the sense that the moon 'plays' with young children, be described as *malineza*. While the celestial beings do not mean to cause harm, the ambiguous figures of the enchanted beings, on the other hand, can be as beneficent as they are maleficent. The evil eye of an animal or its dart can be produced by the pure wickedness of the enchanted beings, and in this way can be seen as *malineza*. The same logic can be applied to all other illnesses or sufferings of a non-natural origin.

Nevertheless, here we must make the distinction between harm provoked by an inner quality of an agent and that conferred by the mixing of external objects. Superficially, these beliefs are similar to the well-known distinction made by Evans-Pritchard (1937) between witchcraft (*bruxaria*) and sorcery (*feitiçaria*). Clearly these concepts are not identical, but they can be approximately translated across cultures, if we are sensitive to the differences.

Thus, the evil eye, *quebranto, panema* caused by jealousy, by mistrust (or refusing food), by a menstruating or pregnant woman, the *parauá* transmitted by a grandmother to a granddaughter, spirit possession, a dolphin assault, the currents of the deep, would all come under the category of witchcraft (*bruxaria*), whether they are considered as *malineza* or not. All the above result from the intrinsic power of a causal agent. Sorcery (*feitiçaria*) is always intentional and malevolent. It does not encompass what is seen, in local terms, as good magic such as curing illnesses. Sorcery would be thought, then, as *malineza* par excellence, making itself known through spells, harassment and some form of *panema*, originating from the manipulation of external objects or the body of the causal agent and always concerned with the practice of evil.

This would be, however, too simple a definition of *malineza*. The concept should be deepened and developed. We have to consider the fact, as informants say, that at the moment the causal agent becomes aware of his previously unknown powers, his actions tend to be intentional. This consciousness makes it difficult to hold on to the difference between the intentional and non-intentional causing of harm and illness through inner powers, such as evil eye, admiration, mistrust and so on. In this sense the suspicion of the cause of *malineza* goes back, somewhat obscurely, to the angry and evil actions, arising from either the manipulation of external substances (which we could call sorcery, *feitiçaria*), or those resulting from the inherent power of the agent (witchcraft, *bruxaria*).

The concept of *malineza*, therefore, assumes a much larger role in the minds of the people that use it. Considering the sophisticated classification encountered in the Brazilian Amazon, it is a more wide ranging concept than that of *panema*, which is in effect only one form of the expression of *malineza*. Despite its more widespread academic attention, *panema* is part of a larger category, *malineza*, which should be the appropriate level of analysis, considering that it can result from sorcery, jealousy, menstruating or pregnant women. Indeed, for the people in Salgado region, the 'guilt' of the person who is a victim of *panema*, no matter how careless, should be qualified. Even in the case of a pregnant woman who eats a fisherman's or hunter's takings, the act of causing *panema* (what does not occurs in all cases) is fundamentally seen as a consequence of a kind of malevolent action of the foetus, as a being who is in process of formation, and whose potential danger is admitted not only in the Brazilian Amazon, but in other parts of the world].[12]

Besides, there are many ways of protecting oneself from evil. A person can recite 'God bless' which will neutralise the regard of others or oneself. This can be combined with various other practices; for example a pregnant woman can bite part of a game or fish catch, while it is still raw, in order to avoid *panema*. In other situations, it is enough to avoid the offending deed: expressions of jealousy and admiration, eating a catch if a woman is pregnant and so on. On the other hand, it is always possible to explain *panema* (and by extension other forms of illness or misfortunes of the same kind) through recourse to *malineza*. This clearly relates to the social system in non-metropolitan areas which is resistant to change, and where the sense of balance between local residents operates on the premise of limited good, the good fortunes of a single person coming at the expense of the majority.[13]

On the other hand, even though *malineza* can be provoked by apparently non-human (or imperfectly human) persons, such as enchanted beings or spirits, it is, at bottom, always a human action, inasmuch that the enchanted beings (even those of the forest) do not abandon their humanity in their world, the enchanted city, which is located at the bottom of rivers, in forests, on beaches and in swamps. The spirits who persecute and possess, as I have emphasised, are always seen as human beings (dead or living). In this sense *malineza* (evil and malevolence) following the cases of misfortune we have analysed (illness and sufferings and other afflictions of a non-natural order, which can also affect animals, plants and material objects) can be thought of fundamentally as diverse and diffuse pervasive forms of action of human beings against other human beings, within a relatively stable social system and one resistant to external influence. The

---

12   See Motta Maues (1993).
13   See Foster (1967); da Matta (1973); Motta Maués (1993); and Velho (1976).

hypothesis, for it to be further tested, should be examined in the light of the ethnographic material from other areas of the Amazon, not just regions dating from post-conquest occupation, but also recently colonised and transformed areas, such as the Amazonian frontier.

Chapter 7

The Peasantry and the Church on the Brazilian Frontier: The Significance of the Alliance and its Repercussions

Neide Esterci

Attracted by low land prices and tax incentives offered by the government, entrepreneurial companies from southern Brazil began to open up huge ranches in Amazonia from the late 1960s. The Friars of the Dominican Order, who had been involved in missionary efforts with the indigenous peoples in the south of the state of Pará since the late nineteenth century, perceived that this new drive for land ownership clashed with their own interests. It threatened both the indigenous communities and clusters of small farmers along the Araguaia River. The missionaries began to work more closely with other Roman Catholic priests and bishops in this region, advising the indigenous peoples and small-holders about the plans of these companies and sometimes supporting resistance against their commercial interests.

The local religious teams had other reasons for their alliance with the smallholders beyond the need to preserve their gains,. On the one hand, the parallel between the image of the smallholders threatened by a large enterprise followed the Biblical model of 'God's People' in search of the 'promised land'. This image was very dear to liberation theology, which began to guide significant sectors of the Church in Brazil and was quickly absorbed by the leading pastoral agents in the area. Drawn up on the basis of the Meeting of Bishops in Medellín (1968) this new theology drew heavily on the Book of Exodus for its inspiration. The manner in which the smallholders worked the land helped burnish this image, as their system seemed to be the opposite of the agrarian capitalist appropriation of land and other natural resources.[1] There were also strong ties between some members of the religious teams and the principles that guided the 'Economics and Humanism Movement', which originated in France and

---

1   In some regions of Brazil, there are groups of small producers whose forms of distribution and relations to the land and natural resources cannot be understood in terms of a notion of private property. Amongst these groups, the term property is used in a very different way, as seen in the rest of this and other chapters in this volume. The sense in this case bears some resemblance to the concepts of property as they have been found in Africa; see, for example, Bohannan (1963).

was active in Brazil. In the present case history, several initiatives were implemented in the sphere of production, although their effects were frequently more symbolic and political than material, helping boost the self-esteem of the smallholders and supporting their land rights' claims.

By returning to the history of this conflict, I try to rethink the basis of the alliance between the smallholders and the religious groups under the Roman Catholic Church which operated in this area. I wish to argue that this alliance played a key role in a broad-ranging network that extended beyond regional borders to reach even the highest echelons of the Roman Catholic Church itself in Brazil. Over the subsequent years this association had a decisive influence on the organisation of rural workers in Brazil, mainly through the Pastoral Land Commission (CPT — Comissão Pastoral da Terra) which was an entity established mainly through the initiative of Bishops and pastoral agents linked to Amazonia.

Peasant Organisations: Communities and Unions

In north-east and south-east Brazil peasants and rural workers had been involved in an expanding process of organisation and political mobilisation since the 1950s. They were supported by the Communist Party, which was striving to stir up local struggles and organise unions, and also by the Roman Catholic Church, which at that time was eager to block communist progress on the eve of Brazil's military coup in 1964. The result was the introduction of the first laws that guaranteed rural workers' and peasants' labour rights and freedom of organisation. There emerged an inclusive form of organisation that attracted members ranging from wage-earning rural workers to sharecroppers. The government of the day was also keen to implement agrarian reform and was supported by certain sectors of the bourgeoisie wanting to modernise rural production relationships in order to create markets for their products and guarantee the output of raw materials for industry and urban markets. A set of laws drawn up for this purpose, regulating access to land, had been under discussion, and in 1964 — during the first military administration — these laws were approved by the National Congress under the title of the Land Act (*Estatuto da Terra*).[2]

As the heavy hand of the dictatorship bore down on union leaders, it became impossible to improve on these laws or even to implement the rights that had been won. Although many trade unions had been set up, by

2   Gryzbowiski (1990); Martins (1985).

the 1980s, when the first commercial enterprises reached the borders of Amazonia, there were no trade union organisations underpinning the struggles of these smallholders and sharecroppers. The first trade unions were only set up later, triggered by the struggles for land, and with the crucial support of the Roman Catholic Church. Consequently, it was the communal networks that formed the foundations on which these smallholders and sharecroppers organised themselves along this economic frontier in order to challenge these new frontier enterprises and ensure they were represented before the authorities. But even after the trade unions were established, the networks played a supplementary role, as an institutional channel of contact with the authorities. The initiative for taking action in their own defence and claiming land fell to the smallholders and sharecroppers organised around their own interests and commitment to the struggle for land.

Background to the Clashes

Since 1955, the government of what was then Mato Grosso state had already begun to sell off huge tracts of government land to entrepreneurs and land dealers. These sales flouted existing laws and virtually ignored the presence of indigenous villages and the hamlets that were home to smallholders and sharecroppers, and even small towns. When incentives were offered to enterprises in the region, several farming and ranching projects were submitted to government agencies. From 1966 until 1970, 66 projects were approved.[3] The earliest clashes flared up in the north-east of the state, with widespread repercussions involving the residents of what was then the village of Santa Terezinha, today the municipal seat of the same name and the headquarters of the Araguaia Development Company (CODEARA — Companhia de Desenvolvimento do Araguaia), which was owned by entrepreneurs from São Paulo linked to the Banco Nacional de Crédito.[4] In 1965, these businessmen bought another enterprise consisting of some 169,497 hectares of land, which also included a village, together with the schools, churches, homes, crop-fields and orchards of its residents.

The disputes began the same year, peaking dramatically in March 1972, when a group of squatters clashed with company employees, leaving several of them wounded, including the ranch manager. This clash took place at the site where the vicar of Santa Terezinha had ordered an outpatient clinic to be built, a challenge to the enterprise which claimed that it was not

3   See Casaldaliga (1971); Davis (1977).
4   Dutertre, Casaldaliga and Balduíno (1986).

located in accordance with planning documents. As a consequence of this clash, army troops occupied the village and almost all its adult men had to flee into the rainforest, where they hid for over a hundred days in order to escape persecution by the military.

Government agents strove to speed up the demarcation process for family plots of land, the size of which was predetermined by regional planners. The enterprise was guaranteed ownership of the vast majority of these lands.[5] The French Roman Catholic priest was accused of subversion and tried in court where he was sentenced by a military tribunal to ten years in prison, and later expelled from Brazil under an agreement reached between the senior Church authorities and the nation's military government. One of the squatter leaders was jailed and beaten in the state capital, but was never taken to court. He was later released and sent back to Santa Terezinha. About a year later the military government turned its repressive tactics on other members of this religious group. Following the arrival of the other enterprises, fresh clashes flared up in other locations within the same prelacy. In these cases residents were also supported by the members of the Church, many of whom were jailed, interrogated and even tortured.

The Peasant Style of Land Tenure: the Meaning of the Alliance

The smallholders and sharecroppers had been living in this area since the early decades of the twentieth century and, until the 1960s, had never been challenged as to their settlement claims. Over time they had developed their own rules for access to and use of the land and its natural resources, including grazing lands, water sources, fruit-bearing plants and native medicines. They felt that dividing the land up into contiguous plots assigned to each family as stipulated in the Land Act of 1964 was an odd practice poorly attuned to their farming, grazing and extractivist activities. Each family took over on a permanent basis only the area where its home was built, together with the yard and orchard, which was the *property* of each family head. Every year small crop fields were prepared in other areas that remained under the control of the family only long enough to harvest the produce. These were the 'service areas' subject to temporary appropriation and could be taken over by other people once the last manioc roots — the plant with the longest cycle — had been harvested. There were also natural grazing lands that no one took over because they were designated as commons (*comuns* — that is they can be used by every household).

---

5   Similar processes occurred in the 1970s and 1980s over the whole of Brazilian Amazonia; see Davis (1975); Ianni (1978).

The squatters of Santa Terezinha were peasants, smallholders and sharecroppers. The word for squatters (*posseiros*) in Portuguese was initially introduced in the 1960s, when the first company arrived to designate a juridical figure subject to a special type of land right defined in the Brazilian Civil Law Code as differing from another type of land title, which is ownership. According to the official legislation in effect at that time, the land in this case would be subject to *de facto* expropriation — known as *posse* in Portuguese — which could develop into tenured ownership providing that a certain period of time went by with no legitimate challenge to this expropriation. However, in the course of these clashes, the meaning of squatter or *posseiro* was reworked into a self-classificatory political category that referred to a struggle over land. People committed to the fight were known as *posseiros* — as might have been expected.

In the peasant form of land tenure the landowners, or *proprietários*, were people whose efforts were reflected in the house, the garden and in larger cultivations that were already well established. The status of landowner or *proprietário* was less the outcome of a commercial transaction than the reflection of assets built up over time: 'This is a landowner (*proprietário*): I live here ... I have the orchard that is already grown, the banana trees and the house where I live — so this is my property.' (Mr Antônio, *posseiro*).

The length of time required to build a house and to plant an orchard and a banana plot matches the developmental cycle of the domestic group, as well as the maturation of social relationships, reflected in alliances of marriage, godparenthoods and neighbours. This process can also been seen as one of transforming a person into a dweller or resident (*morador*) of a place. Thus, a landowner was someone who had built up this status over time and through work, but people who arrived from outside claiming land obtained by purchase were called the owners of the land (*donos de terra*) and these capitalists, who had many assets, fenced everything in.

The idea of ownership (*propriedade*) in the code of the smallholders and sharecroppers also had its own specific characteristics in terms of the manner in which land was demarcated. Although more vague than the official code of fixing land boundaries, the mutually agreed boundaries to a plot of land among the smallholders and sharecroppers of Santa Terezinha was sufficient to establish the tenure rights of each of family. In addition to the house, the garden and crop plots, the orchard and the fallow area that had already been worked, a property also included areas that had not yet been worked but were kept aside for the future, as well as for logging the timber needed to repair the house and build fences. But no one should take over any tract of land and forest, including uncultivated areas, kept aside as reserves. These were subject to the calculations of residents who assessed their use according to the number of mouths they had to feed and the labour power in the domestic unit able to work. So if a family head attempted to keep more land than was rated necessary, the others would often say that he was 'devouring' or 'ruining' the forest.

This model was certainly shaped by local discourses, and advocated by the smallholders and sharecroppers through their spokespersons in the midst of the clashes with the outsiders. It was also reflected in linguistic categories and practices that followed an alternative to selfishness and exploitation associated with private property. This was certainly one of the reasons why this adapted so well to the Biblical models and the political and ideological ideals of the pastoral groups working in that area.

Closing off the Fields and Roads between the Village and the *sertão* Scrublands

Due to the type of agriculture they preferred, the *posseiros* of Santa Terezinha initially settled in the riverbank forests where they built their homes and planted their first crops. As the land lost its initial fertility and the forests grew sparser, they shifted further inland. On the lands that had already been worked, the village began to appear, set back from the riverbanks in the drier *sertão* scrublands, where other properties were being built.

Some *posseiros* began to plant in the *sertão* scrublands while keeping their old houses in the area where the village was developing, ensuring easier access to schools and shops. Others moved completely into the *sertão* scrublands, where they organised themselves into hamlets consisting of domestic units interconnected by links of godparenthoods and other relationships. This network of relationships served as a basis for sharing and exchange and provided mutual help and labour cooperation. Within the context of the conflict, the hamlets — each known by the name of the head of the domestic unit around which the others clustered — were strategic factors in organising resistance. Their importance varied according to various objective factors and their inhabitants's willingness to resist the threats of the company. All the hamlets spread out from the hub of the village were linked to it by roads and paths that were kept cleared by the residents.

The first clash was triggered by a fence that the enterprise built around the area left empty between the village and the *sertão* scrublands, blocking the traffic and forcing local residents to travel far longer distances from their *sertão* plantations to the trading centre in their home village. The *pos-*

seiros were angry, but seemed to accept the need to walk around the fence until the day when some brave soul decided to cut away the fence and leave a clear passage. The company called in the police, who tried in vain to force witnesses to reveal the person behind this action. In fact, it turned out to be the leader of the group.

The *posseiros* always found the fences built by the company to be inconveniently placed, and as a consequence some were cut. Many fences remained however, prompting disputes that dragged on for years. A full decade after the conflict ended the ranch fences were still perceived as a symbol of the domination of the company: 'There are gates and more gates ... This is the ranch dominating, it takes over everything, there are sentry-boxes everywhere.'[6]

The dispute over the area between the village and the *sertão* scrublands became even fiercer for other reasons. The squatters had left this land free, as it provided the main source of water for local residents, together with natural grazing lands and coconut groves. This was considered to be the 'richest land' and was defined as a common area where everyone grazed their cattle during the dry season and gathered straw to roof their houses, as well as berries and medicinal plants.

The company fenced in this area in order to build the ranch house there, but the squatters and the priest were willing to fight for it. With the help of a small French NGO, the priest acquired some equipment and the squatters got together to establish a huge plantation in the nearby forest, as a way of legitimising their claims over this desirable area.

In fact, many of the representatives of the state agencies who visited Santa Terezinha acknowledged that the claims of the squatters were reasonable and fair. There were some 140 families with around 400 registered head of cattle. Handing over the grazing lands and the water source to private ownership by the company would have impeded the productive activities of these small farmers and ranchers, but the correlation of forces favoured the company. The law was interpreted to guarantee *posseiros* only the right to family-sized plots of land. This meant they lost access to their main source of water, which was taken over by the company, together with natural grazing lands and the coconut groves, in addition to common forest. The only area of common use that was guaranteed was the village, and even so this space was very constrained, due to the company's eagerness to control access to the river.

6   Former Chairman of the Squatter Cooperative (1983).

The Struggle for Urban Space: Peasants Invade the Street

In 1967, tensions reached a peak when it was time to clear land to plant the new crops. According to the squatters, they were frequently involved in direct clashes with the company, generally defused by the priest who always attempted to settle disputes through legal means. The priest was also well aware that holding back on violence served the squatters well in negotiations with the state. Consequently, he went to the authorities and issued a threat: the squatters were 'desperately' awaiting government intervention and could interpret the silence of the authorities as permission to 'take matters into their own hands'.[7]

In June 1967, the mayor of the Municipal District that was home to the village of Santa Terezinha declared that 'felling was suspended ... not only by CODEARA but also by the squatters'.[8]

The accusations against the priest by the owners of the company prompted representatives of the senior security agencies to travel to the region this same year, and the priest wrote to his friends in France:

> Suddenly the peace of the sky above the Tapirapé village was broken by two bomber fighters flying low. It was 13 June 1967. Grasping a machine gun, a sergeant was ordered to keep watch over the aircraft parked on the ground. The terrified Indians fled. And an interrogation began immediately ... directed by an Officer of the Armed Forces sent by the Political Police and the National Security Service'.[9]

The owners of the enterprise were unhappy with the delays because, as already noted, they also had to stick to the schedule of activities that would give them the right to fresh cash instalments for investment, as stipulated in the contract they had signed with the State Credit Agency (the Amazonia Development Superintendency, SUDAM — Superintendência do Desenvolvimento da Amazônia),[10] so they turned to the authorities, particularly the National Information Service (SNI — Serviço Nacional de Informação), which was a powerful agent of repression during the years of the dictatorship, and active locally.[11]

7   See the report by Padre Francisco (François) Jentel; June 1967, archives, Santa Terezinha Parish.
8   Announcement of Tender issued by the Luciara Mayor's Office, 1 June 1967; archives, Santa Terezinha Parish.
9   Archives, Santa Terezinha Parish.
10   For a political analysis of SUDAM see Bandeira (1975); Cardoso and Müller (1977).
11   During the dictatorship guerrilla warfare linked to a breakaway group of the Brazilian Communist Party that sprang up not far away in Pará State (report by the company's directors to the SNI, 14 July 1967, archives of Santa Terezinha Parish).

Later in 1967, the conflicts remained unresolved and the squatters had not been able to plant their crops for the following year. The company then began to impose more pressure as it attempted to take over the urban area. Right from the beginning of the clashes it had become clear that in addition to the strategic value of access to the river port, everyone involved in this conflict also gave it political and symbolic value. The Church had its most important buildings (school, chapel, monastery) located at a point that was targeted by the company, on top of the only hill in the neighbourhood, right on the riverbank. It was suggested that the Church and all the residents of the village and the *sertão* scrublands should move upstate, leaving vacant the areas alongside the river. The company offered them a cleared area called the Jatobá Settlement Hub (Núcleo de Colonização Jatobá) that included an urban area and rural plots of land. The squatters and their allies turned this suggestion down flat, for reasons that are easy to understand. In addition to the material losses, the distance from the only access to and from the village, the river, was too great. It would also mean giving up the place that bore the name of the local patron saint, which the company had taken over, calling its ranch the Fazenda Santa Terezinha. Finally they would forfeit their status as *posseiros*, which they had used to their advantage in the course of their struggle, instead of being mere settlers (*colonos*).

In 1968, soon after the first clashes in the rural area, the company registered a plan for the future town of Santa Terezinha at the mayor's office and signed an agreement over town planning works with the local authority.

Local residents were banned from repairing their homes in any way. At the same time the company began to offer small amounts of cash in compensation for leaving the village. This coercion began along the two streets offering access to the river ports, which were the only routes for goods to enter and leave the village. In one of these streets almost all the residents bowed to this intimidation and left their homes. In the other, which had a few shops and older residents with more resources and stronger roots in the area, these pressures failed to produce much effect. For instance, one of the squatter leaders lived in this street. He had moved to this region as an employee with the first company back in the 1950s and had stayed on, and he had become a friend of the priest. In fact, after the priest, he was the person held in highest regard by the *posseiros* and identified as the ringleader by the company. At one point, there was an encroachment on his property. The priest reacted as expected, in view of the importance of the leader: he chartered a small aircraft like those habitually used by the ranchers themselves and flew many kilometres to seek a judge in order to block this intrusion.

Power of Priest

As the pressures on the local residents continued, the priest decided to transfer the outpatient clinic and the school from the top of the hill in the old church building to a plot of land he had acquired in one of the main streets of the village. The company opposed the construction of these facilities, claiming that they did not conform to their plans for the future town. In February 1972, as soon as the cement foundations of the project had been poured and the building materials stored on the plot of land, a group of company employees, including the manager, broke into the premises and destroyed the foundations and all the equipment.

The priest then had to accept the will of the people, which was to defend the construction project by force. At the same time, he forwarded a signed petition to the judge, justifying the protection of the project under the claim that he was advancing the interests of the local residents. Immediately, messages began to fly back and forth across the village, claiming that the squatters were going to protect 'the Padre's building' and that CODEARA would destroy the project as often as required.

For the first time the squatters left the forests to face up to the company in the village with their hunting and agricultural tools, encouraged by the members of the pastoral team. They were steeled to spend five or six long and tension-filled days waiting for the announced invasion by the company employees. With some of them hiding behind a banana grove and others crouching behind two empty kerosene drums, others dug a trench for protection. On 3 March 1972, two military police captains arrived at the construction site, together with five soldiers, the CODEARA manager and a further ten or 12 armed employees. The police issued a warrant for the arrest of the construction workers and were about to tie them up when shooting broke out. Which of the two sides was the first to shoot, who among the trespassers was armed, how many men had dug into the building yard are matters that are still controversial. But the fact is that a squatter organisation took the trespassers by surprise, ensuring that no one was hurt among the building site guards, although there were several people injured among the invading forces.[12]

This episode plays such a leading role in the experience of the squatters that many of them said that it was the most important event in their lives. Every squatter talks about this episode in the first person, placing themselves in the centre of a small scene and expanding their narratives, based on their own experience.

12 Canuto (1972), p. 33.

A Church on the Frontier

Until the late 1960s, north-eastern Mato Grosso and southern Pará states formed the vast territory of the Conceição do Araguaia Prelacy. It was only later divided up to form the new São Felix do Araguaia Prelacy in what is now Mato Grosso State. As stated earlier, missionaries belonging to the Dominican Order had built the facilities needed to support their work converting local indigenous tribes. These facilities were built on the lands where the village of Santa Terezinha was forming, on a hill known as the *Morro de Areia* on the bank of the river. In 1954, when the first company arrived and acquired the Santa Terezinha land, the area where these facilities had been built was disputed by the company, due to its strategic location near the river port. This dispute was only settled ten years later when another company took over the lands and once the Church had managed to ensure that its property rights to the buildings were recognised in a court of law.

The Church was soon to become involved in another dispute, this time over the lands where the Tapirapé indigenous village was built. A group of missionaries from the Order of Foucault, who had long been working with the Tapirapé, was joined in 1954 by a priest who was to become famous, Padre François Jacques Jentel. At that time the Tapirapé were severely debilitated in physical, social and cultural terms. Many of them had died while others had scattered into the rainforest, under attack from another indigenous nation — the Kaiapó. When the survivors finally gathered together near an outpost run by the Indian Protection Service (SPI — Serviço de Proteção aos Índios, which later became FUNAI) on the bank of the Tapirapé River, this tribe had shrunk to a mere 30 people.

The priest had a definite way of exercising his skills. A deft mechanic, he enjoyed assembling and dismantling engines and machinery and soon began to introduce initiatives designed to improve the living conditions of the Tapirapé — a farming people who were finding it hard to survive. The style of this priest was well adapted to the purposes of the Economics and Humanism movement (Economie et Humanisme) established during the 1940s by another French priest, the Dominican Louis Lebret, who visited Brazil on many occasions and set up an office for the movement in São Paulo. Its target was to find a type of economic development offering an alternative to both capitalism and communism — a Roman Catholic 'third way'. In order to bring in the funding needed to underwrite his project (in the indigenous village and later in the hamlet of Santa Terezinha as well), this priest called on his friends in France, who were able to establish a small association to bring in the funds needed for the project. In Brazil physicians, engineers and other practitioners linked to the Economics and Humanism movement organised the Association for the Development of the Araguaia Valley (ADEVA — Associação para o Desenvolvimento do Vale do Araguaia) in São Paulo for the same purpose. Padre Francisco was praised in the Brazilian press for his entrepreneurial spirit and dedication to fostering economic progress and improved living conditions for the local residents.[13]

However, the lands on which the Tapirapé village was built were all included in the area of 1.3 million hectares that was claimed by the Rio de Janeiro-based Araguaia Village Real Estate Company (CIVA — Companhia Imobiliária do Vale do Araguaia), on the grounds that it had been acquired from the State of Mato Grosso. This was the start of a merciless battle, initially with the directors of the company in Rio de Janeiro and the authorities in Brasília, fighting to acknowledge the legal status of Indian lands and to demarcate their borders. Padre Francisco drew up maps that he took to the National Indian Foundation (FUNAI — Fundação Nacional dos Índios), the government agency that replaced the old Indian Protection Service (SPI). As nothing was resolved, he began to demarcate the indigenous lands on his own initiative, in conjunction with the tribespeople.

A Brazilian bishop who had studied in France, the Reverend Tomás Balduíno worked closely with the French priest during this struggle, initially as the Apostolic Administrator of the Conceição do Araguaia Prelacy and then as the bishop of a nearby diocese in neighbouring Goiás State. Having become aware of the plans of the company, the Reverend Tomas Balduíno, who by then had already been appointed bishop, suggested to Padre Francisco that he should move to Santa Terezinha. Once installed, the priest then managed to cut a narrow road through the forest between the indigenous village and the hamlet where the *posseiros* established the Araguaia Mixed Farmers' Cooperative (Cooperativa Mista de Produtores do Araguaia) in 1965, and had 128 members by the following year. This cooperative played an important role in the dispute with the company and, with the support of his ecclesiastical superior, the priest attempted to strengthen local economic development, also making good use of his French friends for this purpose.

Political and Institutional Repercussions

Meanwhile, Bishop Balduíno was building up links with other pastoral groups in the region. A small four-seater aircraft had been donated for his travel requirements, giving him access to the immense area that constituted

13   *O Estado de São Paulo* newspaper, 29 August 1964.

the three neighbouring ecclesiastic administrative units: São Felix do Araguaia (Mato Grosso State), Conceição do Araguaia (Pará State) and Old Goiás (Goiás State). A Spanish priest, Pedro Casaldaliga, was appointed to the São Felix do Araguaia Prelacy in 1968, with no intention whatsoever of getting involved in matters that were not strictly religious. However, Padre Casaldaliga was soon converted to the cause of the indigenous peoples, smallholders and sharecroppers. With Bishop Balduíno and other bishops a group was formed that challenged the policy of Brazil's military government and denounced the practices of the new large-scale landowners in this region, not only in terms of the smallholders and sharecroppers, but also in terms of the manner in which they treated labourers such as ranch hands.

The efforts of these priests and bishops soon became famed both nationwide and internationally. The charisma of priests such as Padre Pedro Casaldaliga, the political dynamism of Bishop Balduíno and the dedication of Padre Francisco (François) Jentel, as well as the significance of the resistance movements among smallholders and sharecroppers soon drew in other religious leaders and leftist lay militants who were welcomed by local groups. During these repressive times, people of diverse political slants found shelter under the protective cloak of the Church, a fact that is reflected in the phrase 'umbrella of the Church'. The manner in which Padre Francisco (François) Jentel acted — striving to create economic alternatives for indigenous peoples, smallholders and sharecroppers, often undertaken on his own initiative and a step ahead of measures undertaken by those more directly connected — was challenged by some who called for local initiatives that were more political and secular.

However, regardless of the pragmatic stance of the priest, matters were somewhat different in the case of the Santa Terezinha Cooperative with weak interest in political activism. The priests's group's importance in these disputes was due far more to its political and symbolic efficacy than to its economic function. In fact, for the smallholders and sharecroppers, the Church offered a space for organising and meeting, where group decisions on their actions during the conflicts could be made. As the group lacked trade unions or any other type of organisation, the Cooperative also served as a form of representation for the group when these smallholders and sharecroppers had to address the authorities and face up to their opponents. The fact that it had 128 members in a hamlet of 200 homes legitimised its status in the eyes of these smallholders and sharecroppers, and insofar as it appeared to increase their productivity, offered proof as to the effort invested in the lands that they claimed as their own.

Despite all this, there was a clash between the purposes of the priests and the way in which these smallholders and sharecroppers viewed the Cooperative. For instance, the priests insisted that the Cooperative should be run by the smallholders and sharecroppers, yet the latter always called it 'the Padre's Cooperative'. Furthermore, they remained tied to a system of giving and receiving personal favours, guided by signs of affirmation or denial of loyalties, as well as trust between themselves and the priests, or the employee responsible for its administration and accounting. Moreover, the Cooperative remained in operation for over 20 years, yet it did not manage to be economically independent during the 'crisis' period, depending on financial support from the association of the French friends of Padre Francisco (François) Jentel.[14]

Another battlefront for the bishops, priests and laypeople involved in these conflicts in Amazonia was within the Church itself. The locally engaged clergy tried to heighten awareness among the members of the religious hierarchy, urging them to take supportive measures, but this was not an easy task. On being consecrated bishop of the São Felix do Araguaia Prelacy in 1970, Padre Pedro Casaldaliga wrote a personal letter in which he denounced the violence of the enterprises and police against the indigenous tribes, smallholders, sharecroppers and workers hired to establish the ranches in this region. This document 'expressed the political and theological grounds and reflection of a pastoral practice already under way'.[15] It prompted indifference from the higher clergy, to the extent that it was only published the following year as part of a larger document, under the title of 'A Church in Amazonia in conflict with large-scale land ownership and social marginalisation'. But the letter written by Bishop Casaldaliga was not an isolated fact, as 'similar pastoral processes were being experienced by other local churches …'[16] Progressive bishops in other regions soon began to take similar initiatives. In 1972 a letter from the south region was released entitled *Testemunho de Paz* (Witness of Peace), followed by letters from the north-east region in 1973, entitled *Eu ouvi os clamores do meu povo* (I Hear the Calls of my People) and the centre-west region entitled *Marginalização de um povo, Grito das Igrejas* (Marginalization of a People, the Shout of the Churches).[17]

---

14   In other papers, I had the opportunity of examining these and other issues related to the practice of the Church in terms of smallholders and sharecroppers, see Esterci (1987).

15   Poletto (1997), p. 31.

16   *Ibid.*, p. 31.

17   Casaldaliga (1997), pp. 79–80.

The more progressive Roman Catholic Bishops in Brazil — who included those mentioned above — formed an active and persuasive minority within the National Council of Brazilian Bishops (CNBB — Conselho Nacional dos Bispos Brasileiros). This was due to the fact that they had elaborated a much superior body of theoretical reflection in both theological and ethical terms. They also gained legitimacy from their first hand experience of the repression (even martyrdom) that was then assailing religious leaders in other regions, some of whom were accused of links to urban guerrilla movements. This generated an increasingly strong feeling of unity within a Church with some of whose internal rifts would lead some to confront the military government. Among the priests and other religious leaders jailed at that time, some belonged to the Dominican Order, like some of the more active bishops in Amazonia (Conceição do Araguaia and Marabá, Pará State) and neighbouring dioceses (Velho Goiás and Porto Nacional, Goiás State). This progressive minority soon became acknowledged and its arguments gained prominence, standing out from the voices of some 250 bishops in the National Council of Brazilian Bishops (CNBB), although they accounted for just over ten per cent of its membership.

In 1972, urged by the bishops and priests of Amazonia, the Indigenous Missionary Council (CIMI — Conselho Indigenista Missionário) was set up in order to handle pastoral activities among the indigenous peoples and defend their lands against the encroachment of companies buying up land in Amazonia. Helping establish this new entity were Bishops Tomás Balduíno and Pedro Casaldaliga. The leaders of the bishops of Amazonia were to take further action in order to obtain the support of the higher echelons of the clergy in the ecclesiastical entities in order to underpin their proposed pastoral activities. Every year the National Council of Brazilian Bishops (CNBB) met (and still meets) in the town of Itaici in São Paulo State. Each year, this assembly issues a document expressing the position of the bishops on social matters that are rated as relevant and on which the bishops feel that the Church should make its position clear. By the time of the 1974 Assembly, Bishop Casaldaliga and his Church were undeniably intimidated by the repressive actions deployed against them. The activist Padre Francisco Jentel had been sentenced to ten years in jail by a military court in 1973, immediately sent to prison in Cuiabá, Mato Grosso State to complete his sentence.

In subsequent years military repression affected the religious and secular alike in the São Felix Prelacy and many citizens were taken prisoner and tortured by government troops. The bishop himself was placed under house arrest. Despite great differences in the social positions, this attack on a senior member of the Church hierarchy led to a greater sense of unity within the Church. It was within this context that the bishops met at Itaici, and heard the evidence of Bishop Casaldaliga of the 'violence against the rights of the people' and the 'repression against pastoral agents'.[18]

During the subsequent decades, the Pastoral Land Commission (CPT) has had a decisive influence on the rural workers' trade union movement. Particularly in areas where conflicts had flared up over land, the CPT has encouraged the introduction of trade unions, or encouraged the emergence of new leaders, who have begun to challenge the boards of the less aggressive trade unions and sometimes replaced them. The CPT and the leaders shaped by their new political experiences soon began to challenge the guidelines of CONTAG, accusing it of reformist attitudes. Established only two months before the military coup in 1964, CONTAG was linked more closely to the struggle of wage-earning field-hands on the sugar-cane plantations rather than *posseiros*. It had developed a stance based more on prudence and a tactic of addressing the higher levels of the organisation itself and the government, in its attempts to settle the conflicts that flared up through legal means. In turn, the CPT was accused of highhandedness and radicalism, while demanding that CONTAG focus its efforts on 'working its bases' in order to become more directly involved in the struggle, and to denounce its trade union practices as legalistic and even negligent.

During the 1980s the presence of the Pastoral Land Commission (CPT) and other pastoral organisations linked to the dioceses proved a powerful factor in the organisation of movements such as the MST, which originated in southern Brazil, as well as those affected by major government projects, such as dams for hydro-power complexes. It should not be thought that the CPT has had equal power and influence in all regions, but as a church body it is linked to the most remote parts of Brazil. Even though the movement consists of different organisations which have sprung up under the auspices of the CPT, it remains today a powerful reference point for rural social movements. But there is no denying the links between the CPT and the region and the specific issues which gave rise to its development. The headquarters of the CPT have always been in Goiás, and its leaders have always included a large number of members of the Church in Amazonia.

Conclusion

I have shown how the disputes between large-scale enterprises and the smallholders and sharecroppers in a region of Amazonia formed the core

18   Poletto (1997), p. 34.

of a broad-ranging network built up among the agents of the Church itself, which had nationwide repercussions in subsequent years. I suggest that there were political and symbolic motives that involved concepts of economic development, the meaning of control over certain tracts of land, the take-over of the names of both saints and places, and above all a new theological concept based on solidarity with the oppressed, in this case, the indigenous peoples and the *posseiros,* instead of the elites with whom the Church had been allied in the past.

If the project drawn up by those working in this area was successful, the same cannot be said about its efforts to train peasant leaders elsewhere in the Santa Terezinha region. Many other land disputes have taken place in Amazonia during the 1970s and 1980s and have shaped leaders among the smallholders and sharecroppers later to become trade union bosses or party-political heads. These developments have taken place in southern Pará, where the Brazilian Communist Party (PCdoB) has been very active, although hidden under the 'umbrella of the Church'; they also occurred in the north of the State in the municipality of Santarém, where an NGO was active, in addition to the Church. More recently, peasant leaders have emerged from rubber-tree groves of Acre State following the martyrdom of rubber-tapper Chico Mendes, as well as others. However, no leaders appeared from the clashes in and around Santa Terezinha. The pastoral agents themselves and the Roman Catholic lay workers who were active in this area, whether or not they belonged to any political organisation, asked themselves why, but sadly no reply is forthcoming. Some people assign this fact to the type of rela-tionship — 'paternalistic' to its detractors — that Padre Francisco Jentel established with the smallholders and sharecroppers. However, others recall that many of these smallholders and sharecroppers were forced off the land when they lost access to their grazing areas and sources of water for their cat-tle, trapped on small plots of land that were at times located on soil that was useless for planting crops. What can be said is that in the municipal elections held in subsequent years, the most progressive candidates, backed by the Church, attracted the votes of the smallholders and sharecroppers. Many of these candidates were elected to municipal positions.

CHAPTER 8

Of Rum and the Amazon:
The Traditional Sugar-cane Industry and its Demise

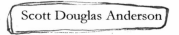

Scott Douglas Anderson

To be master of a sugar mill is a title to which many aspire, for it brings with it being served, obeyed, and respected.

Antonil (1711)

Introduction

Sugar-cane entered the Amazon with the first Portuguese colonists and it has been grown and processed in the region since that time. Despite this long history, the sugar-cane industry in Amazonia has largely gone unnoticed and unstudied, except for the mention of sugar-cane mills, or rum, by travellers and local chroniclers. The inconspicuousness of the industry may be due to the attention drawn to more dramatic events, such as the *Cabanagem* revolt and the Rubber Boom. Its persistence in the face of those events is due to the ongoing need it steadily met in the region over centuries.

The sugar-cane industry has historically been a significant presence in its own right in Amazonia. It employed a system of production remarkably adapted to the particular natural environment and social demands of the region. Its influence extended far beyond the local rural society that it directly sustained. Its recent history elucidates processes occurring throughout the region.

This study presents an overview of the sugar-cane industry in traditional Amazonia. To begin with, it highlights basic features of the production system as it emerged in the 1930s and 1940s after the rubber boom. Drawing on written and archaeological evidence, it calls attention to the important role that the industry played in the region. In this context, the recent history of the industry is traced, from its rapid expansion and brief period of classic production to its demise. Finally, the chapter seeks underlying causes for the decline of the industry and then relates them to the end of traditional Amazonia itself.[1]

---

1   This chapter is based largely on fieldwork carried out between 1985 and 1989. For fuller documentation and references, see Anderson (1993).

The Production System

The sugar-cane production system was shaped by features of the natural environment, customary economic and social relations in the industry and the historic demand in the region for rum.

The Natural Environment

The high floodplains along rivers and streams near the mouth of the Amazon offer unusual conditions in which to grow sugar-cane. Because of the immense volume of water flowing into the ocean from the Amazon, lands near its mouth are flooded by freshwater and not saltwater tides. Flooding of the high floodplains occurs some 20 to 30 times in the rainy season, near the March equinox and, in some years, five to ten times in the drier season, near the September equinox. During these periods, the high tide covers the land with up to 50 cm of water, generally for less than two hours. This tide-driven flood regime is distinct, therefore, from the great annual rain-driven flood along the main stem of the Amazon, which can be metres in height and last for months.

This regime combining freshwater and tide-flooding has a number of consequences. Floodwaters deposit sediments on the soil surface that contribute to maintain its fertility. The large volume of rain and tide water that flows off the floodplains creates a dense system of streams that cuts through them. These streams facilitate drainage, so that the soil does not become saturated even after flooding. On the other hand, when the tide does not cover the land, it still penetrates the floodplain through these streams twice a day and maintains the humidity of the soil even in drier periods. And by channelling the inflow and outflow of the tide, these streams provide access and facilitate transport to and from all parts of the floodplain. Taking advantage of these natural conditions, farmers have planted sugar-cane on these lands since colonial times.[2]

The Growing of Sugar-cane

In the 1930s and 1940s, production of sugar-cane was concentrated in the municipalities of Igarapé-Miri and Abaetetuba (See Figure 8.1.) There, on the high floodplains, farmers cleared fields in forest or regrowth with axes and machetes. They used the usual slash-and-burn techniques of the Amazon, except that before burning they removed much of the wood to

2   Daniel (1757-76), vol. 1, p. 384; vol. 2, p. 25.

sell to cane mills for fuel. Fields ranged in size from patches to nearly a hectare. Farmers planted the fields with cane tops inserted in the ground irregularly, roughly a metre apart. The variety of cane they planted, known locally as *caña branca* or *cana caiena,* was Bourbon cane, dominant throughout the world in the nineteenth century. Farmers limited cultivation to one or two weedings with a machete and partial replanting after harvest. Generally, farmers kept a field in production for three to six or more harvests, until yields fell and weed problems grew, and then left the area fallow for at least five years (See Figure 8.2.)

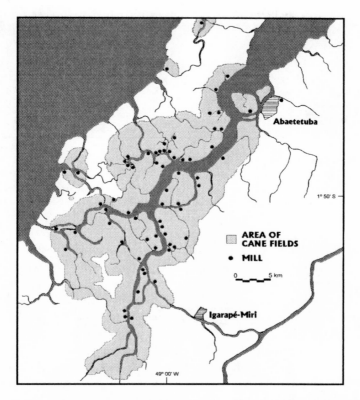

Figure 8.1: Map showing the extent of lands used to plant sugar-cane on high, freshwater-tide-flooded lands in Igarapé-Miri and Abaetetuba. Not all land eventually used was under cane at any one time because of fallowing and changing demand. The extent of land used for cane was determined from air photographs taken in 1977. Also shown is the location of sugar-cane mills when their number peaked at about 65 around 1960. The distribution of mills in the 1930s and '40s was roughly the same, but with less than 30 mills. Mill locations were determined by field surveys.

Figure 8.2: A sugar-cane farmer in front of one of his fields at high tide. The cane is plant-ed on the high floodplain bordering the stream. The variety of cane is the traditional one, Bourbon cane, known locally as *cana branca* or *cana caiena*. It is about six to seven months old and 'closing in'. It will be ready for cutting at 12 to 18 months. (Shown is 'Zecão' Pinheiro near the mouth of the Uruá River in 1987.)

To cover the expenses of preparing and cultivating a field, farmers could obtain advances from the owner of a sugar-cane mill. Millers made advances in goods, available at the mill store, to maintain the farmer and pay his day labourers. In exchange, the miller expected the farmer to deliver all the pro-duction of the field whenever requested. Being a personal relationship that required considerable integrity as well as management skills, only around a tenth of the farmers received such advances, which enabled them to produce about half of the cane, overall. Those farmers without advances or resources of their own, except time to plant small plots of cane, were relegated in large part to working as labourers in the fields or mills.

Access to land was not a constraint on farmers. In contrast to major cane-producing areas in Brazil, millers did not control suitable land, which was abundant. The many small landowners in the region sought rents, and it was common for farmers, even when landowners, to use the land of oth-ers. By custom, the farmer compensated the landowner with a third of the cane produced at each harvest, less its cutting costs.

Harvest, Transport and Settling Accounts: the Frasqueira

Farmers harvested sugar-cane year-round. Unlike other parts of Brazil, there is no season on the floodplain sufficiently dry or cool to curtail the growth of cane, stimulate the concentration of sugar in the stem and improve its quality significantly for processing. Because of this continuous harvest, the agricultural population was stable with its activities and income distributed throughout the year.

A cane field was ready for harvest every twelve to eighteen months. At harvest, any reliable farmer could get a short-term advance to cover the costs of cutting from a miller who needed cane. Farmers never burned fields before cutting, as is common elsewhere in Brazil, because fallen cane leaves retain sediments and keep down weeds. Rather, workers with machetes cut down the stalks, stripped them of their leaves, removed the tops for planting, and chopped the stems into pieces four spans in length. They then laid the pieces into standard-size piles, containing the volume of one hundred pieces of first-cut cane, and were paid by the farmer according to the number of piles they prepared. Ten such piles made a *frasqueira* of cane.

Cane was transported in open wooden boats, which the miller sent out with the tide. Workers guided the boats to the field with sweep oars. On arrival, the workers carried each pile of cane from the field on their shoulders, loaded the piles into the boats until full, and then guided the boats back to the mill with the return tide. The miller paid them according to the number of *frasqueiras* of cane they delivered to the mill.

Each boat used for transport was identified by name and rated as having the capacity to carry a certain number of *frasqueiras* of cane. Millers rated a new boat publicly by loading it with standard *frasqueiras* until full and then chiselling marks amidships at the water line that corresponded to that load. From that time on, farmers and workers in the field used the marks to determine when a boat was loaded to its rated capacity in *frasqueiras*. This was essential to know, because a *frasqueira* of cane was the unit of measure for settling accounts between the farmer and the miller.[3]

Settling accounts between the farmer and the miller rested on the acceptance in the region that 'the miller has right to half the cane' processed in the mill. This meant that the farmer and the miller should

---

3   Measurements in cane fields and mills indicate that a *frasqueira* of cane weighs in the order of 500 kg. This is useful for comparing this production system with others, but is not for understanding the exchanges within the system, in which a *frasqueira* of cane might best be thought of as an *amount* of cane, which can be measured in terms of volume, weight or even number.

divide the final product equally. Possibly this practice dates to colonial times in Pernambuco and Bahia, when owners of mills were obliged to process the cane of farmers without mills and were compensated usually with half of the sugar obtained from each batch.[4] Such batch-division in kind, in equal parts, still occurs today in small raw-sugar mills in Ceará, an important source of migrants to the Amazon during the Rubber Boom.

In the Amazon, since the principal product was rum, not sugar, it was not convenient, or always possible, to follow the processing of a batch of a particular farmer's cane and measure its output. Processing took about a week and the miller might need to use the juice from the cane of more than one farmer to fill a fermenting tank completely. Thus, to divide the final product, it would be convenient, if not necessary, to determine a standard relation between a given amount of cane loaded in the field and the quantity of rum produced. Since farmers planted only one variety of cane and grew it under similar natural conditions, and since its quality did not vary seasonally, such a standard relation would be plausible to expect; since cane was transported in boats, it would be possible to measure the amount.

To facilitate the customary settling of accounts between farmer and miller, it is hypothesised here that at some time in the past they established a standard relation between cane and rum. This would explain the fact that farmers and millers in the region accepted that a *frasqueira* of cane produces 24 litres of rum, a quantity also known as a *frasqueira*. Thus, for each *frasqueira* of cane loaded in the field the farmer received half a *frasqueira of rum*, half of its standard yield. The farmer took his part in kind from the miller or, optionally, in credit at the mill store based on the current price of rum. From the farmer's part, a third, less cutting costs, would go to the landowner, if that were the case, and the miller would deduct whatever advances he had made to the farmer. By this customary arrangement, half of the product of the traditional production system was distributed to farmers, landowners and labourers in the fields.

The Manufacture and Marketing of Rum

Millers processed sugar-cane in small mills, generally located along principal waterways to give easy access to buyers who took their product (See Figure 8.1). The principal equipment of a mill consisted of a horizontal three-roller mill to crush the cane, open wooden tanks to hold the cane juice while fermenting, a copper and steel column-still, wooden vats to store rum, and a

4   Antonil (1711), p. 75; Boxer (1957), p. 141; Schwartz (1985), pp. 20, 296.

boiler and steam engine. The roller mills and stills used down to the present were state-of-the-art in the 1880s.[5] While steam powered the roller mill and still, human labour moved sugar-cane through the mill.

When the cane boats arrived at the mill, the workers who had brought them back unloaded the cane by tossing it, piece by piece, onto the river bank in front of the mill. There it was left in disorder to await grinding, usually done once a week (See Figure 8.3). On the day of grinding, mill workers re-piled the cane and carried it on their shoulders, as in the fields, into the mill. There, a worker hand-fed the cane, piece by piece, into the roller mill. Then one or two workers stuffed the ground stalks into baskets and carried them to sheds for drying. Some weeks later, workers carried this material back to the mill to use, along with wood from newly cleared cane fields, to fire the boiler. The juice extracted from the cane was pumped directly from the roller mill to tanks for fermenting.

Figure 8.3: Cane boats and cut sugar-cane thrown onto the bank in front of a mill to await grinding. These boats each have the capacity to carry five *frasqueiras* of cane. A *frasqueira* is the unit of measure for the transaction between the farmer and the miller. (Shown is the Engenho São Raimundo on the Maracapucu River in 1987.)

5   See Lock et al. (1885), plates II, III and figure 204.

Fermentation of the cane juice was a spontaneous process, that is, done by yeasts found naturally in the air, on the cane or in the tanks, and millers gave it little attention. When this ended, after four to six days, the resulting liquor was pumped to a column still. There, a skilled operator, often the miller himself, fed the still slowly and monitored its operation continuously. The standard strength for rum was 50 per cent alcohol. On leaving the still it flowed into a container so that the operator could measure and control output.[6] When the container was full, the operator tallied it and poured the raw rum into a closed vat, ready for sale.

Millers marketed their rum in bulk. The usual containers were bottles or casks of one, one-and-a-half, or two *frasqueira* capacity. Some millers sold part of their production in Belém, where it entered the long-distance trade up the Amazon carried in steamboats remaining from the rubber boom. But small-scale river traders took much of the rum right at the mills. They travelled in sailboats and took advantage of the flow and ebb of the tide near the mouth of the Amazon to reach their customers. As with cane farmers, river traders also received advances from millers, only in this case in rum. In exchange, they brought back agricultural products such as manioc meal and tobacco produced on uplands near the floodplains, salted fish from the lower Tocantins, jerked beef from the grasslands of Marajó Island, and additionally, manufactured goods that came by way of Belém, all of which millers used to stock their stores.

The Traditional Sugar-cane Industry

The participants in this industry pursued specialised activities and therefore were mutually dependent. Farmers depended on millers for advances, on landowners for access to land and competed among themselves for day labourers, who also had the options of working in the mills, planting cane at their own expense or exploiting local extractive products. Likewise, millers, who rarely owned land or planted cane, depended on farmers for their raw material and also depended on the traders to dispose of their product, selling in bulk largely at their port.

Still, the role of the millers in the industry was crucial because of their central position in the two cycles of exchange that drove it. In the external cycle, the miller exchanged rum with traders for food and manufac-

---

6   This also allowed the miller to determine, for his purposes only, the specific yield of the cane ground some days before; generally, one *frasqueira* of cane yielded 1.2 *frasqueiras* of rum, well above the standard relation.

tured goods to stock the mill store. In the internal cycle, the miller advanced those stocks to farmers and in return received sugar-cane to produce rum. These cycles were closed insofar as most of their resources, activities and products had their source in, and were destined to, the region near the mouth of the Amazon. In this way, the traditional sugar-cane industry, driven by these two cycles of exchange, operated in considerable ecological and economic equilibrium.

This industry, quite defunct in the 1930s and '40s, sustained a similarly isolated rural society. People paddled to town, in many cases less than once a week, and transport to leave the region was limited to slow sailboats or to steamboats that made only a few stops a month. Communication was by word of mouth, informed by an occasional newspaper for those who could read, with mail and telegraph service restricted to the two small towns of the region. Cut off in this way, some millers, despite personal and paternalistic traditions, were able to exploit farmers and workers without recourse in ways resented long after. However, it is important to note, in retrospect, that the difference in the quality of life between the town and the rural areas was *not* marked at this time: neither had medical assistance nor electricity. It was common for a woman to lose half her children to disease, if not her own life in childbirth, and malaria was present, especially in the towns. Certainly the city was a more lively place to live, but there everything had to be paid for with money. In compensation, in rural areas resources were largely unexploited and, so old people say, game, fish, shrimp and the fruit of their staple, *açaí*, were all plentiful.

Rum in the History of Amazonia

One of the most distinctive features of the sugar-cane industry in Amazonia was that it produced rum as its principal product rather than sugar. In major sugar-cane regions in Brazil and elsewhere in the world the chief object is to produce sugar, and rum is merely a by-product. Nevertheless, a number of historical references to the industry support the primacy of rum in Amazonia. A census in 1751 found, along with 42 small mills for making rum, some 22 full-size sugar-cane mills in private hands in Pará and 'that almost all are occupied in making rum'.[7] In 1849, on a visit to a plantation on the Rio Capim, Wallace observed that the owner 'made sugar and caxaça [rum], but most of the latter, as it paid best'.[8] Referring to Igarapé-Miri in 1898, a resident reported that the 27 steam-

7   Pinheiro (1751), p. 346.
8   Wallace (1889), p. 81.

powered, seven water-powered and five animal-powered sugar-cane mills there had produced at least 42,166 *frasqueiras* of rum that year [slightly over one million litres], but no sugar.[9]

Moreover, remains of old mills powered by the tide, some perhaps dating from colonial times, are witness by their number and size to the wealth and importance of the industry in the past. Some 14 have been found near Belém with extensive ruins of cut stone.[10] More recent remains of wood, at some 13 sites in Igarapé-Miri, attest to the existence of a later generation of less sumptuous mills.[11]

Yet, from statistical sources, the production from sugar-cane mills would appear to be relatively unimportant. Export records from Belém between 1756 and 1777 show sugar or rum as present in 15 of the 22 years but only in two anomalous years did their value exceed two per cent of the total.[12] A source for the years 1773 to 1818 indicates that the important products of the region, those that were exported at least, were *cacao* and rice, with some coffee and cotton, while sugar and rum were grouped with extractive production as secondary products.[13] Later in the nineteenth century, all other export products were gradually overwhelmed, of course, by rubber.

The output of the mills appears to be insignificant because the rum they produced was *not* principally for export. Rather, it was used to pay, in part, for the labour that produced the *cacao*, rice, coffee and cotton, and products extracted from the river and forest, including rubber. For example, before the expulsion of the Jesuits in 1759, a missionary observed of indigenous peoples that

> what they like best is fire water [*ágoa ardente*] distilled from cane, and for a bottle they will make great efforts. For this reason the best good that a white man can take on a mission to trade for [manioc] meal, etc., is *ágoa ardente* because the Indians will take [the meal] out of their mouth just to buy it...[14]

Nearly a hundred years later, in 1849, travelling up the Amazon with a river trader, Bates reported that

9   Oliveira (1899–1904), vol. 1, pp. 25–6.
10   Marques (1993).
11   Anderson and Marques (1992).
12   Dias (1970), vol. 1, pp. 317–59.
13   Barata (1915), pp. 3-10.
14   Daniel (1757–76), vol. 1, p. 216.

> just before dinner ... according to the universal custom on the
> Amazons,... we each took a half a teacupful of neat *cashaça*
> [rum]... and set to on our mess... [15]

Seen in this light, rum has been a constant presence since the formation of
Traditional Amazonia because it was something traders could offer indigenous peoples that they wanted, but could not make for themselves: the
Indian could be lured and cajoled with rum and brought into the commercial system of Traditional Amazonia, and then, along with iron tools
and weapons and other new needs, be kept there as a *caboclo*.

Thus, regionally-produced rum was an important instrument for the creation and maintenance of the economic system of traditional Amazonia. It
was one of the basic trade goods steadily going upriver, at least from the
1700s to the beginning of this study in the 1930s, and exchanged for what
the market happened to want that the *caboclo* could produce. Because of this
essential economic and social function, the sugar-cane industry in
Traditional Amazonia was able to adapt to changes in technology, labour
regimes and governments and to survive revolts, booms and depressions.
The sugar-cane industry of Igarapé-Miri and Abaetetuba was, for better or
worse, heir to that long and important tradition.

The Recent History of the Sugar-Cane Industry

From the 1940s the sugar-cane industry and region underwent changes that
closely paralleled those occurring elsewhere in Amazonia. The striking expansion of the industry followed by its even more abrupt decline is shown graph-
ically in Figure 8.4. When viewed from the perspective of participants in the
industry itself, key events in this process fell into three phases.

Expansion (c. 1945-1960)

During the Second World War, Amazonia was the target of two Allied
campaigns: the 'rubber war' to increase the production of that strategic
material, and, in support of the first, the combat of diseases with the
establishment of a rural public health service. These initiatives had a direct
effect on rural residents throughout the region. They resuscitated the
regional economy and population growth, following the decades of
decline and stagnation after the end of the Rubber Boom, and were maintained by the Brazilian government after the war.[16] This upturn was in

15   Bates (1892), p. 141.
16   Wagley (1964), pp. vii, 53–55, 301–2.

itself favourable to increased production in the sugar-cane industry and established the context for other changes that followed.

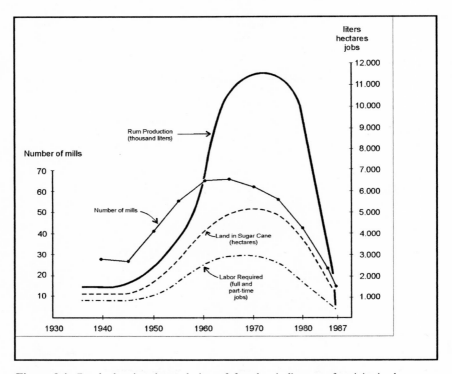

Figure 8.4: Graph showing the evolution of four key indicators of activity in the sugar-cane industry of Igarapé-Miri and Abaetetuba from the 1930s through the 1980s. The marked expansion and decline of the industry are evident. These figures are estimates based on tax records and on individual mill histories and capacities obtained from informants in the field. Published federal and state data on production based on aggregated estimates were considered to be less reliable regarding these indicators.

Expansion of the industry further accelerated in the late 1950s as river traders installed diesel engines in their boats and began to extend their operations up the river, encroaching on the long-distance trade carried in steamboats. At the same time, upriver, rural producers were increasing the exploitation of wild animal skins as well as production of a new, cultivated product, jute. The river traders, when going upstream, offered agricultural and manufactured goods from the lower Amazon, including rum, to local merchants as a short-term advance; when going downstream, they received other products, especially highly profitable skins, in exchange.[17] On returning to negotiate for rum with the millers, the traders now offered new products for the mill store, such as salted caiman and *capybara* meat, by-products of the trade in skins, and, thanks to sales to exporters, more manufactured goods and payments in cash.

The river traders steadily demanded more of the millers' rum because of their expanding operations, and the millers, in turn, demanded more cane. In response, farmers intensified their use of land, cutting existing cane fields more often and keeping them in production for more harvests. When farmers sought to bring more land under cane, millers could finance this from the steadily increasing flow of goods from the traders. This expansion also required and attracted additional labourers, who moved from the nearby uplands to work in the fields and mills.

To increase production of rum, millers had only to expand the capacity of fermenting tanks in existing mills to be able to grind cane more often than once a week. Nevertheless, at the same time, many people also took the opportunity to establish new mills. In particular, families in the region, even some who already had sugar-cane mills, worked throughout the period to build a number of small mills in succession, one of each for a father and sons or for several brothers. As a result, by about 1960 the number of mills had more than doubled, but, grinding just twice a week, they were operating only at half capacity. People insisted on building new mills that were underused, rather than allowing existing ones to expand production in step with demand, because of what it meant to be a miller in local society at that time. In this part of traditional Amazonia, millers with their crucial economic role and paternalistic authority had the highest social position, except for the priest and mayor, that could be conferred. Certainly it was the chance to achieve the status of a miller that had motivated so many people to build new mills.

Thus, in response to increased demand for rum, the industry realised remarkable sustained growth of over ten per cent per year for 15 years as output more than quadrupled. The capital for expansion came from the growing volume of business in the region, since there was no government or bank support for the industry. This did not require or employ technological innovations; farmers and millers simply increased the number of units in production without changing the nature of the industry.

During this period, Amazonia began to receive attention from other parts of Brazil. The federal government created a regional development

17 McGrath (1989), pp. 159–65.

agency (SPVEA later SUDAM), with funding guaranteed by the constitution, and reformed the war-time Rubber Bank as a regional credit bank, and later development bank (BASA). Most significant was the inauguration of the Belém–Brasilia Highway in 1960, which marked the beginning of the Brazilian effort to occupy its part of Amazonia effectively and incorporate it into the national economy. However, these events did not yet have a noticeable impact on the sugar-cane region. Rather, as part of the general economic upswing in traditional Amazonia, it was the expansion, of the sugar-cane industry that most affected local rural society, and the effect was certainly perceived as a positive one. Growing in size without changing its nature, the industry offered a steady, rapid increase in jobs and income for half a generation, distributed in the customary way among millers, farmers, landowners and labourers.

Classic Production (c. 1960–1975)

Beginning around 1960 some millers expanded the commercial scope of their operations by bottling the rum they produced. It was an easy innovation to put into practice, one that required only manual labour to fill and cork retail-sized bottles and to glue distinctive labels on them. This permitted millers to advance their rum to traders ready for the consumer, which added value to their output. Also, it gave the miller some control over quality, since traders could not easily dilute or mix it, as with rum sold in bulk.

The initiative of millers in bottling individually indicated a certain pride in product and an attempt to attract repeat customers. This occurred at a time when rural life was as yet largely unchanged, the relations between farmers, millers and workers were still close, and the income of all was growing. Marketing their product directly to traders under their own label, millers reached the height of their identity and independence, yet within the norms of the traditional mode of production. It marked a classic period of the sugar-cane industry and of the mills.

In contrast, two initiatives in the commercial area were taken to bottle collectively. First, a number of millers formed a cooperative to receive their product in bulk and bottle it, and eventually most millers became members, at least nominally. Later, individuals began to buy rum from millers in bulk, bottle it under their own labels and advance it to traders. By the end of the 1960s four such bottlers in Abaetetuba had become important buyers of rum.

Finally, in the late 1960s, the end of the isolation of the market was signalled when rum produced and bottled elsewhere, particularly in São

Paulo, was brought up by truck and became available in the region. This rum, which was sweetened, was not necessarily a better product, but was consistent. This was *not* a characteristic result of the spontaneous fermenting process used by the millers, which gave inconsistent results. To make things worse, millers would distil badly fermented batches, rather than take the immediate financial loss of discarding them, and the poor-quality rum produced, even if not bottled under the miller's own label, would eventually make its way to consumers through traders, the cooperative, or a local bottler. Given these practices, bottled rum from outside the region could certainly compete with local rum in terms of quality, if not initially in terms of price, and traders began to carry it.

Still, demand for regionally produced rum continued to increase. Millers met this now, not by building new mills, but by expanding their overall physical capacity and grinding cane more often, three or more times a week. To obtain the necessary cane, it had to be sought further from the mill, and millers installed diesel engines in boats to tow cane boats to and from the fields. However, the advantage of processing bigger batches was limited to a reduction in costs of about ten per cent obtained during the distilling stage of manufacture, since in the earlier stages handling cane continued to be a labour-intensive activity and fermentation technology, despite its manifest problems, continued unchanged. Because of these economies of scale, it became more difficult for individuals to start or operate small mills successfully.

Changes also took place in the agricultural sector as farmers adopted new varieties of sugar-cane, obtained by millers from the agronomic research station in Belém. These varieties, bred in the 1920s on Java, had the advantages to the farmer of requiring less weeding and replanting, of being easier to cut and pile, and of yielding up to 50 per cent more cane per area. This innovation did not prove to be advantageous to the millers, since their thinner and woodier stalks were harder to grind and yielded somewhat less rum. In any case, millers negotiated these varieties on the same terms as the traditional one, compensated in part by the smaller advances they had to make to farmers to produce the same amount of cane.

Overall, this period saw the continued growth in the output of the industry, at a reduced, but still respectable rate of 3.5 per cent per year. During this time the industry was physically restructured, as the number of mills passed its peak when many of the small mills closed while half increased their capacity. The modest economies of scale that millers could realise without technical change did not fully compensate for the decline in the yield of rum from cane, and a fall of nearly 20 per cent in the real price of rum. The decline in price suggests that the millers were also being challenged in these terms by rum produced and bottled outside the region, which traders increasingly carried.

During this period rural society began to notice outside influences as well. In the towns, electricity and running water were installed, as was a telephone service. Television arrived with programmes from 'the South'. Transport from the towns to Belém was no longer limited to trips three times a week, sleeping overnight in a boat; rather the trips became daily, by bus and ferry, and eventually took only three hours with the improvement of local roads. The tuition-free federal university in Belém increased enrolment, so that even children in the towns could aspire to study there, if their families could support them and afford their preparatory schooling. For the first time there was a marked difference between the towns and the rural areas in terms of quality of life and opportunities, and the rural areas had been left behind. There, the most noticeable change was in health, a consequence of government programmes and the appearance of wonder drugs available at pharmacies in town. As a result, the rural population continued to grow, but no longer because of migration, and at rates that now approached those of the sugar-cane industry itself.

Decline (c. 1975-1987)

In the mid-1970s the continuous expansion of the sugar-cane industry over the previous 30 years reversed abruptly. Practices of the millers were altered and their options constrained in ways beyond their immediate control. Traditional relations in the industry were broken, production virtually ended and most of the mills closed in just a little over ten years (see Figure 8.5).

The first imposition on the millers occurred after a Federal Labour Board was installed in Abaetetuba in 1973. The Board had the authority to act on the complaints of industrial workers against employers regarding payment of the minimum monthly wage and mandated benefits. Some workers now had recourse and between 1974 and 1981 mill employees made over 200 complaints against more than half the millers, who were brought before the Board and made to comply with the law. This increased labour costs in labour-intensive mills. To hold costs down in the short run, many millers deferred maintenance on their mills.

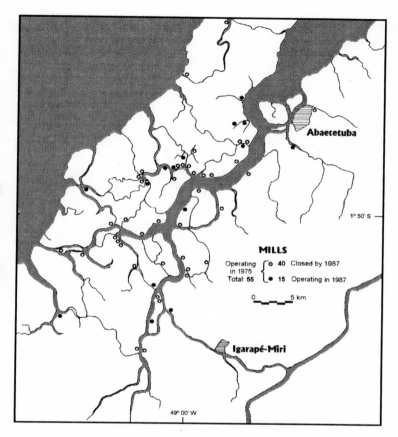

Figure 8.5: Map indicating mills that closed between 1975, when production was near its peak, and 1987. Of the 55 mills operating in 1975, 40 (open circles) had closed by 1987. The 15 mills (solid circles) still operating in 1987 were producing at about one-quarter of their capacity. By the early 1990s the industry has essentially ceased to function, resulting in the loss of almost 3,000 jobs in agriculture and industry.

More insidiously, high inflation rates began to undermine the exchange relations in the industry, driven as they were by advances in goods and product by the millers. Inflation worked to de-capitalise the millers, who were accustomed to settle accounts with historic values. With inflation rates over 100 per cent per year beginning in 1980 they could no longer compensate their loss by mark-ups at the mill store and profits on rum. The effects were graver in the agricultural sector, insofar as the amount of credit and time of repayment were greater. There, as millers lost working capital, they reduced advances to farmers for preparing new fields in favour of maintaining existing ones and eventually gave advances only for cutting cane.

Compounding these problems, in the commercial sector millers lost three of the four options they had to market their product. First, their sales in bulk to traders dwindled as consumers demanded a bottled product. Then, at the end of the 1970s the bottling cooperative expired, never having received effective support from its members during the heady days of expansion. Finally, and most critically, millers who bottled their own rum did not adhere to federal government regulations drawn up in 1975 for hygiene and mechanisation in bottling plants. These regulations were increasingly enforced after 1980 and culminated in the prohibition of the sale of tax stamps to millers who did not comply, none of whom did. Thus, by the early 1980s millers stopped bottling their own product, as all were forced to sell in bulk to local bottlers. This ended the last vestige of classic production with its possibilities of concern for quality.

Local bottlers, however, did not depend only on the millers for the rum they needed. Because they could not compete with outside rum in terms of quality, local bottlers attempted to compete in terms of price and sought only the cheapest available product. By the end of the 1970s this included buying rum in bulk in São Paulo and trucking it to the Amazon to be bottled. This reduced their demand for the millers' product. Moreover, as the commercial options of the millers became limited, local bottlers were able to impose depressed prices on them.

Adding to the millers' marketing problems was the general decline in the 1980s of the river traders, who moved almost all locally bottled rum, wherever produced. This happened as merchants along the Amazon became physically accessible to southern Brazil by means of roads and ferries and commercially accessible through the expanded telecommunications network and banking system. As a result, the traders' customers began negotiating products and payments directly with suppliers outside the region, without river traders as necessary middlemen.[18]

Finally, and most significantly, faced with rising costs and falling sales, the millers turned to the agricultural sector for relief and broke the traditional relations based on the *frasqueira*. In the late 1970s millers gradually managed to dissociate the price of a *frasqueira* of cane from that of rum, and began to pay lower prices for cane. Millers were facilitated in this imposition by rapidly changing prices during inflationary times, by diminished credit ties to farmers and by the existence of stocks of ripe cane that

18 *Ibid.*, pp. 304–14.

farmers had to sell. With this change, sugar-cane became a mere commodity, and farmers, landowners and labourers no longer had a guarantee to half of the nominal product of the industry. This marked the end of the traditional production system.

Appropriating more of the shrinking income of the industry for themselves did not address the basic problems the millers faced and could not keep them in business. Under these conditions, mills began to close, especially in the early 1980s as bottling requirements were enforced and millers were limited to selling to local bottlers. By 1987 almost three-quarters of the mills had stopped operating and total production was only five per cent of the peak. And by the early 1990s, although some mills might still be physically intact and occasionally be used to produce some contraband rum to sell in bulk in town or supply the few traders who were left, the industry had essentially ceased to exist.

The decline of the sugar-cane industry devastated the rural society that it had sustained. As many hundreds of jobs in the cane fields and the mills were lost each year, thousands of people moved to town to try their luck. Of those who stayed, some found informal jobs in improvised sawmills and brick factories that were expanding, in part to meet the demand for the construction of housing in town. Others gathered *cacao* and tapped rubber trees despite very low prices. Whole families dedicated themselves to making crude baskets from palms, sold to traders for insignificant prices, to be used in urban supermarket checkouts. Not surprisingly, rural residents exploited traditional food resources intensively: game became practically extinct; fishing yielded little; shrimp, instead of a complement to family diets, was captured to sell without regard for breeding season or size; and whole stands of *açai* palms were cut down to sell their hearts to canneries. The old abundance was over.

An Analysis of the Decline

Millers attributed the decline of the sugar-cane industry to the entry of rum produced outside the region with which they could not compete successfully. As to reasons for this failure, some millers cited the difficulties of grinding the new varieties of cane. Many millers were adamant that their problems started or were made much worse after the installation of the Labour Board in the region. Others felt that a key problem was the attempt of the local bottlers to compete only in terms of price with no regard for quality.

In seeking causes that lay behind this decline, it should be made clear at the outset that the industry did *not* decline because it could no longer physically produce rum or because there was insufficient demand for it. There is no evidence that the industry suffered from any type of internal collapse due to depletion of natural resources or to debilitating attacks from disease, pests or weeds. Land was abundant, naturally replenished by sediments, and its discontinuous use would tend to check biological competitors. Moreover, there was no external crisis due to a decreasing market for rum. Even if Amazonian consumption per capita were only half the national average, there would still have been regional demand for nearly twice the production of the industry at its peak.

In these terms, if the industry had stayed in isolation, it conceivably could have continued to meet regional demand indefinitely on its sustainable natural resource base. Thus, the building of the Belém–Brasília Highway, which opened the region to competitors' products, was a key factor that led to the decline of the industry. But the road was not sufficient in itself. After all, it is not immediately evident, or inevitable, that a bulky, inferior good like raw rum could simply be trucked almost 3,000 kilometres and compete successfully in a market because it was marginally superior in quality. This is even more problematic if the millers' competitors had to contend with the same kind of problems — technical, regulatory and commercial — that the millers themselves cited.

To unravel this historical process, it is necessary to identify the specific factors that led to the decline of the industry with the end of the isolation of the region. These include government actions or omissions that possibly affected the millers and their competitors unequally, the production and marketing situation of both in that context, the range of technical and commercial options available to the millers and finally the millers' response to the new reality.

The Role of the Government

Government intervention in the sugar-cane industry ignored the production of rum. Rather it was directed, from the mid 1960s, to an increase in the production of sugar and, from the mid-1970s, the production of alcohol to power automobiles. To do this the federal government centralised sugar-cane breeding and extension under the existing sugar and alcohol authority, subsidised production credit and upgraded mills. The objective was to sustain the traditional industry in the north-east and then stimulate the more dynamic one in São Paulo, while other parts of Brazil were left out. As a result, the meagre sugar-cane research and extension ended in Amazonia, while rum producers in São Paulo benefited from spin-offs such as abundant, good-quality cane and inexpensive second-hand mill equipment, which producers in the Amazon did not.

Other government activities, such as the installation of the Labour Board, touched on the rum industry more incidentally. This was the direct government measure which millers felt first and perhaps resented most, but actually traced its origins to urban industrial conflicts in the south-east in the 1930s and '40s and was applied there first. When competitors' rum began to appear in Amazonia in the late 1960s, producers in São Paulo were already paying up to the value of three minimum wages to their mill workers. Although this legislation raised the millers' cost for labour to at least one minimum wage per worker in the late 1970s, this was still well below the cost in the south.

Likewise, inflation was a product of government policies independent of the sugar-cane industry, but which began to impinge on those who financed crop production after the mid-1960s. Since such financing was done by banks in São Paulo, which had access to government loan subsidies, this did not burden rum producers there or limit sugar-cane production. In the Amazon, the reduction of advances to farmers by the millers, due in part to inflation, was potentially a serious limit on the industry; but, in practice, it did not affect rum production, since the rate of decline in the industry for other reasons was more rapid than the decrease in the availability of cane.

Finally, national beverage legislation, implemented in 1975 nominally to protect the consumer, certainly benefited major brand-name bottlers of both liquor and soft drinks based in the south. The federal inspectors who enforced the legislation sought only to prohibit unregulated bottling, as done by millers. They did not attempt to stop the millers from producing and selling rum to the bottlers in town, who were the points of concentration for inspectors to verify beverage quality. Non-compliance with beverage legislation removed the millers from the classic mode of production and relegated them to dependence on purchases by bottlers, but that situation also existed, by and large, for rum producers in São Paulo.

Perhaps the most puzzling thing about government posture during the decline of the industry, and the consequent loss of several thousand jobs, was the general indifference of officials within the region itself. Apparently only the low-level federal inspectors who prohibited bottling by the millers were concerned about the precarious situation of the mills and the serious economic and social consequences that their closing would have. They specifically alerted the mayors of the two towns to the gravity of the situation in the early 1980s but, to their surprise, this provoked little interest and no action on the part of local officials. At a state level, the planning and development agency, IDESP, virtually ignored the sugar-cane industry, and later its problems, in three different diagnostic reports touching on the region.[19] And federal sugar policies notwithstanding, the regional development agency and the development bank, as far as is known, never during this entire period gave any assistance, directly or indirectly, to cane farmers or to millers.

Production Systems Compared

A principal source of the rum that entered the Amazon region was produced in the state of São Paulo near Piracicaba. The sugar-cane industry there serves as a referent to attempt to discover why the millers failed to compete successfully with those in the 'south'.

In the agricultural sector, both land and labour were more expensive in the south and the technology employed to produce sugar-cane was quite different. Farmers used land more intensively and maintained fertility chemically. They made labour more productive by partially mechanising planting and weeding and, although cutting was still done by hand at harvest, by fully mechanising the loading and unloading of trucks used to transport cane to the mills. Although production per hectare was 35 to 50 per cent greater in the south, the final cost per ton of cane delivered to the mill was ten to 15 per cent higher, which actually placed the extensive agriculture of the traditional system in Amazonia at a slight advantage.

However, the higher cost of producing cane in the south was more than compensated for by the quality of the cane ready for processing. As measured by the concentration of sugar in the cane juice, in the traditional system in the Amazon, the *cana branca* varieties had about 11.5 per cent sugars and the new varieties only ten per cent; in the south with other varieties the value was in the order of 14.5 per cent. Thus, when millers were competing with producers in the south, the cane they received had only about 70 per cent as much sugar in the juice.

In the industrial sector, the difference in the quality of the raw material was accentuated by more efficient processes in the south to convert cane into rum. These included the use of three or more roller mills in tandem to grind cane, as opposed to single roller mills in Amazonia, which extracted only 80 per cent as much juice. But the most striking difference between the industries was in the method of fermentation. Unlike the spontaneous method used in the Amazon, the industry in the south used baker's yeast to start the process. This reduced the time of fermentation from between four and six days to 14 hours, yielded a more consistent and therefore higher quality prod-

19   Pará (1968, 1970, 1977).

uct and converted virtually all of the sugar initially present to alcohol, compared with only about 75 per cent in the traditional system. Because of these
factors, millers in the Amazon obtained only 40 to 45 per cent of the amount
of rum that producers in the south did from a ton of cane.

Given their technical efficiency, along with mechanisation in the mills
that offset higher labour costs, producers in the south manufactured rum
for about 35 per cent of the cost of millers in Amazonia. On the other
hand, the price of rum in the south was only about 40 to 50 per cent of
that obtained by the millers in the late 1970s. As a result, millers in the traditional system, despite higher costs, made a much greater margin per litre
than those in the south, because of the much higher regional price. But
that left them vulnerable if the price of rum were to fall and approach
competitors' levels. This is of course what happened when the millers were
forced in the early 1980s to sell to local bottlers who had already begun to
buy less expensive rum in bulk in the south.

In the marketing sector, bottlers, both in the south and in Amazonia,
faced problems of consistency and quality. One large bottler in São Paulo,
whose only concern was for the large, nearby markets in the south,
attempted to deal with this by purchasing rum in bulk from a limited number of the same producers every year, mixing, and incidentally aging, the
rum in storage before bottling, and, as mentioned, sweetening it. The bottlers in the Amazon, as far as is known, did not attempt any of these practices, but, by buying in the south, they may be seen as attempting to obtain
the same kind of rum as was becoming popular in the region, besides
obtaining a cheaper product. Moreover, in terms of cost, by shipping in
bulk and bottling locally, they could put rum from the south on the
Amazon market more cheaply than that transported in bottles from the
south. But what they bought was not of the same quality and consistency as
could be obtained by established bottlers in the south, so that their problems
along those lines continued and they opted just to compete in terms of price.

The demise of the sugar-cane industry in Amazonia was hastened by
local bottlers who discarded legal niceties and any concern for consequences: with the abundance of automotive alcohol in the south in the
1980s, some local bottlers began to buy it to concoct rum. This use of
alcohol was patently illegal and cannot be formally confirmed, but has
been reported so widely by knowledgeable individuals that the practice is
taken here as certain, despite federal beverage inspection. By doing just
that, bottlers could cut their transport costs by about half in relation to
rum brought up in bulk from the south. Ironically, this use of alcohol actu-

ally created a limited, but urgent, demand for the rum of the millers who were still in business, since, after diluting alcohol with water to obtain standard rum strength, the bottlers used local rum (and, it is said, black pepper) to flavour the final product. At this point there was of course no pretence to quality or of attracting repeat customers and the sales of the local bottlers, and so of the remaining millers, spiralled downwards, relinquishing the small, distant Amazonian market to outside producers.

Options Available to the Millers

Between technical inefficiency and domination by local bottlers, it would appear that the millers had little control over their destiny and the decline of the industry. Nevertheless, at the end of the period of 'classic' production in the 1970s, when the industry was still strong but competitors' products were beginning to appear on the regional market, were there no improvements that would have allowed the millers to become more efficient converters of sugar-cane to rum, and even to better quality rum? And later, was there no way they could have restructured their commercial relations, lessening their dependence on the bottlers, and so have continued in operation?

Introducing other varieties of sugar-cane was a possible improvement. To investigate this, a trial plot was established in 1987 in a long-fallow cane field with varieties of cane easily obtained at a research station in the north-east. Of 15 varieties tested, none showed signs of damage caused by pests, disease or over-wet conditions. Despite the poor conditions for ripening typical of the floodplain, three varieties had sugar concentrations above 14.5 per cent, the standard reported for São Paulo. Although these results are not conclusive, they do suggest that varieties adaptable to conditions of the floodplain and with higher concentrations of sugar in the juice, did indeed exist.

Improvements in fermentation offered the greatest return. Based on a study of a mill in operation, chemists at the Federal University of Pará recommended cleaning fermentation installations regularly to reduce contaminating 'natural' yeasts and starting the process with commercial baker's yeast, which is easily available in the towns of the region.[20] Such practices are commonly used by small and medium-scale rum producers elsewhere throughout Brazil.[21] The potential benefits would be great, both in raising overall conversion of sugar to rum and in improving the quality and consistency of the final product.

20   Menezes, Anderson, and Braz (1988), p. 16.
21   Valsechi (1960), pp.38–50.

New varieties of sugar-cane and baker's yeast are biological means that multiply naturally and would be inexpensive to implement. If they increased efficiency in the mill to standards common in the south they could have almost *doubled* the return from each ton of cane delivered and improved the quality of the rum produced at virtually *no* additional cost. The installation of roller mills in tandem would have been a more expensive innovation, but no more than installing motors in cane boats and certainly within the means of the millers at their peak. Clearly there were technical and financially viable improvements that could have brought the mills of the region to levels of efficiency similar to producers of rum in other regions. With the implementation of these innovations, and protected by lower transport costs, millers could have delivered rum to local bottlers with quality and consistency comparable to producers in the south and at a competitive price.

In terms of restructuring their commercial relations in order not to be dependent on the bottlers, the millers had three options. The first was an industry-wide bottling cooperative, which millers had formed and which, apparently by coincidence, closed shortly before the bottling regulations began to be enforced. The second was a more tightly controlled bottling arrangement formed among a limited number of millers, reminiscent of the time when family members supported each other to establish mills. The third was to continue independently and concentrate on quality, after meeting the government's requirements for bottling standards, which would have been less costly than the expansion of mill capacity that they had already realised.

There are examples of such successful independent rum producers, but not in the Amazon. For instance, in 1989, an agronomist in the state of São Paulo had been making high-quality rum, on a very small scale, for about five years. He did not produce his own cane, but bought it from suppliers. His continuous fermenting process, based on a 'start' of baker's yeast, was held to offer the means to guarantee not only quality but also consistency in the final product. After distilling, the rum was aged for a year, with two months in oak barrels to give flavour and colour. He produced throughout most of the year and his annual production was limited to 100,000 litres, that of a mill in Amazonia in the 1930s. He also satisfied the government bottling requirements. Even though his costs, including luxury packaging, might easily be double those of common bottlers in São Paulo, he was able to sell the high-quality rum he produced for almost 12 times more. He thus maintained himself in a situation comparable to the classic one of the traditional millers, in which he bought cane, manufactured and bottled rum individually with control over quality, and sold to distributors.

Thus, there were a number of viable technical and commercial options open to the millers. And it should be remembered that millers as a group had been the innovators in the industry before outside competitors appeared, establishing and expanding mills, seeking out new varieties of cane, and initiating the bottling of their own product. If millers had put into practice one or some combination of the innovations discussed above, and none was beyond their capacity, they could have reduced their costs, improved the quality of their product or lessened their dependence on the bottlers.

The Response of the Millers

The process of innovation by the millers came to a halt when it was all the more urgent to preserve their wealth and income in the face of outside competition. Innovation stopped because of changes in the way many mills were managed and as a result of conflicting demands among the millers.

Traditionally, mills were managed directly on a day-to-day basis by their owners, who lived at the mill with their families. This insured the active attention of the person with the greatest long-term interest in the mill and fullest knowledge of its ongoing operations and problems. However, when the industry began to confront the consequences of outside competition in the late 1970s, only about one-fifth of the mills were being managed in the traditional way by millers whose families lived with them. Roughly a third were managed directly by millers whose families resided away from the mills. The remainder, nearly half, were managed indirectly by millers who lived away from the mills with their families and who hired managers to run them. The managers were paid with a share of the profits on operations and had short-term, and quite possibly short-sighted, interest in the mills.

The transition to indirect management was the result of a process of migration from the mills that occurred in stages. It is widely reported that many families of millers first left the mills to live in nearby towns, and later Belém, while millers stayed behind; later millers began to spend more and more time with their families away from their mills; finally, millers left their mills to be run by managers and lived permanently with their families. On two points, this process is curious. If migration occurred because millers saw the industry as not being viable, it seems that the millers themselves might have left first in order to seek economic opportunities elsewhere, while their families stayed behind holding things together as best as possible. In addition, when the millers did leave they did not dispose of their mills, as might be expected if they saw them in decline. Nevertheless, by the late 1970s, this process was advanced and had begun some years earlier, when the industry was still at its peak. Wealthy as they were, and perhaps even 'served, obeyed, and respected', many millers had apparently turned away from their mills.

To understand this change in many millers' perspective, it is necessary to consider what it meant to be a miller in the broader society of Traditional Amazonia. There, one's status was often associated with where one lives, in a downward cascade from large, urban centres to remote rural areas.[22] In these terms, the status of millers, despite their wealth and local power, was at best that of the first class in the towns, well inferior to the elite in the city. That urban elite was traditionally dominated by individuals who had access to the restricted university training available in medicine, law and, later, engineering, and who, upon graduating, received the title of 'Doutor'. In addition, the millers were perhaps burdened by a certain stigma attached to the source of their wealth, the result, no doubt, of rum's long history as a fetter on *caboclos*. Such a situation may have been tolerable for the millers or their fathers at one time, but as the cane-producing region came to have more contact with the outside, the disparity between the millers' wealth and their lesser status became more obvious and less tolerable.

In addition, at the local level, in the mills themselves, the position of the millers had changed. The mill was no longer the centre of a community focused on the personal, paternalistic authority of the miller. Rather, after the Labour Board had been installed, there was an objective, impersonal power over the millers and workers in the mills, which the millers strongly resented since it diminished their status and authority. Even more, many millers felt betrayed by complainant workers who, by their lights at least, they had treated correctly and fairly over the years. For millers, this made their already arduous routine — grinding cane day after day, fixing leaky caneboats and sudden breakdowns in the mill, and now dealing with recalcitrant workers — even less bearable for themselves and desirable for their children.

In this context, but certainly before the problems the millers perceived in the mills were aggravated by the Labour Board, their families had begun to move to the two nearby towns. This might be understood, ironically, as the millers' turn to be lured and cajoled, taking advantage of urban benefits that were beginning to appear, especially television, which, with its prime-time programming directed at women, would have been immediately enjoyed by millers' wives. But along with urban amenities, the move by the millers' families to the towns, where there were secondary schools, offered the opportunity to further the education of their children.

22   Wagley (1953), pp. 104–5.

Beginning in the mid-1960s, well before the industry was in crisis, the number of university courses and enrolment expanded greatly in Belém, and many millers desired, and had the means, to have their children study there. Confirming this is the fact that, rather remarkably, over half of the millers with mills in operation in 1975 had children who had studied or were currently studying at university level.

The possibility of a university-level education and the custom of children living with their parents until marriage can explain in large part the move first of millers' families to town and then to the city. It also explains why, even after millers themselves left, they held on to their mills: throughout the period of educating their children, those millers needed a certain, and probably growing, source of income. However, this combination — indirect management and urgent need for income — gave rise to a critical dilemma, impinging directly on the process of innovation, that the industry was unable to resolve.

As a result of the large proportion of millers and their families who left the mills, the millers as a group were divided in terms of their interests and of their knowledge to deal with the problems that the industry confronted. In terms of interest, the millers whose most pressing need was income outnumbered by about four-to-one the millers who had less pressing income needs and could think more in traditional terms of maintaining their mills and building their equity. This explains some responses of millers in the face of outside competition. The deferral of maintenance of mills, which allowed them to operate for a time at an apparently lower cost, and the untying of the price of cane from rum, which appropriated more of the shrinking income of the industry to the millers, were changes that favoured income-oriented millers and could be imposed, since the others would have to adopt them if they wished to meet their local competitors. Also, with immediate income as a priority for a great majority of the millers, there was no widespread support for their bottling cooperative, which would have required investments, and good management, to sustain it as an alternative to domination by the local bottlers.

On the other hand, two inexpensive innovations that would have addressed problems faced by the industry on a permanent basis — new varieties of sugar-cane and the use of baker's yeast in the fermentation process — were not introduced. In this case however, there was no division of interests among millers, since, by reducing costs and increasing quality, these innovations would address the demands both of millers who were income-demanding and of those who were equity builders. This again raises the question of why the process of innovation stopped.

In the traditional industry, innovations implemented by some soon became known and available to all, given the proximity of fields and mills, the fluid use of skilled and unskilled labourers and contacts between millers through family and traders. When competitors from the outside put their products on the regional market, it was as though some producers had monopolised certain innovations for their own benefit. And indeed they had, since without an extension service or other external source of information there would be no way for millers to learn about them from the day-to-day operations in the industry.

To gain knowledge of practices of outside competitors it was necessary to go at least as far as the research station and the university in Belém. But this did not happen despite the fact that the trip to Belém from most mills could be made in half a day, that many millers already lived in Belém and that many more sent their children to the university there to study. On the question of technical innovation, the millers had become divided in a second way, about equally in numbers, between those who still actively managed their mills, and were aware of the growing problems of the industry, and those who did not manage directly and were ever more distant from it.

For the millers who still lived at their mills, and were familiar with their industrial and commercial problems, it was difficult to seek out solutions: they were concerned, year-round, with the day-to-day problems of their mills. Moreover, any attempt by those millers who were equity builders to deal with long-term problems of the industry was discouraged by the climate in the mills of being abandoned, both by other millers, who had gone to enjoy the good life in town, as well as by the government, which seemed to offer benefits only to people there. Moreover, the end of the bottling cooperative marked the end of any organisation that could look after or represent collective interests of the millers. Isolated and divided as they were, millers who still managed their mills never managed, or perhaps attempted, to mobilise even local political support for the continuance of the industry.

For the millers who left, the problems of their mills were ever more remote, not to mention concern for their solutions. Many of these millers engaged in other activities, and in some cases were quite successful, but this talent and effort were no longer directed to the industry. Although they were close to sources of solutions for the problems of the industry, if they were aware of such solutions, they showed no inclination to return to their mills and implement them. Likewise, children of millers studied agronomy, chemistry and business administration, but none saw fit to apply that knowledge in a significant way to the benefit of their family's mill. For the continuance of the industry this was unfortunate, since the successful implementation of a necessary innovation in just one mill likely would have become known and benefited all.

It was this division among millers that gave rise to the dilemma that the industry could not resolve: the millers who knew and were interested in the long-term problems of the mills did not have the means to obtain the necessary solutions, while the millers who had the means did not have the knowledge or interest. There is no reason to conclude that the decline of the industry was inevitable; it was a consequence of a failure to deliver solutions to its underlying problems. Once the division of interest and knowledge among the millers was established — based not directly on economic considerations, but rather on cultural and social ones — the range of action that millers could or would take was limited and, when faced with outside competition, the denouement was clear.

The End of Traditional Amazonia

The decline of the sugar-cane industry was directly involved with a number of critical changes witnessed at a local level: government intervention to develop the region and integrate it into the national economy; the distribution of social benefits that favoured the town more than the country, the elite more than the masses; migration from rural areas; the end of ecologically balanced ways of life; and the increasingly inadequate use of natural resources. All of this occurred in a small part of the Amazon that hardly measures 20 by 50 kilometres. But this was not an isolated case. These events have all become familiar during the recent process of change occurring throughout Traditional Amazonia that led to its demise.

Historically, traditional Amazonia comprised that part of the basin dominated since colonisation by Europeans and their descendants. It was essentially limited to areas accessible by rivers. This imposed a structure on the region, with the main stem of the Amazon as its backbone. Within this area, traditional Amazonia extended upstream as far as trade opportunities at any time justified exploiting (and overexploiting) the resource base of the floodplains and nearby uplands. The seasonal pulse of goods taken upriver and dispersing over the region and the return flow of products concentrating at the mouth gave a functional, some might say an organic, unity to traditional Amazonia.

As a result of trade flows, there was a clear hierarchy of places in traditional Amazonia, with Belém, and later also Manaus, at the top. Smaller towns for breaking and bulking were nodes at middle levels strung along the Amazon and its principal tributaries. Surrounding them were the lower-level rural areas which were dependent on the towns for goods and supplied them with products. Reflecting this hierarchy and the flows of wealth, power and information, social attention in the region was focused downstream and eastward on Belém, and to a lesser extent Manaus, as the principal economic, political and cultural points of reference.

As long as the mouth of the Amazon continued to be the effective point of entry and exit from the basin, the flow of goods and products channelled there would support the historic relations of places and people in Traditional Amazonia. It was not the case, then, that the completion of the Belém–Brasília Highway fundamentally altered this situation, although, as in the case of the sugar-cane industry, it did make competing goods from outside the region more accessible. However, the consequences of later roads, reaching out from the south to Santarém, Manaus, Porto Velho and Rio Branco, were very different, because these roads effectively sectioned the Amazon River for the first time. As a result, the regional transport structure was superseded and the flow of goods and products was redirected. Places at which roads met the river became collection and distribution points where outside products and regional goods were transferred between trucks and boats. Long distance trade along the Amazon dwindled. The relation of places was reordered as the old hierarchy in traditional Amazonia decayed. Cities that had been regional nodes were now just at the end of the road.

In parallel with the sectioning of the Amazon River, there was a shift in the focus of social attention in Traditional Amazonia. As urban centres were bypassed in the transfer of goods and products, concern in the region was drawn to their origins and destinations controlled largely to the south. As the power of state and local officials was constrained, especially during the military regime, and development plans were imposed on the region, interest of the urban elite turned to obtaining influence and largesse at the federal level. As television broadcasting penetrated the region, a part of national integration policy, it potentially affected people in their daily lives at all levels and places. Since programming was dominated by productions from the south-east, they reflected interests and social patterns there, which offered and set new models and standards for viewers in the region. Reception, and thus direct influence, was at first limited to larger urban areas in the 1960s, where programmes were re-transmitted and which had electricity. But, by the 1980s, nearby rural residents were using car batteries to power sets, and subsequently, with satellite transmission and parabolic antennas, programmes could be, and were, received anywhere in the region. As a result of these changes, São Paulo, Brasília and Rio de Janeiro became in many ways the principal economic, political and cultural points of reference for people in the region.

The process of change in social referents in Traditional Amazonia was signalled by migration from rural areas and small towns. This was a widespread phenomenon, reflected in census figures and characterised in studies of three quite different lower or middle level towns, Gurupá, Limoeiro de Ajuru and Itacoatiara, carried out at different times from the 1950s to the 1980s. Each mentions the improvement in the quality of urban life in its study area, two specifically citing the availability of radio or television and pointing to better schools as an important inducement to rural-urban migration.[23] More striking is the fact that each of the studies also makes specific reference to the exodus of the children *from* the town of its study area, particularly those of the local elite, to pursue better educational opportunities in a larger town or city.[24] These observations indicate that throughout Traditional Amazonia the rural and small-town elite were attracted to the new comforts of urban life and educational opportunities for their children in towns near them, as was the case with the millers. This is not surprising since it was a culturally appropriate response to ascend Wagley's cascade by moving to a town or city and assume the benefits and status of living there.

With the migration of the local elite from small towns and rural areas, presumably they also gradually turned away from involvement with traditional livelihood activities, as was also the case with the millers. Similarly, the lack of an interested elite also revealed itself as critical when important rural livelihood activities were threatened and needed support. This happened with both rubber and jute, which were produced widely throughout traditional Amazonia despite chronic problems of low quality and high cost. Although it might be argued that there was no viable technical fix for those problems, as there was in the case of the sugar-cane industry, in practice the fix that was critical for those products was political, that is, maintaining the legislation that protected Amazonian producers from foreign imports. Thus, when the federal government sought to remove import protection for rubber and jute, which would benefit industrial processors in the south, there was no effective resistance in the region to maintain it, such as might have

23   Wagley (1964), p. 299; Parker (1981), pp. 219, 377–8; Wesche and Bruneau (1990), pp. 9, 26.
24   Wagley (1953), p. 122; Wagley (1964), pp. 297, 302; Miller (1977), p. 298; Parker (1981), pp. 399, 414; Wesche and Bruneau (1990), p. 46.

been initiated and sustained by an informed and concerned local elite. With the entry of cheaper, better quality foreign imports, production of rubber and jute in the region became untenable and was extremely reduced by the 1990s. Likewise, effective political pressure from within the region was not brought to bear to mitigate the results of government actions on rural producers nor were other options implemented to use the rich resource base of the floodplains in other, sustainable, ways.

As a result of the lack of support for rural producers, after the direction of economic flows had been changed by roads, the flows themselves largely dried up. With this, the ties between towns and rural areas became ever more tenuous, since rural areas offered little to them economically and thus had little to receive in return, and the last remnants of trade relations in Traditional Amazonia withered. Rural residents fell back on expedient uses of resources and devastated *açai* and marketable timber in the floodland forests. Conflicts, sometimes violent, arose over fishing rights among fishers and over lake use between them and water buffalo ranchers. By this point, the rural economy was driven more by the desperation of hunger than by the ambition of trade.

Thus, Traditional Amazonia ended, as did its sugar-cane industry, in much the way it had begun: with the breaking of old barriers and the creation of new needs. Likewise, this has led to a pervasive dilemma similar to the one that could not be resolved in the sugar-cane industry. Faced with general economic decline, the rural producers who formed the economic base in the region, the cane farmers, rubber tappers, jute planters, fishers and other Amazonians who have an interest there, can hardly make a living, much less take initiatives to deal with their underlying problems. The members of the local elite who left for the towns and cities showed little interest in the rural areas and have abandoned their sway over them. Those who now have the means to influence the region take few initiatives and are insulated from the reality of rural life by an urban elite which seeks to interpose itself to mediate between them but cannot do so knowledgeably. The separation of interest and knowledge from means and power in what was Traditional Amazonia has been raised to a national level. It is a barrier to meaningful action and a basic cause of stagnation in a region that has lost its unity, identity and autonomy. In short, the Amazon River has become a backwater.

CHAPTER 9

Regatão and *Caboclo*:
Itinerant Traders and Smallholder Resistance in the
Brazilian Amazon

David McGrath

Introduction

The *regatão* is an itinerant river trader who travels between regional centres and upriver communities, trading manufactured goods and household staples to *caboclo* smallholders and interior merchants in exchange for 'traditional products', extractive and agricultural. The *regatão* has a long and controversial history in Amazonia: on the one hand regarded as a heroic pioneer bringing civilisation to isolated forest settlers,[1] on the other, as an unscrupulous interloper exploiting the rural poor and robbing local merchants of their business.[2] But, whatever the opinion, there was no doubting the importance of the *regatão* to Amazonian society and economy, for together with the *caboclo* and his *patrão* he formed the basis of the *aviamento* system, and the nexus of the struggle for control of the economic surplus it generated. Playing both sides of the struggle between *caboclo* and *patrão*, the *regatão* has been a decisive force in various periods in Amazonian economic history, helping to both construct, maintain and later dismantle the mercantile system that dominated Amazonia through the mid-twentieth century.

The debate over the *regatão*'s role in the regional economy is a reflection of what has been called 'the Janus-face of merchant capitalism': on the one side its revolutionary role transforming systems of production as it incorporates them into the expanding world market, on the other, its conservative character as merchants monopolise exchange to appropriate ever more economic surplus from impoverished producers.[3] Based in urban centres and trading in isolated areas of the interior, *regatões* were regarded by many writers as agents of urban merchants, both a mechanism of unequal exchange between centre and periphery, and of accumulation by the cen-

---

1   Goulart (1968).

2   Ferreira Penna (1973).

3   Fox-Genovese and Genovese (1983).

tre. Others, by contrast, saw the *regatão* as an innovative force, breaking down the debt-based commercial relations that sustained the *aviamento* system and facilitating the penetration of modern commercial relations. Underlying these different faces is the relationship between *regatão* and *caboclo*, for it was largely through their role in *caboclo* resistance that *regatãos* were able to survive and at times prosper within the *aviamento* system.

This chapter examines the *regatão* and his role in the development of the Amazon regional economy, concentrating on the relationship between *regatão* and *caboclo*, and especially on the *regatão*'s role in *caboclo* resistance. The chapter is divided into four parts. The first part examines the *aviamento* system, the second describes the role of the *regatão* within it, the third *regatão* and *caboclo* resistance under the *aviamento* system and the fourth the evolution of that relationship up to the present.

The *Aviamento* System

While differing superficially from most other regional economies in Latin America, the *aviamento* system, the traditional Amazonian economic system, shared virtually all the principal features associated with merchant capitalism in Latin America. Though based on forest extraction rather than agriculture or mining, the logic of the system was essentially that of debt peonage. Forest and animal products were extracted by independent producers who were bound to individual merchants and land owners by long-term, debt-based commercial relations. Here, the relative isolation of individual producers made labour control difficult and facilitated individual, if not collective, resistance.[4]

Aviamento means supplies or provisions. It comes from the verb *aviar*, to supply or furnish. Within the context of the *aviamento* system, *aviar* is to provide someone with goods on credit with the understanding that payment will be made in extractive products within a specified length of time. The supplier of the goods is the *aviador*, the person being supplied is the *aviado*. As these relationships imply, there are two components to the *aviamento* system. On the one hand, it is the commercial system in which transactions are based primarily on barter and credit, and rarely involve cash. On the other, it is the commercial network, based on these kinds of relationships, through which individual producers are linked to specific urban trading houses, *casas aviadoras*, by means of a chain of intermediaries.

The principal actors within the *aviamento* system have changed over time. Typically, it included: the extractivist, who may be a rubber tapper

4 Weinstein (1983b).

(*seringueiro*), brazil nut collector (*castanheiro*), hunter, varzea fisher or some combination of all four; the local trading post (*barracão*) operator, who may or may not own the rubber groves (*seringais*) or brazil nut groves (*castanhais*) where the extractivists live and work; the merchant in a nearby town, often on a major river boat line, who supplies the trading post operators and local land owners with the goods and receives forest and animal products from them in return; and finally, the trading house (*casa aviadora*), located in Belém or Manaus, which supplies interior merchants and receives whatever local products they have obtained from their customers. The other set of actors are the *regatões*, or itinerant river traders, who operate at a variety of levels within the system, depending on whether they are supplied by the *aviadora* houses, the town merchants or local trading post operators.

The *aviamento* system evolved in response to a variety of circumstances related to the difficulty of organising and maintaining systems for extracting widely dispersed forest and aquatic resources from a vast and thinly populated wilderness.[5] Rubber, brazil nuts and many other forest and animal products are extracted by isolated producers who may visit the local trading post only once twice a month. Under these circumstances, there is virtually no way of supervising production, so that, within limits, collectors are free to do as they please. As a result, collectors of forest products have operated largely as independent producers. Rather than being paid for their labour, they are paid for what they produce. As Russan, a British rubber estate manager at the time of the rubber boom put it.

> When a man or company buys an agricultural estate or other landed property in a foreign country such as Spain or France, or even Mexico, the produce of that estate belongs to, and is the property of the owner ... In the rubber regions of Brazil, the produce does not belong to the owner of the estate. It belongs to the collector — rubber cutter — who sells it to the owner.[6]

The *aviamento* system, then, like most systems operating according to the principles of merchant capitalism, is a system for appropriating producer surplus through exchange rather than production. This is the critical element in the relationship between *caboclo* and *patrão*. The fact that local merchants have only indirect control over producers and the productive process puts them at a disadvantage. They must rely on these producers, who have physical control of the product, to turn it all over to them. This

5   Weinstein (1983a); Murphy (1955).
6   Russan (1902), p. 6.

step should not be taken for granted, for it is the Achilles' heel of the merchant capitalist, and the basis of *caboclo* resistance to the pressure exerted by local merchants.

Credit, and its corollary debt, have been the main strategies employed by Amazonian merchants for obtaining control of producer output, and have been ubiquitous features of traditional Amazonian commerce since the beginning of Portuguese colonisation. Wallace, who spent several years in the Amazon prior to the rubber boom, wrote that,

> There is, I should think, no country where such a universal and insecure system of credit prevails as here. There is hardly a trader, great or small, in the country, that can be said to have any capital of his own. The merchants of Pará, who have foreign correspondents, have goods out on credit; they sell on credit to the smaller merchants or shopkeepers of Pará; these again supply on credit the negociantes in the country towns. From these last the traders up the different rivers get their small parcels of goods to half-civilised Indians, or to any one who will take them, to go among the wild Indian tribes and buy up their produce. They, however, have to give credit to the Indians who will not work till they have been paid sarsaparrilha or oil, which is still in the forest or the lake.[7]

Credit and debt, as the passage above suggests, have been highly functional in the context of the *aviamento* system. By obtaining goods on credit, traders were able to finance expeditions or bring new areas into production with minimum capital outlays, and therefore little financial risk. Furthermore, as observed, the entire extractive economy is set in motion by the initial advance of goods on credit. Without this flow of goods down the commercial hierarchy from urban trading firms to isolated trading posts in the interior, the collection of forest products would grind to a halt. As a trader asserted in an article on business practices during the rubber boom, 'the Indians will not bring rubber if I can't furnish supplies, and if I do not get rubber I can't pay what I owe'.[8]

The extension of credit, or more precisely indebtedness, serves as a bond through which creditor and debtor insure each other of access to supplies and forest products. For those who live in the interior, where transport and communication are slow and unreliable, indebtedness is a form of security, a way of building continuity into sporadic and unpredictable exchanges. For traders based in the main urban centres, indebted-

7   Wallace (1889), pp. 262–3.
8   India Rubber World (1890), p. 105.

ness means access to supplies which they can then exchange for forest products. As Weinstein observes, 'local traders regarded their debts to the large aviadores not as financial millstones that stymied their attempts at upward mobility but rather as the key to their very existence'.[9]

Indebtedness also serves as a mechanism for the control of labour and exchange. In this sense, then, indebtedness both complements land ownership and serves as an alternative to it in the control of exchange. In the case of the former, indebtedness ties the collector to the land. So long as he is in debt to the landowner, he can be prevented from leaving until all outstanding debts had been repaid.[10] Where the trader does not own the land, indebtedness is a means of controlling exchange and of insuring access to locally collected forest products. Because the collector is in debt to the trader, the trader has the moral, if not strictly legal, authority to demand that the collector sell all his produce to him. Through these strategies, then, traders and landowners attempted to monopolise access to the collectors of local forest and animal products.

Regatão

The *regatão*'s role in the Amazon economy dates back to the beginnings of European settlement in the region. During much of the colonial period, a major share of the commerce between Belém and the interior was conducted by itinerant traders known as '*comissários volantes*'.[11] Many of these traders were drawn from the ranks of colonist smallholders who, unable to obtain sufficient Indian labour for farming, turned to trade as the best alternative. These traders, whose operations often consisted of just a canoe and a supply of *cachaça*, did a lucrative, if illegal, trade with the government-operated Indian villages, buying forest and agricultural products from corrupt village directors and Indians. Despite repeated attempts, the colonial authorities were never able to eradicate, or even successfully regulate, this form of commerce, so that by the end of the colonial era itinerant traders were a ubiquitous element of Amazonian trade.[12] With Independence and the decline of what organised commerce and transport there had been between Belém and the interior, the number of itinerant traders apparently increased.[13]

9   Weinstein (1983a), p. 25.
10   Teixeira (1980).
11   MacLachan (1972).
12   *Ibid.*
13   Wallace (1889), p. 261.

With the growth of the rubber trade after 1850, *regatões* assumed an increasingly important role in the development of the *aviamento* system. Travelling further and further upstream, the *regatões* extended the influence of the Belém-based trading firms far into the interior, incorporating local trading networks into the expanding commercial empires of Belém-based merchants. In the process they came into direct conflict with the interior merchants who controlled local economic activity. The local merchants fought back, using their control of local politics to levy prohibitive taxes on *regatões* trading within their municipalities.[14]

The *regatões* were supported in their struggle with interior merchants by the *aviador* firms that supplied them. Weinstein (1983) cites the example of Breves, which in 1877 imposed a tax on *regatões* and trading posts outside the city limits.[15] In response, a group of firms petitioned the Chamber of Commerce protesting at the tax. The signatories included three of Belém's oldest and most powerful *aviador* houses, indicating, as Weinstein points out, that the *regatões* 'were neither marginals nor mavericks; rather, they operated in the vanguard of the commercial penetration for the aviador houses in Belém'.[16] As agents of these *aviador* houses, *regatões* played a critical role in breaking up the existing commercial system and reorganising economic activity in the interior to bring it under the control of Belém-based merchants.

The interior merchants found their allies in the planter class, the dominant group within the *paraense* elite until the 1880s.[17] This agrarian-based elite bitterly opposed the growth of the rubber trade, which they regarded as inimical to the social and economic development of the region. For this elite, *regatões* were not just a symbol of urban interests, but a major force in the destruction of rural agriculture and industry, and consequently of rural settlement and society in general. As Manoel Gomes Correa de Miranda, vice-president of Pará, put it in a 1852 speech justifying his support for a law prohibiting *regatões* in the state of Pará,

> This manner of trading is not just immoral, but very much contrary to the civilisation of the people; in addition to being one of the principal reasons why many villages have disappeared, and some towns are to be found almost abandoned.[18]

---

14   Goulart (1968); Monteiro (1958).
15   Weinstein (1983a), p. 52.
16   *Ibid.*
17   Anderson (1976), p. 165.
18   In Goulart (1968), p. 52.

With the development of the rubber economy and the introduction of steamships and large-scale trading firms during the latter half of the nineteenth century, *regatões* were incorporated into the evolving commercial structure in a variety of ways. At the long-distance, wholesale level, *regatões* supplied by the urban-based *aviador* houses traded primarily with interior merchants, trading post operators and rubber grove owners, and operated in ways that were probably little different from the trading firm's own steamboats. Other *regatões* operated primarily at the retail level trading with rubber tappers and other forest and animal products collectors. Some of these were supplied by the *aviador* houses, while others were supplied by the interior merchants and trading post operators.

By the 1880s the *aviamento* system was well established. Large trading empires developed, monopolising resources, controlling economic activity in the interior and reducing opportunities for small-scale accumulation. In Belém a relatively small number of firms dominated the rubber trade, while in the interior, local landowners monopolised rubber extraction, closing entire river basins to outsiders and preventing entry at gunpoint. With these changes in the structure of the regional economy, the *regatão* was increasingly marginalised within local trading networks, forced to operate in the interstices of the system.

The *regatão*, however, did not disappear in the face of the growing monopoly power of local merchants, he simply changed trading strategies to adapt to the new conditions. Where before he had operated relatively openly, now his activities were more covert. 'The open, lucrative and easy commerce of the past,' wrote Reis (1953), 'assumed the character of a dangerous contraband trade.'[19] Taking advantage of tapper resistance to the increasingly coercive measures employed by rubber grove owners, *regatões* penetrated rubber properties to purchase the '*sobras da safra*' (harvest surplus) direct from the rubber tappers. In this way, tappers and small-scale traders put up a formidable resistance to the monopolisation of economic activity by the local and regional elite. Earning the enmity of local merchants and landowners, *regatões* were often referred to as 'river pirates' by English-speaking writers of the time and castigated for the problems they caused rubber grove owners and interior merchants.

As a result of their activities, *regatões* have had an ambiguous reputation in Amazonian culture and history. Some writers have argued that *regatões* play a destructive role in Amazonian commerce, cheating unsuspecting

19   Reis (1953), p. 126.

caboclos and stealing the customers of legitimate businesses, while others maintain that they have played a progressive role, introducing an alternative to traditional commercial relationships based on debt peonage. Those who took the former position characterised the *regatão* as a greedy, unscrupulous individual who would stop at nothing to obtain a profit. 'There is no immoral act,' wrote the Bishop of Pará, 'which these greedy adventurers do not practice'.[20] Wallace explained this behaviour as being the result of the intense competition between traders for 'an amount of business which would not generally be sufficient for one-third the number'. 'This led,' he reasoned, 'to the general use of trickery and lying of every degree, as a fair means to be employed to entrap a new customer or to ruin a rival trader'.[21]

This ambiguous view of the *regatão* as both the salvation and downfall of the *caboclo* is exemplified in Ferreira Penna's description of a typical encounter between a *regatão* and a *caboclo* family during the early years of the rubber boom;

> The *regatão* is a mercantile providence: always late but never missing a visit. He arrives at the dock, his presence causing shouts and cheers of happiness from the family which has awaited him, anxiously or hungrily.
>
> The old *seringueiro* buys fish, *farinha*, dried meat, cider and canned butter. The wife or mistress buys calico for dresses, scarves, cheeses and sweets for the table and playthings and trifles for the children. The boys buy fish hooks, line, a shotgun, powder, lead shot and *cachaça*. The girls buy gold rings, pieces of fine muslin or silk for dresses, lace, sheets of cambric. He adds up the bill: rubber is the coin. The *seringueiro* complains about the high price of the goods he purchased and the low price offered for the rubber; but in the end not having anyone to appeal to he pays, handing over all the rubber he has produced. The *regatão* takes his leave satisfied with the good reception he received, especially from the daughters who, in return for the dishonour in which he leaves them, he has favoured with cloth for dresses, the value of which he later added to their father's bill.[22]

Those who viewed the *regatão* as a negative element in Amazonian commerce also maintained that *regatões* were rarely able to do anything constructive with the proceeds of their shady business dealings. Despite the

---

20   In Bastos (1937), p. 355.
21   Wallace (1889), p. 264.
22   Penna (1973), pp. 140–1.

exorbitant prices they charged their customers, these writers claimed that few *regatões* succeeded in accumulating any capital because their high profit margins were nullified by low sales volume. As Wallace remarked, 'it seems a very nice and easy way to make a living, to sell goods at double the price you pay for them, and then again to sell the produce you receive at double what you pay for it; but as the greater part of the small traders do not get rid of more than a hundred pounds' worth of goods in a year ... they are almost all of them constantly in debt to their correspondents'.[23]

These authors also maintained that far from contributing to frontier development, the activities of *regatões* actually prevented it. This argument was embedded in a broader debate between extractive and agricultural interests over the course of Amazonian development.[24] This debate, which surfaced initially during the eighteenth century, has been an important issue right up to the present.[25] Those who favoured development based on agriculture rather than extraction argued that the expansion and intensification of extractive activities would lead to the dispersal of rural population and the decline of rural settlement and industry. The rise of the rubber industry, asserted Ferreira Penna,[26] had stolen labour from agriculture, discouraged useful enterprises, depopulated villages, dispersed commerce and reduced the rural inhabitants to nomads. 'The Eldorado of the seringueiro', he intoned, 'is the cemetery of civilisation'.[27]

Other writers, both then and now, defend *regatões*, arguing that they played a progressive role in Amazonian trade, not only opening up frontier areas to commerce, but also helping to break the monopolistic control which rural merchants exerted over local economic activity.[28] *Regatões* may have exploited *caboclos* and Indians, wrote Bastos (1937), but there is little reason to believe that local merchants treated their customers any better.[29] He maintained that much of the invective aimed at *regatões* was prompted more by the interior merchants' resentment of competition than by any real concern for the wellbeing of the rural population. Bastos pointed out that *regatões* provided a valuable service to rural producers, relieving them of the necessity of travelling to market and thereby enabling them to

23   Wallace (1889), p. 263.
24   Anderson (1976); Weinstein (1983a); Barata (1973); Penna (1973).
25   Homma (1989); Allegretti (1995).
26   Penna (1973), p. 141
27   *Ibid.*, p. 143.
28   Goulart (1968), p. 53; Reis (1953).
29   Bastos (1937), pp. 352–3.

devote more time to directly productive activities. If some *regatões* abused their customers, then the solution was to punish those individuals, not to outlaw this form of commerce.

Regatão and *Caboclo* Resistance

Caboclo resistance in the struggle over division of his product took various forms. One strategy involved adulterating rubber with objects which added volume and weight, but involved little labour.[30] In this way tappers recovered some of the value appropriated by their *patrãos*. Another important strategy was to sell part of their output to passing *regatões*. While prices might be worse than those of the *patrão*, trade with the *regatão* represented a net gain, because the *patrão* would simply deduct most of the value of his output from his outstanding debt. Therefore, sale to the *regatão* was an opportunity to extend his purchasing power and obtain goods unavailable from the *patrão*. In this sense, the *regatão* offered *caboclos* an alternative to the commercial ties imposed by debt peonage. As Teixeira (1980) writes, 'the *regatão* presented himself as an alternative, perhaps the only one by which the poor population of the interior could escape from the control of the rubber grove owners'.[31] Trade with the *regatão*, then, was an act of resistance, part of the continuing struggle between merchants and tappers over the control of labour and extraction of producer surplus.[32]

Consequently, the *caboclo*'s relationship with the *regatão* was completely different from his relationship to the *seringalista* or local merchant. The *regatão* could not exert any coercive or monopoly control. For the seringueiro, trade with a *regatão* was a voluntary exchange between two independent equals, while trade with the local merchant was an involuntary exchange between unequals, a subordinate and his *patrão*. Because of this, trading with the *regatão*, as even Ferreira Penna admits, was a festive occasion for the tapper and his family, an opportunity for them to assert their independence in the face of the oppressive, all-encompassing web of debt peonage. This contrast between the *seringueiro*'s relations with the *regatão* and the *patrão* is nicely illustrated in the following passage.

> In contrast to the man of the *barracão*, the man of the river boat made him offers instead of reducing his request; attended to his desires rather than repressing them; satisfied his needs instead of deprecating

30   Weinstein (1983a).

31   Teixeira (1980), p. 93.

32   Weinstein (1983a, 1983b, 1985); Reis (1953); Goulart (1968).

them. From the *regatão*, the customer bought what he wanted and what
he didn't want ...

The *regatão* also differed from the *seringalista* in his social treatment of
the *seringueiro*.

He was affable instead of rude; happy instead of severe; conversation-
al instead of reticent ... for the *regatão* that old commercial axiom prevailed, which said, 'the customer is always right'. [33]

Although the *regatão* is the tapper's partner in crime, it would be a mistake
to consider him the tapper's ally. While the *regatão's* style was very different
from that of the interior merchant, the net result was much the same. The
tapper paid dearly for his resistance, both in terms of the price paid for
goods obtained from the *regatão* and it terms of the opportunity foregone
to reduce his indebtedness. The *regatão* exploited the struggle between local
producer and *patrão* for his own benefit, extracting from the producer the
economic surplus which would otherwise have gone to local merchants.
Consequently, this form of tapper resistance, while damaging to the interests of the *patrão*, actually reinforced the set of relationships which per-
petuated the system. As long as these diversions were relatively small, isolated occurrences, they did not constitute, a threat to the system.

However, in certain situations this resistance could be formidable. One
measure of its effectiveness is that together, tappers and *regatões* were able to
frustrate foreign penetration of rubber extraction. The British rubber estate
manager, Russan, for example, wrote in 1902, that 'all the companies that
have been formed in Europe to work rubber estates in Brazil have lost their
working capital and have either ceased to exist or are in considerable difficulty'.[34] Russan gives the example of the Rubber Estates of Pará, which
averaged 250 tons per year under Brazilian ownership, but only 50 tons per
year under two successive British firms. 'What has become of the balance,
the 200 tons?' Russan asks. 'There is little doubt,' he continues, 'that something like that amount of rubber each year was sold to the rubber pirates.'[35]

It was only by constant vigilance and readiness to, in Russan's words,
'remove the offender from the face of the earth', an option not as available to foreign firms, that Brazilian rubber estate owners were able to keep
tapper and *regatão* resistance down to acceptable levels. Thus, despite the

33   Goulart (1968), pp. 121–2.
34   Russan (1902), p. 6.
35   *Ibid.*, p. 7.

fact that *regatões* did not play a significant role in trade or in capital accumulation during this period, they did have a considerable impact on the character of the *aviamento* system and on the course of Amazonian development. The tappers and *regatões* constituted a barely controlled revolutionary force which greatly increased the cost of an extractive system based on debt-peonage.

The *Regatão* and *Caboclo* Resistance since the Rubber Boom

With the end of the rubber boom in the early twentieth century, the Amazon economy collapsed. The commercial empires which had monopolised extraction and trade during the rubber boom broke apart. As the *aviamento* empires disintegrated, the *regatões* multiplied to fill the void. As the Bulletin of the Commercial Association of Amazonas reported in 1926, 'during the crisis, when many gaiolas [large steamboats] stopped travelling the upper rivers, many canoes and boats began to render splendid service, transporting the merchandise necessary to keep the seringais functioning and bringing the rubber to the lower rivers, to the ports where the steamboats were contractually obligated to stop'.[36] Although the social and economic geography of the basin was profoundly different, the resulting commercial system had, in many respects, reverted to its pre-boom state, when itinerant traders roamed the interior more or less freely, but with little opportunity to accumulate capital.

With the implementation of regional development programmes, such as SPVEA and later SUDAM in the mid-twentieth century, Amazonia entered another period of change, this time marked by the continuing decline of the *aviamento* system and the gradual spread of modern capitalist institutions and commercial relations. Here again, the *regatão* acted as an agent of change, transmitting to the interior the forces of change emanating from the centre. Travelling through the interior, poaching customers from local merchants, *regatões* made debt-based commercial relations increasingly untenable. Diverting producer output from local merchants to urban trading firms, *regatões* contributed to the breakdown of traditional commercial networks in the interior. But instead of reorganising interior trade to tie it more closely to urban trading firms, *regatões* simply opened up traditional commerce. Here, then, *regatões* were functioning as a truly revolutionary force. As Teixeira observes, 'to the extent that he pushed the domination of open commerce, [the *regatão*] was without doubt a progressive factor'.[37]

36   ACA (1926), p. 23.
37   Teixeira (1980), p. 102.

Finally, in the last quarter of the twentieth century the process of change that began a few decades earlier reached its logical conclusion, the transformation of the extractive economy. Under the wave of frontier expansion following the construction of the Amazon highway system in the 1970s and '80s, *seringalistas* are selling out to pioneer ranchers. Taking advantage of government credit programmes, ranchers are converting forest to pasture, thereby eliminating the basis of the extractive economy which has sustained the *caboclo* way of life. The struggle now is not over the division of surplus generated by the system, but over the survival of the extractive system itself. What had been an individual struggle between *caboclo* and *patrão* over division of surplus, is now a collective struggle for economic survival.

In response to this new threat, *caboclos* have changed their resistance strategy. Reflecting both the collective nature of the threat and union and church organisational efforts, resistance strategies have changed from selling to the *regatão*, a covert individual action, to the '*empate*', a directly confrontational collective action aimed at stopping ranchers from cutting down the forest. Organised by union and community leaders, rubber tappers have invaded *seringais* where workers were cutting down forest for pasture to persuade them to stop and leave the area.[38] With this change in strategy, the locus of resistance has changed from the sphere of exchange to that of production. Since he operates in the sphere of exchange, the *regatão* is now largely irrelevant to *caboclo* resistance. In fact, to the extent that *caboclo* survival depends on collective organisation, especially of economic activities, the *regatão* represents a threat to *caboclo* resistance. Siphoning off product that would otherwise be marketed through local cooperatives, *regatãos* weaken the economic power of these *caboclo* organisations and reduce their ability to compete in the developing frontier economy.

With the decline of the extractive economy and the mercantile system on which it was based, the world in which the *regatão* operated is rapidly disappearing, relegated to the isolated basins of the Amazon where extractive activities and traditional commercial relations still predominate. Now local merchants obtain goods direct from major wholesalers in the south at prices *regatãos* cannot match. At the same time, the proliferation of roads and ferry boat lines facilitates access to markets for rural producers reducing dependence on itinerant traders. Even in those areas which have not yet been integrated into the evolving commercial system, opportunities for *regatões* are decreasing. The declining availability and value of extractive products is reducing the major source of income in the *regatão*'s trading

38   Allegretti (1995).

strategy, while rural-urban migration and the spread of cattle ranching into areas of former *caboclo* settlement are eliminating the rural populations *regatãos* once serviced. As a result of these changes, the survival of the *regatão* is no longer dependent on producer resistance, but on the functionality of his trading strategy in the evolving commercial system. A generalist in an increasingly specialised commercial economy, the *regatão's* survival now depends on his ability to compete with local merchants, providing goods at prices and conditions of payment comparable with theirs.

Conclusion

The relationship between the *regatão* and the *aviamento* system is a good example of the complexity of commercial relations under merchant capitalism. In this regard perhaps the central point of this chapter is that the tendency to view itinerant traders as simply agents of larger-scale merchants in the extraction of producer surplus misses a fundamental characteristic of mercantile systems and of the role played by small-scale itinerant traders within these systems.

First, one of the main failings of the conventional view of merchant capitalism is that it overestimates the ability of local merchants to control exchange and extract producer surplus. In the Amazon, at least, *caboclos* are smallholders who control the means of production and the product of their labours, and are generally outside the surveillance of local merchants and landowners. Under these conditions, there is nothing automatic about the transfer of smallholder output and the value it represents to local merchants. On the contrary, it is precisely through the process of exchange that *caboclo* resistance takes place, and itinerant traders play a critical role in making at least one form of this resistance possible.

Second, the conventional interpretation of merchant capitalism tends to treat all traders alike, failing to recognise the diversity of traders involved in regional marketing systems. In particular, this approach fails to recognise that large-scale sedentary and smaller-scale itinerant traders have very different capabilities and interests that are reflected in their different trading strategies. While the former employ monopolistic strategies aimed at controlling exchange, the latter, without the economic or coercive power to monopolise local smallholders, adopt opportunistic strategies, exploiting economic opportunities as they arise.[39] Thus, while there is a certain 'functionality' to the role played by itinerant traders, in terms of surplus extraction within the

39   McGrath (1989).

system as a whole, on the local level itinerant traders and local merchants are frequently competing for access to the same product. As the example of the *regatão* shows, depending on the circumstances, this competition can merely redirect a portion of producer surplus or lead to the breakdown of the mercantile system. In this sense, then, the *regatão*, perhaps more than any other figure, embodies the 'Janus-face' of merchant capitalism.[40]

---

40   Fox-Genovese and Genovese (1983).

BIBLIOGRAPHY

Acevedo Marin, R. and Castro, E. (1993) *Negros de Trombetas: guardiães de matas e rios* (Belém: UFPa/NAEA)

Adams, R. (1952) 'Un análisas de las creencias y practicas médicas en un pueblo indígena de Gautemala,' *Publicaciones Especiales de Instituto Indigenista Nacional*, no. 17 (Guatemala).

Albuquerque, Milton (1969) *A Mandioca na Amazônia* (Belém: Sudam).

Alden, D. (1976) 'The Significance of Cocoa Production in the Amazon Region during the Late Colonial Period,' *Proceedings of American Philosophical Society*, no. 120, pp. 103–35.

Allegretti, M. (1995) 'Reservas extrativistas: parâmetros para uma política de desenvolvimento sustentável na Amazônia,' in *O destino da floresta* (Rio de Janeiro: Dumará), pp. 17–47.

Almeida, A. (1995–96) *Quilombos: repetorio bibliografico de uma questão redefinida*, mimeo

Anderson, R. (1976) 'Following Curupira: Colonization and Migration in Pará, 1758 to 1930,' PhD. Dissertation, Department of History, University of California–Davis.

Anderson, Scott Douglas (1993) Sugar-cane on the Floodplain: a Systems Approach to the Study of Change in Traditional Amazonia,' PhD dissertation, University of Chicago.

Anderson, Scott Douglas and Tavares Marques, Fernando Luiz (1992) 'Engenhos movidos a maré no estuário do Amazonas: vestígios encontrados no município de Igarapé-Miri, Pará,' *Boletim do Museu Paraense Emílio Goeldi*, série Antropologia, vol. 8, no. 2, pp. 295-301.

Andrews, Christopher (1990) 'The Ornamental Fish Trade and Fish Conservation,' *Journal of Fish Biology*, vol. 37(Supplement A), pp. 53–59.

Andrews, Christopher (1992) 'The Ornamental Fish Trade and Conservation,' *INFOFISH International*, vol. 2, no. 92, pp. 25–9

Antonil, André João [João António Andreoni] (1711) *Cultura e opulência do Brasil*, texto confrontado com o da edição de 1711 (São Paulo: Ed. da Universidade de São Paulo, 1982).

Araújo, A.M. (1979) 'Medicina rústica,' *Brasiliana*, vol. 300 (São Paulo: Ed. Nacional).

Associação Comercial do Amazonas (ACA) (1926) 'Transporte e navegação,' *Revista da Associação Comercial do Amazonas*, vol. 136(August), pp. 23–4.

Atz, James and Faulkner, Douglas (1971) *Aquarium Fishes: their Beauty, History and Care* (New York: Viking Press).

Ayres, Deborah de Magalhães Lima (1992) 'The Social *Caboclo*: History, Social Organization, Identity and Outsider's Social Classification of the Rural Population of an Amazonian Region (The Middle Solimões),' Unpublished PhD dissertation, University of Cambridge.

Balée, W. (ed.) (1999) *Advances in Historical Ecology* (New York: Columbia University Press).

Balée, W. (2000) 'Antiquity of Traditional Ethnobiological Knowledge in Amazonia: the Tupí-Guaraní Family and Time,' *Ethnohistory*, vol. 47, no. 2, pp. 399–422.

Bandeira, M. (1975) *Cartéis e desnacionalização: a experiência brasileira (1964–1974)* (Rio: Civilização Brasileira).

Bannister, Keith (1977) *Aquarial Fish* (New York: Crescent Books).

Barata, Manuel (1915) *A antiga produção e exportação do Pará: estudo histórico-econômico* (Belém: Typ. da Livraria Gillet).

Barata. M. (1973) 'A antiga produção e exportação do Pará,' in *Formação Histórica do Pará* (Belém: Federal University of Pará), pp. 301–30.

Barth, F. (1984) 'The Nature and Variety of Plural Units, in David Maybury-Lewis, *The Prospects for Plural Societies* (Washington: American Ethnological Society), pp. 77–88.

Bastos, A.C. Tavares (1937) *O Valle do Amazonas* (São Paulo: Editora Nacional).

Bastos, A.C.T. (1975) (original 1866). *O vale do Amazonas: a livre navegação do Amazonas, estatística, produção, comércio, questões fiscais do vale do Amazonas* (São Paulo: Ed. Nacional, Brasília: INL).

Bates, Henry Walter (1892) *The Naturalist on the River Amazon* (New York: D. Appleton & Co).

Benchimol, S. (1966) *Estrutura geo-social e economica da Amazonia* (Manaus: Edicoes Governo do Estado do Amazonas).

Benchimol, Samuel (1994) *Manáos-do-Amazonas: Memória empresarial* (Manaus: Emprensa Estaual do Amazonas, Universidade do Amazonas, Associação Comercial do Amazonas).

Benchimol, Samuel (1997) *Exportação da Amazônia brasileira:1996/1995* (Manaus: Universidade do Amazonas; SEBRAE/Amazonas).

Benchimol, S. (1999) *Eretz Amazônica: Os Judeos na Amazonia*

Bentes, Abrahim Ramiro (1987) *Das Ruinas de Jerusalém à Verdejante Amazonia: formação da primeira comunidade israelita brasileira* (Rio: Edições Bloch).

Bernstein, Henry. (1990), 'Taking the Part of Peasants,' in H. Bernstein, B. Crow, M. Mackintosh and C. Martin (eds), *The Food Question: Profit versus People* (London: Earthscan), pp 69–79.

Blaut, J.M. (1993) *The Colonizers Model of the World: Geographical Diffusionism and Eurocentric History* (New York and London: Guilford Press).

Bloch, M. (1975) 'The End of Affinity,' in M. Bloch (ed.) *Marxist Analysis and Social Anthropology*. (London: Malaby).

Bloch, Maurice (1984) 'Property and the End of Affinity,' in M. Bloch (ed.), *Marxist Analysis and Social Anthropology* (London: Tavistock Publications), pp. 203–28..

Bohannan, P. (1963) 'Land, Tenure and Land Tenure,' in *African Agrarian Systems* (London, Oxford University Press).

Boxer, C.R. (1957) *The Dutch in Brazil: 1624–1654* (Oxford: Clarendon; reprint Hamden, Connecticut: Archon, 1973).

Boyer-Araujo, V. (1994) 'Do "mau-olhado" à "coisa feita" ou o caminho para a mediação do filho-de-santo,' in M.A. D'Incao and I.M. da Silveira (eds), *A Amazônia e a crise da modernização* (Belém: Museu Goeldi), pp. 207–12

Brass, Tom (1986) 'Unfree Labor and Capitalist Restructuring in the Agrarian Sector: Peru and India,' *The Journal of Peasant Studies*, vol. 11, no.1, pp. 76–88.

Brown, P. (1981) *The Cult of the Saints* (London: SCM).

Câmara Cascudo, L. (n.d.) *Dicionário do folclore brasileiro* (Rio de Janeiro: Edições de Ouro).

Canuto, A. (1972) 'Histórico de Santa Terezinha,' unpublished manuscript.

Cardoso, F.H. and Müller, G. (1977) *Amazônia: expansão do capitalismo* (São Paulo: Brasiliense).

Carvalho, José. C. Melo (1952) *Notas de viagem ao Rio Negro* (Rio de Janeiro: Universidade do Brasil).

Casaldaliga, P. (1971) *Uma Igreja na Amazônia em conflito com o latifúndio e a marginalização* (Petrópolis: Vozes).

Casaldaliga, P. (1997) 'Nos 20 anos desta menina-moça,' in *A luta pela terra—A comissão pastoral da terra 20 anos depois* (São Paulo: Paulus).

Chao, Ning Labbish (2001) 'The Fishery, Diversity, and Conservation of Ornamental Fishes in the Rio Negro Basin, Brazil — A Review of Project Piaba (1989–99),' in Ning L Chao, Paulo Petry, Gregory Prang, Leonard Sonneschein and Michael Tlusty (eds), *Conservation and Management of Ornamental Fish Resources of the Rio Negro Basin, Amazonia, Brazil: Project Piaba* (Manaus, Amazonas: Editora Universidade do Amazonas), pp. 161–204.

Chayanov, Alexander V. (1966) *The Theory of Peasant Economy*, D. Thorner, B. Kerblay and R.E.F. Smith (eds) (Manchester: Manchester University Press).

Chernela, Janet M. (1989) 'Managing Rivers of Hunger: The Tukano of Brazil,' in Darrell A. Posey and William Balée (eds), *Resource Management in Amazonia: Indigenous and Folk Strategies. Advances in Economic Botany*, vol. 7 (New York: New York Botanical Garden), pp. 238–48.

Chibnik, M. (1994) *Risky Rivers: the Economics and Politics of Floodplain Farming in Amazonia* (Tucson: University of Arizona Press).

Chute, Walter H. (1934) 'Tropical Fish Immigrants Reveal New Nature Wonders,' *National Geographic*, vol. 65, pp. 93–109.

Cleary, D. (1993) 'After the Frontier: Problems with Political Economy in the Modern Brazilian Amazon,' *Journal of Latin American Studies*, vol. 25, no. 2, pp. 331–349.

Cleary, D. (1999) '"Lost Altogether to the Civilised World": Race And The Cabanagem in Brazil, 1750–1850,' *Comparative Studies in Society and History*, vol. 40, no. 1, pp. 109–35

Coates, Christopher W. (1933) 'A Fish Story,' *Asia*, vol. 33, pp. 18–24.

Da Matta, R. (1973) 'Panema: uma tentativa de análise estrutural,' in *Ensaios de antropologia estrutural* (Rio de Janeiro: Vozes).

Daniel, João (1757–76) 'Tesouro descoberto no rio Amazonas,' offprint from *Anais da Biblioteca Nacional* 95, 2 vols. (Rio de Janeiro: Biblioteca Nacional, 1975).

Davis, S. (1977) *Victims of the Miracle. Development and the Indians of Brazil* (Cambridge: Cambridge University Press).

Dawes, John (2001) 'International Aquatic Industry Perspectives on Ornamental Fish Conservation,' in Ning L Chao, Paulo Petry, Gregory Prang, Leonard Sonneschein and Michael Tlusty (eds), *Conservation and Management of Ornamental Fish Resources of the Rio Negro Basin, Amazonia, Brazil: Project Piaba* (Manaus, Amazonas: Editora Universidade do Amazonas), pp. 109–121..

Dean, W. (1987) *Brasil and the Struggle for Rubber: a Study in Environmental History* (Cambridge: Cambridge University Press).

Derby, O. (1898) *O rio Trombetas.* Boletim do Museu Goeldi, Belém, no. 5

Descola, P., Lenclud, G., Taylor, A.C. and Seveir, A. (eds.) (1988) *Les idées de l'antropologie* (Paris Armand Colin).

Dias, Manuel Nunes (1970) *Fomento e mercantilismo: a companhia geral do Grão Pará e Maranhão (1735–1778),* 2 vols. (Belém: Universidade Federal do Pará).

Duncan, I. and Rutledge, S. (eds) (1977) *Land and Labour in Latin America* (Cambridge: Cambridge University Press).

Durrenberger, E. Paul (ed.) (1984) *Chayanov, Peasants and Economic Anthropology* (Orlando: Academic Press).

Duterte, A. Casaldaliga, P. and Balduíno, T. (1986) *Francisco Jentel — defensor do povo do Araguaia* (São Paulo: Paulinas).

Eisenstadt, Todd A. (1992) 'The Rio Negro Basin's Aquarium Fish Trade: Harbinger of Sustainable Development, or the "One that Got Away?"' unpublished manuscript (Manaus: Fundação Vitória Amazônica).

Emperaire, Laure and Pinton, Florence (1993) 'Ecological and Socio-economic Aspects on the Middle Rio Negro,' in .M. Hladik, A. Hladik, O.F. Linares, H. Pagezy, A. Semple, and M. Hadley (eds.) *Tropical Forests, People and Food: Biocultural Interactions and Applications to Development-Man and the Biosphere Series,* vol. 13 (Paris: The Parthenon Publishing Group), pp. 783–88.

Ennew, Judith, Hirst, P. and Tribe, K. (1977) '"Peasantry" as an Economic Category,' *Journal of Peasant Studies*, vol. 5, pp. 295–322.

Esterci, Neide (1987) *Conflito no Araguaia: peões e posseiros contra a grande empresa* (Petrópolis: Vozes).

Evans-Pritchard, E.E. (1937) *Witchcraft, Oracles and Magic Among the Azande* (Oxford: Clarendon Press).

FAO Fishstat Plus (2001) *Commodities Production and Trade, Ornamental Fish, 1976–1999*, vol. 2, no. 30 (Food and Agriculture Organization of the United Nations).

Fernando, Audrey A. and Phang, Violet E. (1994) *Freshwater Ornamental Fish Aquaculture in Singapore* (Singapore: Singapore Polytechnic).

Ferreira, Aurélio B.H. (1975) *Novo dicionário da língua portuguesa* (Rio de Janeiro: Editora Nova Fronteira).

Figueiredo, N. (1976) 'Pajelança e catimbó na região Bragantina,' *Revista do Instituto Histórico e Geográfico de Alagoas*, vol. 32, pp. 41–52

Figueiredo, N. and Vergolino e Silva, A. (1972) 'Alguns elementos novos para o estudos dos batuques de Belém,' in *Atas do Simpósio sobre a Biota Amazônica, Vol 2, Antropologia.*

Fitzgerald, Sarah (1989) *International Wildlife Trade: Whose Business is it?* (Washington, DC World Wildlife Fund).

Forman, S. (1975) *The Brazilian Peasantry* (Colombia: Colombia University Press).

Foster, G. (1953) 'Relationships between Spanish and Spanish-American Folk Medicine,' *Journal of American Folklore*, vol. 66, pp. 201–18

Foster, G. (1967) 'Peasant Society and the Image of the Limited Good,' *American Anthropologist*, vol. 67, pp. 293–315

Fox-Genovese, E. and Genovese, E. (1983) *The Fruits of Merchant Capital* (Oxford: Oxford University Press).

Friedman, H. (1980) 'Household Production and the National Economy: Concepts for the Analysis of Agrarian Formations,' *Journal of Peasant Studies*, vol. 7, no. 2, pp. 154–84.

Furtado, L. et al. (1993) *Os povos das águas* (Museu Goeldi: Belém).

Gabriel, C. (1980) *Communications of the spirits: Umbanda, regional cults and the dynamics of a mediumistic trance*, PhD dissertation, McGill University

Galvão, E. (1952) *The religion of an Amazon community: a study in culture change*, PhD dissertation, Columbia University.

Galvão, Eduardo (1955) *Santos e visagens: uma estudo da vida religiosa de Itá Amazonas*, Brasiliana, volume 284 (São Paulo: Companhia Editora Nacional).

Galvão, Eduardo (1979a) 'Aculturação indígena no Rio Negro (1959),' in *Encontro de sociedades; índios e brancos no Brasil* (Rio de Janeiro: Paz e Terra), pp. 135–92.

Galvão, Eduardo (1979b) 'Encontro de sociedades tribal e nacional no Rio Negro, Amazonas (1962),' in *Encontro de sociedades; índios e brancos no Brasil* (Rio de Janeiro: Paz e Terra), pp. 257–71.

Galvão, Eduardo (1979c) 'Mudança Cultural na Região do Rio Negro (1954),' in *Encontro de sociedades; índios e brancos no Brasil* (Rio de Janeiro: Paz e Terra), pp.120–5.

Géry, Jacques (1994) 'Neon,' *Aqua Geõgraphia*, vol. 7, pp. 82–5.

Goodenough, Ward H. (1969) 'Yankee Kinship Terminology: a Problem in Componential analysis,' in S.A. Tyler (ed.), *Cognitive Anthropology* (New York: Holt, Rinehart & Winston), pp. 225–88.

Goodman, D. and Redclift, M. (1981) *From Peasant to Proletarian* (Oxford: Blackwell).

Goodman, D. and Watts, M. (eds) (1997) *Globalising Food: Agrarian Questions and Global Restructuring* (London: Routledge).

Goulart, J. (1968) O *regatão* (Rio de Janeiro: Conquista).

Goulding, M., Smith, N. and Mahar, D. (1996) *Floods of Fortune: Ecology and Economy along the Amazon River* (New York: Columbia University Press).

Goulding, Michael and Smith, Nigel (1997) 'The Amazon Wetland Conservation: the Need to Conceptualize River Basin Ecology and Urban-Driven Economies,' unpublished report for EIDEN Department, World Bank. June 4.

Gryzbowiski, C. (1990) 'Rural Workers Movement and Democratization in Brazil,' *Journal of Development Studies*, vol.26, no. 4.

Gudeman, Stephen (1976) *Relationships, Residence and the Individual: a Rural Panamenian Community* (London and Henley: Routledge & Kegan Paul).

Gudeman, S. and Rivera, A. (1990) *Conversations in Columbia: the Domestic Economy in Life and Text* (Cambridge: Cambridge University Press).

Harris, M. (2000) *Life on the Amazon* (Oxford University Press: Oxford).

Harris, Mark (1998) '"What It Means to Be *Caboclo*": Some Critical Notes on the Construction of Amazonian *Caboclo* Society as an Anthropological Object,' *Critique of Anthropology*, vol. 18, no. 1, pp. 83–95.

Harris, Mark (2000) *Life on the Amazon* (Oxford: Oxford University Press).

Harris, Phillip and Petry, Paulo (2001) 'Preliminary Report on the Genetic Population Structure and Phylogeography of the Cardinal Tetra (*Paracheirodon axelrodi*) in the Rio Negro Basin,' in Ning L Chao, Paulo Petry, Gregory Prang, Leonard Sonneschein and Michael Tlusty (eds) *Conservation and Management of Ornamental Fish Resources of the Rio Negro Basin, Amazonia, Brazil: Project Piaba* (Manaus, Amazonas: Editora Universidade do Amazonas), pp. 205–25.

Harrison, Mark (1975) 'Chayanov and the Economics of Russian Peasantry,' *Journal of Peasant Studies*, vol. 2, pp. 389–417.

Hiraoka, Mario (1992) 'Caboclo and Ribereno Resource Management in Amazonia: a Review,' in K. Radfor. and C. Padoch (eds) *Conservation of Neotropical Forests: Working from Traditional Resource Use* (New York: Columbia University Press).

Homma, A. (1989) 'Reservas extrativistas: uma opção de desenvolvimento viável para a Amazônia?' *Pará Desenvolvimento*, vol. 25, pp. 38–48.

Hughes-Jones, Stephen (1992) 'Yesterday's Luxuries, Tomorrow's Necessities: Business and Barter in Northwest Amazonia,' in Claude Humphrey and Stephen Hughes-Jones (eds), *Barter, Exchange and Value: an Anthropological Approach* (Cambridge: Cambridge University Press), pp. 42–74.

Ianni, O. (1978) *A luta pela terra: história social da terra e da luta pela terra numa área da Amazônia* (Petrópolis: Vozes).

IBGE (Institúto Brasileiro de Geografia e Estatística) (1991) *Censo demográfico 1991. Características Gerais de População e Instrução*. Fundação Instituto Brasileiro de Geografia e Estatística. Ministério do Planejamento e Orçamento. Resultado da Amostra no. 4. Amazonas.. Censo Demográfico. Rio de Janeiro.

IBGE (Institúto Brasileiro de Geografia e Estatística) (2000) *Resident Population, in Absolute and Relative Values, Total, Urban or Rural Situation in the Municipal Seat, Total Area and Population Density, according to Federative Units and Municipalities,* Accessed 18 August 2001; available from: <http://www.ibge.gov.br/english/estatistica/populacao/censo2000/sino pse. php?tipo=21&uf=13>

India Rubber World (1890) 'Business Customs at Pará,' *India Rubber World,* 15 February.

Ingold, T. (1995) 'Building, Dwelling, Living,' M. Strathern (ed.), *Shifting Contexts* (London: Routledge).

Institúto Brasileiro do Meio Ambiente e dos Recurso Naturais Renováveis (IBAMA) (1999) *Relatório de Exportação de Peixes Ornamentais [1998]* (Manaus: MMA, IBAMA, DIRFA).

Jackson, J. (1975) 'Recent Ethnography of Indigenous Northern Lowland South America,' *Annual Review of Anthropology,* vol. 4.

Keller, W. (1971 [1966]) *Diaspora: the Post-Biblical History of the Jews* (London: Pitman).

Klee, Albert J. (1987) *A History of the Aquarium Hobby in America. Special Publication No. 1* (Guy D. Jordan Endowment Fund. American Cichlid Association).

Ladiges, Werner (1956) 'Einig Ergänzende Bemerkungen zu Hyphessobrycon cardinalis Myers and Weitzman,' *Die Aquarien und Terrarien Zeitschrift,* vol. 9, no. 5, p. 116.

Ladiges, Werner (1978) 'Keeping and Breeding Fish: Some Reminiscences,' *Aquarium Digest International* (English Edition), vol. 20, pp. 4–6.

Laslett, Peter N. (1972) 'Introduction: the History of the Family,' in Peter Laslett and Richard Wall (eds), *Household and Family in Past Time* (Cambridge: Cambridge University Press), pp: 1–89.

Lathrap, D. (1968) 'The 'Hunting' Economies of the Tropical Forest Zone: an Attempt at Historical Perspective,' in R.B. Lee and I. Devore (eds), *Man the Hunter* (Chicago: Aldine).

Leonardi, V. (1999) *Os historiadores e os rios: natureza e ruína na amazonia brasileira* (Brasília: Ed. Universidade de Brasília).

Lescure, Jean-Paul and Pinton, Florence (1993) 'Extractivism: a Controversial Use of the Tropical Ecosystem,' in C.M. Hladik, A.

Hladik, O.F. Linares, H. Pagezy, A. Semple, and M. Hadley (eds), *Tropical Forests, People and Food: Biocultural Interactions and Applications to Development-Man and the Biosphere Series*, vol. 13 (Paris: The Parthenon Publishing Group), pp. 767–74..

Lescure, Jean-Paul, Emperaire, L., Pinton, F. and Renault-Lescure, O. (1992) 'Nontimber Forest Products and Extractive Activities in the Middle Rio Negro Region, Brazil,' in Mark J. Plotkin and Lisa M. Famolare (eds), *Sustainable Harvest and Marketing of Rain Forest Products* (Washington DC: Island Press), pp. 151–7.

Lima Ayres, Deborah de Magalhães (1992) 'The Social Category *Caboclo* — History, Social Organisation, Identity and Outsider's Social Classification of the Rural Population of an Amazonian Region (the middle Solimões),' Unpublished PhD dissertation, University of Cambridge, UK.

Lima, Deborah (1999) 'A construção histórica do termo *caboclo*. Sobre estruturas e representações sociais no meio rural Amazônico,' *Novos Cadernos do Naea*, Belém, UFPa, vol. 2, no. 2, pp. 5–32.

Lock, Charles, Warnford, G., Wigner, G.W. and Harland, R.H. (1885) *Sugar Growing and refining* (London: E. & F.N. Spon.).

MacCreagh, Gordon (1985) *White Waters and Black* [1926] (Chicago: University of Chicago Press).

McGrath, D. (1989) 'The Paraense Traders: Small-scale, Long Distance Trade in the Brazilian Amazon,' PhD dissertation, Department of Geography, University of Wisconsin-Madison.

McGrath, D., Castro, F., Futemma, C., Amaral, B. and Calabria, J. (1993a) 'Fisheries and the Evolution of Resource Management on the Lower Amazonia Várzea,' *Human Ecology*, vol. 21, no. 3, pp. 167–96

McGrath, D., Castro, F., Futemma, C., Amaral, B. and Calabria, J. (1993b) 'Manejo comunitário da pesca nos lagos de várzea do Baixo Amazonas,' in Furtado, L. et al. (eds) *Os povos das aguas* (Belém: Museu Goeldi).

McGrath, David Gibbs (1989) 'The Paraense Traders: Small-Scale, Long Distance Trade in the Brazilian Amazon,' PhD dissertation, University of Wisconsin–Madison.

MacLachan, C. M. (1972) 'The Indian Directorate: Forced Acculturation in the Portuguese Amazon, 1700–1800,' in Dauril Aulden (ed.) *Colonial Roots of Modern Brazil* (Berkeley: University of California Press).

Maclachlan, C. (1973) 'The Indian Labour Structure in the Portuguese Amazon 1700–1800,' in D. Alden (ed.), *Colonial Roots of Modern Brazil* (Berkely: University of California Press), pp. 199–230.

McLarney, Bill (1988) 'Still a Dark Side to the Aquarium,' *International Wildlife*, vol. 18(Apr/May), pp. 46–51.

Margolis, M. and Carter, W. (eds) (1979) *Brazil: Anthropological Perspectives, Essays in Honor of Charles Wagley* (New York: Columbia University Press).

Marques, Fernando Luiz Tavares (1993) 'Engenhos de maré em Barcarena, Pará: arqueologia de seus sistemas motrizes,' MA thesis, Pontífica Universidade Católica do Rio Grande do Sul.

Martins, José de Souza (1980) *Expropiação e violência (a questão política no campo)* (São Paulo: Hucitec).

Martins, J.S. (1985) 'A Igreja face à política Agrária do Estado,' in V. Paiva (ed.) *Igreja e a Questão Agrária* (Rio: Loyola).

Martins, José de Souza (1997) *Fronteira (a degradação do Outro nos confines do humano)* (São Paulo: Hucitec).

Marx, K. (1976) *Capital, volume 1* (Penguin: Harmondsworth).

Maués, A.E. Motta (1989) 'A questão étnica: índios, broncos, negros e caboclos,' in V. Loureiro (ed.), *Estudos e problemas amazônicos: história social e econômica e temas especiais* (Belém: IDESP).

Maués, Heraldo (1977) 'A Ilha Encantada: medicina e xamanismo numa comunidade de pescadores,' unpublished Master's dissertation, Universidade de Brasília.

Maués, R.H. (1990) *A Ilha Encantada: medicina e xamanismo numa comunidade de pescadores* (Belém: UFPa).

Maués, R.H. (1992) 'Catolicismo popular e pajelança na região do Salgado,' in P. Sanchis (ed.), *Catolicismo: unidade religiosa e pluralismo cultural* (São Paulo: Loyola), pp. 197–230

Maués, R.H. (1995) *Padres, pajés, santos e festas: catolicismo popular e controle eclesiástico* (Belém: Cejup).

Maybury-Lewis, B. (1996) 'Land and Water: Agrarian Politics and the *riberinhos* of Amazonas,' Paper presented to the Third International conference of the Brazilian Studies Association (BRASA III), Cambridge, September 1996.

Medeiros, L.S. (1989) *Movimentos sociais no campo* (Petrópolis: Vozes).

Meira, Márcio (1993) 'O tempo dos patrões: extrativismo da piaçava entre os índios do Rio Xíe (Alto Rio Negro),' Masters thesis, Universidade de Campinas.

Mellen, Ida (1931) 'Tropical Toy Fishes,' *National Geographic*, vol. 59, pp. 286–317.

Menezes, Lúcia Beckmann de Castro, Anderson, Scott Douglas and Braz, Vera Nobre (1988) 'Avaliação e apoio técnico-econômico das microdestilarias da região de Abaetetuba e Igarapé-Miri,' research report submitted to the Universidade Federal do Pará, Departamento de Operações e Processos Químicos, Belém, Pará, typewritten.

Miller, Darrel (1977) 'Itá em 1974: um epílogo,' in *Uma comunidade amazônica: um estudo do homem nos trópicos* por Charles Wagley, traduzida por Clotilde da Silva Costa. 2nd ed. Brasiliana vol.290 (São Paulo: Companhia Editora Nacional).

Mintz, S (1989) *Caribbean Transformations* (Chicago: Aldine).

Mintz, S. (1996) 'Enduring Substances,' *Journal of the Royal Anthropological Institute (inc. Man)* (June), vol. 2, pp. 289–311

Mintz, Sidney W and Wolf, Eric R. (1950) 'An Analysis of Ritual Co-parenthood (*Compadrazgo*),' *Southwestern Journal of Anthropology*, vol. 6, pp. 341–68.

Monteiro, M.Y. (1958) O *regatão* (Manaus: Sergio Cardoso).

Moore, D. and Balée, W. (1991) 'Similarity and Variation in Plant Names in Five Tupi-Guarani Languages (Eastern Amazonia),' *Bulletin of the Florida Museum of Natural History*, vol. 35, pp. 210–62.

Moran, E. (1974) 'The Adaptive System of the Amazonian *caboclo*,' in C. Wagley (ed.), *Man In the Amazon* (New York: Columbia University Press).

Motta-Maués, Angélica (1977) 'Trabalhadeiras e camaradas: um estudo sobre o status das mulheres numa comunidade de pescadores,' unpublished Master's dissertation, Universidade de Brasília.

Motta Maués, Maria Angélica (1989) 'A questão etnica: índios, broncos, negros e caboclos,' in IDESP (Instituto do Desenvolvimento Econômico-Social do Pará), *Estudos e problemas amazonicos: história social e econômica e temas especiais* (Belém: IDESP).

Motta Maués, A. (1993) *Trabalhadeiras e camarados: relações de gênero, simbolismo e ritualização numa comunidade amazônica* (Belém: UFPA).

Muniz, P. (1907) *Registros das terras: Estado do Pará* (Belém: Imprensa Oficial).

Murphy, R. (1955) 'Credit Versus Cash: a Case Study,' *Human Organization*, vol. 4, pp. 26–8.

Murrieta, Rui S.S. (2001) 'Dialética do sbor: alimentação, ecologia e vida cotidiana em comunidades ribeirinhas da Ilha de Ituqui, Baixo Amazonas, Pará,' *Revista de Antropologia* (São Paulo: USP), vol. 44, no. 2, pp. 39–79.

Netting, Robert (1993) *Smallholders, Householders: Farm Families and the Ecology of Intensive, Sustainable Agriculture* (Stanford: Stanford University Press).

Nugent, S. (1993) *Amazonian Caboclo Society: an Essay on Invisibility and Peasant Economy* (Berg: Oxford).

Nugent, S. (1997) 'The Coordinates of Identity in Amazonia: at Play in the Fields of Culture,' *Critique of Anthropology*, vol. 17, no. 1, pp. 33–53.

Nugent, S. and Athias, R. (2000) 'Where's the Rabbi? Jewish Communities in the Lower Amazon' (ethnographic film) (London: Department of Anthropology, Goldsmiths).

Nugent, Stephen (1981) 'Amazonia, Ecosystem and Social System,' *Man*, NS 16, pp. 62–74.

Nugent, Stephen (1993) Amazonian Caboclo Society: An Essay on Invisibility and Peasant Economy (Oxford: Berg Publishers).

Oliveira, Adélia Engrácia de (1975) 'São João, Povoado do Rio Negro (1972),' *Boletim de Museu Paraense Emílio Goeldi*, Serie Antropologia, vol. 58, pp. 1–55.

Oliveira, Adélia Engrácia de (1979) 'Depoimentos Baníwa sobre as Relações entre os Índios e "Civilizados" no Rio Negro,' *Boletim de Museu Paraense Emílio Goeldi*, Serie Antropologia, vol. 72, pp. 1–31.

Oliveira, Agostinho Monteiro Gonçalves d'. (1899–1904) *Chronica de Igarapé-Miry*, 3 vols. (Belém: Typ. da Imprensa Official).

Oliveira, Ana Gita (1995) *O mundo transformado: um estudo da cultura de fronteira no Alto Rio Negro* (Belém: Museu Paraense Emílio Goeldi).

Oliveira, Ana Gita, Pozzobon, Jorge and Meira, Márcio (1994) *Relatório Antropológico: Área Indígena Rio Negro, Área Indígena Rio Apapóris, Área Indígena Rio Téa* (Brasília: FUNAI).

Overing, J. (1981) 'Amazonian Anthropology,' *Journal of Latin American Studies*, vol. 13, no. 1.

Padoch, C., Ayres, J. M., Pinedo-Vasquez, M. and Henderson, A., (eds) (1999) *Várzea: Diversity, Development and Conservation of Amazonia's Whitewater Floodplains* (New York Botanical Gardens: New York).

Pará. IDESP [Instituto do Desenvolvimento Econômico-Social do Pará] (1968) *Zona Guajarina: diagnóstico sócio-econômico preliminar*, Estudos Paraenses no. 15 (Belém: IDESP).

Pará. IDESP [Instituto do Desenvolvimento Econômico-Social do Pará] (1970) *Relatório preliminar de desenvolvimento integrado: município de Abaetetuba*, elaborated by IDESP for SUDAM and SERFHAU (Pará: Falangola).

Pará. IDESP [Instituto do Desenvolvimento Econômico-Social do Pará] (1977) *Diagnóstico do município de Abaetetuba*. Relatório de Pesquisa no. 6 (Belém: IDESP).

Parker, E. (ed.) (1985) *The Amazon Caboclo: Historical and Contemporary Perspectives*. Studies in Third World Societies, vol. 32 (Williamsburg, VA: College of William and Mary).

Parker, Eugene Philip (1981) 'Cultural Ecology and Change: a *caboclo várzea* Community in the Brazilian Amazon,' PhD dissertation, University of Colorado.

Patnaik, Utsa (1979) 'Neo-Populism and Marxism: The Chayanovian View of the Agrarian Question and its Fundamental Fallacy,' *Journal of Peasant Studies*, vol. 6, pp. 375–420.

Penna, D. S. Ferreira (1973) *Obras completas: Volume I* (Belém: Conselho Estadual de Cultura).

Penna, D.S.F. (1973) (original 1867). *Obras completas de Domingos Soares Ferreira Penna* (Belém: Conselho Estadual de Cultura), 2 vols.

Pinheiro, A. de Souza (1994) 'A Vision of the Brazilian National Security Policy on the Amazon,' *Low Intensity Conflict & Law Enforcement*, vol. 3, no. 3 (London: Frank Cass), pp. 387–409.

Pinheiro, João Antonio da Cruz Diniz (1751) 'Noticia do que contém o Estado do Maranhão ...,' in J. Lúcio D'Azevedo(ed.), *Os Jesuitas no Grão Pará* (Lisbon: Tavares Cardoso & Irmão, 1901), pp. 343–7

Polleto, I. (1997), 'A terra e a vida em tempos neoliberais. Uma releitura da história da CPT,' in *A luta pela terra: A comissão pastoral da terra 20 anos depois* (São Paulo: Paulus).

Porro, A. (1996) *O povo dos aguas: ensaios de etno-historia Amazonicas* (Petropolis: Editora Vozes).

Prang, Gregory (2001) '*Aviamento* and the Ornamental Fishery of the Rio Negro, Brazil: Implications for Sustainable Resource Use,' in Ning L Chao, Paulo Petry, Gregory Prang, Leonard Sonneschein and Michael Tlusty (eds), *Conservation and Management of Ornamental Fish Resources of the Rio Negro Basin, Amazonia, Brazil: Project Piaba* (Manaus, Amazonas: Editora Universidade do Amazonas), pp. 43–73.

Price, R. (1994) *Les premiers temps: la conception de l'histoire des marrons saramaka* (Paris: Seuil).

Ramos, A. (1999) *Indigenism: Ethnic Politics in Brazil* (Madison and London: University of Minnesota Press).

Reis, A. C. Ferreira (1953) *O Seringal e o Seringueiro* (Rio de Janeiro: Serviço de Informação Agrícola).

Reis, A.C.F. (1979) *História de Óbidos* (Rio de Janeiro: Typ. Nacional).

Reis, Arthur Cesar Ferreira (1997) *O Seringal e o Seringueiro*, 2nd ed. (Manaus: Editora da Universidade do Amazonas/Governo do Estado do Amazonas).

Reminick, R.A. (1974) 'The Evil Eye Belief among the Amhara of Ethiopia,' *Ethnology*, vol. 13, no. 3, pp. 279–91

Ribeiro, Darcy (1970) *Os indios e a civilização* (Rio de Janeiro: Editora Civilização Brasileira).

Ricardo, Alberto Carlos, ed. (2000) *Povos indígenas no Brasil, 1996/2000* (São Paulo: Institúto Socioambiental).

Rodrigues, J. Barbosa (1875) *Exploração e estudo do Vale Amazonas* (Rio de Janeiro).

Roosevelt, A. (ed.) (1994) *Amazonian Indians: from Prehistory to the Present: Anthropological Perspectives* (Tucson and London: University of Arizona Press).

Roosevelt, A. (1999) 'Twelve Thousand Years of Human-Environment Interaction in the Amazon Floodplain,' C. Padoch et al (eds) *Várzea* (New York: New York Botanical Gardens), pp. 371–92

Roseberry, W. (1995) 'The Cultural History of Peasantries,' in J. Schneider and R. Rapp (eds), *Articulating Hidden Histories: Exploring the Influence of Eric R. Wolf* (Berkeley: University of Californian Press), pp. 51–66.

Ross, E. (1978) 'The Evolution of the Amazon Peasantry,' *Journal of Latin American Studies*, vol. 10, pp. 30–62.

Roth, N. (1995) *Conversos, Inquisition and the Expulsion of the Jews from Spain* (Madison: University of Wisconsin Press).

Rubel, A.J. (1960) 'Concepts of Disease in Mexican-American Culture,' *American Anthropologist*, vol. 62, pp. 795–814

Russan, A. (1902) 'Working Rubber Estates on the Amazon,' *India Rubber World*,(October), pp .5–7.

Sahlins, Marshall (1988) *Stone Age Economics* (London: Routledge).

Salles, V. (1976) 'Cachaça, pena e maracá,' *Brasil Açucareiro*, vol. 27, no. 74 (Rio de Janeiro), pp. 46–55.

Salles, V. (n.d.) 'Ritos populares: pajelança e catimbó,' mimeo

Saloman, Frank and Schwartz, Stuart (eds) (1999) *The Cambridge History of the Native Peoples of the Americas, Vol. III, South America Parts 1 & 2* (Cambridge: Cambridge University Press).

Santos, Roberto (1980) 'História Econômica da Amazônia (1800–1920),' *Estudos Brasileiros*, vol. 3 (São Paulo: Biblioteca Básica de Ciências Sociais).

Schmink, M. and Wood, C. (eds) (1992) *Contested Frontiers of Amazonia* (Florida: University Press).

Schneider, David M. (1969) 'American Kinship Terms for Kinsmen: a Critique of Goodenough's Componential Analysis of Yankee Kinship Terminology,' in S.A. Tyler (ed.) *Cognitive Anthropology* (New York: Holt, Rinehart & Wiston), pp: 288–311..

Schwarcz, L. (1996) 'Questão racial no Brasil,' in L. Schwarcz and L. Vidoar de Souza Reis (eds), *Negras Imagens* (São Paulo: University of São Paulo Press).

Schwarcz, L. (1999 [1993]) *The Spectacle of the Races: Scientists, Institutions and the Race Question in Brazil, 1870–1930* (New York: Hill and Wang).

Schwartz, Hans W. (1961) 'A Journey into Cardinal Country,' *Tropical Fish Hobbyist*, vol. 9, no. 11), pp. 5–12.

Schwartz, Stuart B. (1985) *Sugar Plantations in the Formation of Brazilian Society: Bahia 1550–1835* (Cambridge: Cambridge University Press).

Seed, P. (1995) *Ceremonies of the Possession in Europe's Conquest of the New World 1492–1640* (Cambridge: Cambridge University Press).

Segalen, Martine (1986) *Historical Anthropology of the Family* (Cambridge: Cambridge University Press).

Seitz, Georg (1963) *People of the Rain-Forests*, translated by Arnold J. Pomerans (London: Heinemann).

Skidmore, T. (1976) *Black into White: Race and Nationality in Brazilian Thought* (Durham and London: Duke University Press).

Slater, C. (1994) *Dance of the Dolphin: Transformation and Disenchantment in the Amazonian Imagination* (Chicago: University of Chicago Press).

Socolof, Ross (1996) *Confessions of a Tropical Fish Addict* (Bradenton, FL: School of Enterprises).

Spooner, B. (1970) 'The Evil Eye Belief in the Middle East,' in M. Douglas (ed.), *Witchcraft Confessions and Accusations* (London: ASA monographs).

Staniford, P. (1973) *Pioneers in the Tropics: the Political Organization of Japanese in Immigrant Communities in Brazil* (London: Athlone Press).

Stedile, J.P. (2002) 'Landless Battalions,' *New Left Review* (May/June), vol. 15, pp. 77–104.

Sternberg, H. (1956) 'A água e o homen na várzea do Careiro,' tese do Concurso a catedra de geografia do Brasil, Rio de Janeiro.

Sternberg, H. (1975) *The Amazon River of Brazil* (Wiesbaden: Franz Steiner).

Stoye, Frederick H. (1936) 'The Discovery of the Neon Tetra,' *The Aquarium*, vol. 5, no. 7, pp. 137–8.

Strathern, Marilyn (1981) *Kinship at the Core: an Anthropology of Eldom, a Village in the North-West Essex in the Nineteen-sixties* (Cambridge: Cambridge University Press).

Taussig, M. (1982) 'Peasant Economics and the Development of Capitalist Agriculture in the Cauca Valley, Colombia,' in John Harriss (ed.), *Rural Development: Theories of Peasant Economy and Agrarian Change* (London: Hutchison), pp 178–205.

Teixeira, C.C. (1980) 'O *aviamento* e o Barracão na Sociedade do Seringal,' Master's thesis, Department of Sociology, University of São Paulo.

Ugarte, Auxiliomar Silva (1992) 'As correspondências manuscritas na dinâmica do *aviamento*,' *Boletim Informativo do Museu Amazônico*, vol. 3, no. 3, pp. 49–62.

Valsechi, Octávio (1960) *Aguardente de cana de açúcar* (Piracicaba, São Paulo: Livroceres).

Velho, O. (1976) *Capitalismo autoritário e campesinato* (São Paulo: DIFEL)

Viveiros de Castro, Eduardo (1996) 'Images of Nature and Society in Amazonian Ethnology,' *Annual Review of Anthropology*, vol. 25, pp. 179–200.

Von Cziffra, Géza (1964) *Lana — Königen der Amazonen* (Lana — Queen of the Amazons) [feature film].

Wagley, Charles (1957) *Uma comunidade amazônica — estudo do homem nos trópicos*, Brasiliana vol. 290 (São Paulo: Companhia Editora Nacional).

Wagley, C. (ed.) (1964) *Man in the Amazon* (Gainesville, FL: University of Florida Press).

Wagley, C. (1976 [original 1953]) *Amazon Town: a Study of Man in the Tropics* (New York: Macmillan) (reprint with a new epilogue by the author, New York: Knopf, 1964).

Wallace, Alfred Russell (1889) *A Narrative of Travels on the Amazon and Rio Negro*, 2nd edition (London: Ward, Lock and Co; reprint New York: Dover Publications, 1972).

Watson, Ian (2000) 'The Role of the Ornamental Fish Industry in Poverty Alleviation,' NRI Report 2504, Project No. V0120 (Natural Resources Institute, Chatham Maritime, Kent, UK)

Weinstein, B. (1983a) *The Amazon Rubber Boom: 1850–1920* (Stanford: Stanford University Press).

Weinstein, B. (1983b) 'Capital Penetration and Problems of Labor Control in the Amazon Rubber Trade,' *Radical History Review*, vol. 27, pp. 121–40.

Weinstein, B. (1985) 'Persistence of *Caboclo* Culture in the Amazon: the Impact of the Rubber Trade, 1850–1920,' *Studies in Third World Societies*, vol. 32, pp. 89–113.

Weitzman, Stanley H. (1956) 'The Cardinal Tetra,' *The Aquarium Journal*, vol. 27, no. 7, pp. 257–9.

Weitzman, Stanley H. and Fink, William L. (1983) 'Relationships of the Neon Tetras, a Group of South American Freshwater Fishes (Teleostei, Characidae), with Comments on the Phylogeny of New World Characiforms,' *Bulletin Museum of Comparative Zoology*, vol. 150, no. 6, pp. 339–95.

Weitzman, Stanley H. and Fink, William L. (1993) 'Changing Courses: The Juruá River, its People and Amazonian Extractive Reserves,' PhD dissertation, Department of Geography, University of California, Berkeley.

Wesche, Rolf and Bruneau, Thomas (1990) *Integration and Change in Brazil's Middle Amazon* (Ottawa: University of Ottawa Press).

Whitehead, N. (1996) 'Amazonian Archaeology: Searching for Paradise?' *Journal of Archaeological Research*, vol 4, no. 3, pp. 241–64.

Whitehead, N. (1999) 'Native People Confront Colonial Regimes in the Northeast South America,' in S. Schwartz and F. Salomon (eds), *The Cambridge History of the Native Peoples of the Americas*, vol. 3, part 2, South America (New York: Cambridge University Press).

Whitesell, Edward (1993) 'Changing Courses: the Jurua River, its People and Amazonian Extractive Reserves,' unpublished PhD thesis, University of California, Berkeley.

Wilson, D. (1999) *Indigenous South Americans of the Past and Present: an Ecological Perspective* (Boulder and Oxford: Westview Press).

Wolf, E. (1966) *Peasants* (Englewood Cliffs, New Jersey: Prentice Hall).

Woortmann, Ellen F. (1995) *Parentes, herdeiros e compadres* (São Paulo/Brasília: Hucitec & Edunb).

Wright, Robin (1981) 'The History and Religion of the Baniwa Peoples of the Upper Rio Negro Valley,' PhD dissertation, Department of Anthropology, Stanford University.

Printed in the United States
22540LVS00005B/67-255